CULTURAL RESEARCH

CULTURAL RESEARCH

Papers on Regional Cultures and Culture-Mixing

by and for

The Institute for Cultural Research

Edited by

TAHIR SHAH

THE OCTAGON PRESS
LONDON

Contents

NOTES:

In each monograph, references to *Notes* are by superscript roman numerals in the running text. Notes appear at the end of each chapter.

BIBLIOGRAPHY:

In each monograph, references to *Bibliography* in the text appear as superscript numerals. *Bibliography* follows each chapter, after *Notes*.

Foreword

We often say that the world has become very small. By this I think we mean that travel and communication, even to the most obscure places on earth have been made possible, if not easy. One hundred years ago no one would have been heard moaning because it had taken an hour longer than expected to travel from London to Tokyo. Few then could have dreamt of a day when going from Paris to New York for lunch would be conceivable. Until recently, the bulk of one society had little or no interaction with another. A few intrepid explorers might have gone to far-flung lands and then returned to describe them. They might have brought with them strange new fabrics, or spices with unknown smells. One hundred years ago a few nations from Europe and the Americas had earnestly begun to influence, not only the countries bordering them, but even those on the other side of the globe.

As countries such as India, Arabia and Japan increased their exposure to the world outside their own borders, there was a direct influence on their societies and cultural systems. Newly introduced products and ideas had an irreversible effect on places from Buenos Aires to Bangkok. There was a knock-on effect as the changes filtered from one community to the next. It became possible to buy a Savile Row suit in Mexico City, or to buy a mango in Bradford.

The 19th century was a time in England when science was at odds with religion. It was an era when 'cults' of all kinds were introduced into English society. This topic is referred to by Robert Cecil in his important paper. Also concerning the last century we will look at the very area from which England set out to influence and change the world: the docklands of London.

The wind of change ripped across each continent in turn, forcing societies which had been isolated for thousands of years, to adapt or to die out. In the papers that follow we shall look at various examples of such societies. We shall see the Gond tribe of Central India, the Ainu of Japan, the Kafirs of the Hindu Kush: each of whom was compelled to leave ancient traditions and beliefs, in an attempt to adapt to the new ways thrust upon them.

The few pure Ainu that still remain have been forced to forget their heritage. They, like the Gonds, have been driven from their lands and become inferior members of society. Or, as in the case of some ancient Kafir tribes (especially those who sought refuge in Pakistan), they have little choice but to eke out an existence selling traditional carvings to tourists.

There are parallels that we can draw between such people as the Gonds, the Ainu and the Kafirs. We see how each was totally autonomous and self-reliant. Their societies had no need for the world beyond the frontier. But as bureaucracy developed and the secluded communities fell under the jurisdiction of others, they were stripped of their own systems of regulation and control. The increased interaction between people of different nations leads, as we shall see, to complex situations. So, when there was conflict, it became necessary to establish which legislative system should preside over a case with one or more foreign elements.

Slaves who were shipped in their hundreds of thousands to the New World tried, although persecuted, to cling to their native beliefs. These convictions, as the paper on *Macumba* outlines, were influenced by all those around them – including the philosophies of Native Americans and others. The principles of certain West African secret societies, dance and cultural ingredients, went with the droves of slaves to the

Americas, where they continued to develop. Certain secret societies, and a fascinating dance known as *The Sokodae*, are discussed in the pages that follow.

The changes of the last century, spurred on substantially by the rise in technology, have brought riches as well as poverty. Many countries of the Arab World happened upon wealth when what was under their land became more important than what was above it. In his inspirational paper on the years that he spent with the Arabs, General Sir John Glubb writes of the simple courtesy and dignity of a people, still relatively unchanged by technology. Peter Brent sums up the mystique that Arabia still holds for many. He remembers the descriptions of early travellers through Arab lands and discusses the changes of late, that have allowed highways to slice through the desert and air-conditioned limousines to speed along them.

At its height, the Arab Empire stretched across Africa and Asia, lasting for some seven centuries. It produced some of the most magnificent architecture, literature and art of any civilization. But each empire comes to an end, and the great Islamic dominion eventually broke up. For those on the boundaries of the Arab empire, persecution followed. The Moors who had taken the Iberian peninsula were defeated and driven into subservience by the Catholic kings. They were forcibly converted to Catholicism and oppressed in every way imaginable. These people, called *Moriscos* ('Little Moors') by the Spanish, managed against extraordinary odds to continue their Islamic beliefs in secret, and even produced a considerable body of literature.

Now that communication has become faster and easier we can learn about cultures in every corner of the earth. Indeed, we *must* learn from them. Our society is riddled with problems of all kinds: problems that are growing, and spreading to those far-off lands that we influenced and changed. There is inner city collapse in sub-Saharan Africa: a place where, until recent times, there were no great cities. Cars are spewing out exhaust fumes in lands where, until a few decades ago, cars were unknown. The papers in this book can help us to understand our own society for they illustrate a certain sense and sensibility that we seem to have lost and must re-learn. Those papers which are presented here without attribution are contributed by members of the *Institute for Cultural Research*.

The world may have *become* small but it will do us no good unless we learn from all of those within it.

Tahir Shah
London, August 1992

1

My Years with the Arabs

GENERAL SIR JOHN GLUBB

Anyone who writes or speaks about Arabs is obliged, first of all, to say what he means by the word – who, in his opinion, the Arabs are. This introduction involves a little history. Basically, of course, the Arabs were the people who lived in the peninsula of Arabia, an area which today includes Saudi Arabia, the west side of the Persian Gulf, Oman and South Arabia and the Yemen. As most of the inhabitants of this area were nomadic, the word 'Arab' also came to have the secondary meaning of nomads.

Let us begin our brief historical review in the seventh century A.D. The world (omitting India and China) was at that time divided between an Eastern and a Western Power Bloc, as it has been for the past fifty years. The Eastern Power in the seventh century was Persia, the Western was the Roman Empire. Six hundred years after Christ, the countries which we call Turkey, Syria, Lebanon, Palestine, Egypt and Algeria had been Greek and Roman for nearly one thousand years. Syria and Egypt were more wealthy, cultured and important provinces in the Roman Empire than were France or Britain.

Iraq, on the other hand, had been part of Persia for a thousand years. In fact, in 600 A.D., the capital of the Persian Empire was in Iraq, on the Tigris not far below Baghdad. The frontier between Rome and Persia ran approximately along the present border between Syria and Iraq.

The Arabs lived in Arabia; most of them were nomadic;

1

and they were in contact with both Power Blocs, with Persia along the Euphrates, with Rome along the eastern borders of Syria.

The Prophet Muhammad began to preach in Mecca, in the Arabian peninsula, in 613 A.D. and he died in 632. A year after his death, his enthusiastic followers burst out of their deserts and within eighty years, conquered an empire extending from Spain and Morocco in the West, to India and the borders of China (in Central Asia north of the Pamirs) in the East.

Now the point which affects us is this. The population of Arabia, most of which is desert, is very small. Even today, the whole peninsula contains only about half as many people as live in the Nile Delta alone. In the seventh century, most of these vast areas were conquered by little Arab armies of fifteen or twenty thousand men. Egypt, with a population of seven million, was occupied by an Arab force of about sixteen thousand men.

It has been estimated that, when all the conquests were over, only about one per cent of the inhabitants of the immense Arab Empire were of Arab descent, or had ancestors who had come from the peninsula. The statements one sometimes reads to the effect that the Arabs 'poured' into Syria, Palestine or Egypt and that, henceforward, the inhabitants of all these countries were Arabs, are mathematically impossible. Moreover, the Arab conquests were not accompanied by massacres, evictions or exile. The original inhabitants remained unchanged.

Eventually, the majority of conquered peoples accepted the Muslim religion and the Arabic language. We may say, therefore, that the countries which we call Arab today share, to a great extent, the same religion, culture and language, but differ widely from one another in their ethnic origin. These racial differences cause them to react in entirely different ways to the events and the crises of life.

I think that the closest comparison we can make to them is South America, where everyone speaks Spanish (or

Portuguese), everyone is Roman Catholic, but hardly anybody is a Spaniard. In both cases, the situation is due to military conquest many centuries ago.

Personally, I served in Iraq and Jordan, and I had some experience of Saudi Arabians, Palestinians, Syrians and Lebanese. All these peoples differed widely from one another. Syria, Lebanon and Palestine form a narrow causeway connecting Asia and eastern Europe, on the one hand, with Africa on the other. Since the dawn of history, these countries have been endlessly invaded from the north and the south, from the desert and by sea across the Mediterranean. Hittites, Hurrians, Philistines from the Aegean, Greeks, Romans, Arabs, Turks, Armenians and many more have added to their racial composition.

No one, on the other hand, ever wanted to settle in Arabia, until the oil-rush in the 1940's. Syria is perhaps the most invaded country in history, Arabia the least such. Not only all races but all individuals are different from one another. There can be no easy and superficial generalizations for those who wish to understand. Human relations are extremely involved, and the sooner we reject sweeping generalizations and try to understand, the better we shall get on.

Courtesy

I do not want today to speak of battles or of political crises, but to try and tell you some of the things I learned in my thirty-six years with the Arabs. When I went out there in 1920, there were virtually no Europeans outside the big cities. Also, there was no B.B.C. Not that I wish to say anything against the B.B.C. but now that broadcasting exists, British people in Asia can daily recover the atmosphere of England. They live, as it were, looking over their shoulders, counting the days till they can go home. This makes it much more difficult to lose yourself whole-heartedly in the country where you are. I was peculiarly lucky to arrive among the Arabs, when communication with home was extremely difficult. Such a situation may perhaps never recur.

What then did I learn? Firstly, two qualities which some may nowadays think unimportant – courtesy and dignity. Courtesy makes all human relations pleasant and easy. It is extremely practical also. Whether you are engaged on high diplomacy or buying a loaf of bread, courtesy will secure you better terms. For some reason, rudeness among us is considered democratic. The idea is erroneous. To be polite is not to be servile, indeed it is quite the opposite, if we are polite to rich and poor alike.

There are two different types of courtesy in the Middle East, which we may, generally speaking, call 'city' and 'Arabian'. The Syrians seem to me to be the most courteous people I have ever known. Their politeness may be outward ritual but it makes life easier all the same. Some say that they learnt the forms from the Byzantines, or from some much earlier period. When you are entering a doorway, you stand back and invite the other man to go first. When coffee comes round, you ask the coffee man to give a cup to someone else before you. If someone calls at your house, you say what an honour he has done you – and innumerable other little courtesies of the same kind.

The second form of courtesy is native to Arabia and has not been learned from foreign invaders. I remember once an American journalist asking if he could accompany me when I went for a drive in a car. We stopped at a small group of ragged tents in the desert and were invited in for coffee. A few rather threadbare carpets were spread and we sat down.

Seeing visitors, the men from other tents dropped in for coffee and the news. As each walked up to the tent, the other occupants all stood up and offered their seats to the newcomer, as they always do. When we were back in the car and driving on, the journalist burst out, 'Say, that has changed my views of life. I would not have believed that such poor people could be so courteous!' I have always remembered this remark, with its unconscious self-revelation of the attitude that the only 'nice' people are those who have money. This native Arabian courtesy characterizes their relations among themselves. The early explorers called them 'nature's gentlemen', but nowadays we despise them because they do not have money.

In all Arab countries, today there are two cultures:

(1) Traditional forms of living and of human relationships.

(2) The 'educated' minority, whose principal aim is to imitate Western customs.

The ways of life to which I shall refer in the rest of this paper are of the old and traditional culture.

Dignity

I said that I had learned from the Arabs not only courtesy but dignity, a quality which is basic to all Middle East cultures. One is often ashamed of Western visitors in the company of the local people. No Arab will lounge back in his chair, stick out his legs, yawn or roar with laughter with mouth wide open, unless it be in the absolute bosom of his family. In company, he will sit up straight, talk in a normal voice and never be loud or conspicuous. Europeans or Americans, scantily clad, who lounge around, shouting and making a noise, seem barbarians to these dignified people.

Western people, at least the more educated, used of course to obey much the same code of manners as people in the Middle East do now. It is presumably the wealth produced by the industrial revolution in the last two hundred years, which has changed the social behaviour of the West.

Religion

To the casual visitor, Arabs do not normally seem very pious. (Those who are trying to impress you with their modernity and Westernization may tell you that they are atheists.)

Muslims are required to pray five times a day, wherever they may be. Many do not do so. Modern ways of life sometimes make it difficult. The prayers are supposed to be preceded by washing the hands, face and feet, but this is difficult, for example, for office-workers or factory workers. It is complicated for people wearing European dress, to take off their socks and shoes. I must admit that I often met men who excused themselves from praying at the set times, owing to the impossibility of performing their ablutions. Few consider that it would be better to pray unwashed, than not to pray at all.

Incidentally, these five daily prayers are not really prayers at all, but little services of praise. There is a different word in Arabic for petitions to God. All the verses and prayers repeated five times a day are glorification of God.

Whether or not they perform all the rites exactly, it is still possible to say that all Arabs (except a few completely Westernized) believe in God. They accept His existence and the fact that He is Almighty and All-Merciful. Perhaps it is illogical to believe completely in God and yet to lead a life not solely dedicated to Him, but most men do that whatever their religion may be.

Among traditional Arabs, God is always present and always on their lips. Any reference to the future is always qualified by the phrase, 'If God wills'. Any enquiry regarding health, status, business conditions and so on, receives the reply 'God be praised'. When saying goodbye to someone going away, you say 'In God's safe keeping'. When your friend tells you he has opened a new business or bought some land, you say 'May God give you success'. If you yourself are setting out to go somewhere, you do not say, 'It is time to start', or 'Let's go', but 'Let's put our trust in God'.

Some of these phrases are conventional and do not mean very much, but I cannot help feeling that this continual mention of God does produce a stabilising effect on their characters.

An implicit belief in the existence of God certainly seems to provide a secure background for life. There are, for example, no suicides among these people. One of the commonest sneers directed against Muslims is that of fatalism. We are asked to think of them sitting inert waiting for fate to decide their lot. This charge seems to me completely misleading. They are as active as we are in pursuing their own affairs or defending their own interests.

The only foundation of which I can think for this charge of fatalism is that they accept their defeats and set-backs calmly. Instead of despairing or shooting themselves, they shrug their shoulders and say that such was God's will. It is a form of acquiescence in the inevitable. When the worst has happened, they do not rage against God and man. They say 'Praise to God; He wanted it that way', and resume their normal activities.

It seems to me that most of our mental breakdowns and suicides are due to our loss of belief in the existence of God. Dr. Jung, the great psychologist, is alleged to have said that the principal need of most of his mental patients was a firm religious faith.

Of course, we like to attribute the constant increase of nervous breakdowns and mental illness to 'the stress of modern life'. But I cannot help feeling that Arabs often live under greater stress than we – for example, the Palestine refugees, driven from their homes and their country by military force, and left to wander homeless and penniless year after year.

In the poorer parts of the Middle East, in the years when the rains fail, I have seen children picking individual undigested grains of barley out of horse and camel dung lying on the road. Tuberculosis is also terribly widespread among the poor and I have seen anguishing little families, the mother obviously coughing herself to death, with three or four children around her breathing in the disease. Yet there are no nervous breakdowns or suicides.

I cannot help feeling that it is their basic faith in the existence of God, which helps them to bear such terrible misfortunes and hardships. When we deny God, we have no remaining object in going on living. A materialist who loses his material wealth has nothing to hope for or live for.

Money

Most of the traditional Arabs among whom I lived presented a phenomenon entirely strange, perhaps incredible, to the modern Western mind – they did not live for money.

Of course, like all of us, they needed money to live, but the accumulation of money was not important to them. This is not intended as a criticism of people in the West – our civilization has developed in a manner which compels us to attach importance to money, and we live in fear of losing it and being left destitute. This situation, however, is also partly due in the West to the break-up of the family. Old people are not cared for and loved by their children, but are often thrust into some public institution, leaving the young to live as they wish without 'encumbrances', until they, in their turn, grow old and are pushed into a 'home' of some kind.

Among Arabs, such things cannot happen. The family automatically undertakes responsibility for all its members, and ageing people need not fear poverty or loneliness, and thus do not feel the constant struggle to accumulate money. I remember an old man saying to me, 'money is like dirt on your hands. One day it's there and the next it is gone'.
He was sitting cross-legged on the ground, boiling up a pot of coffee, on a little fire of twigs. He shrugged his shoulders philosophically – why worry about money?

One advantage of this lack of interest in money is that the poor are not jealous of the rich, as they are in the West. In general, Arabs are jealous people but not about money.

Lack of appreciation of this factor has led the Western Powers, particularly the United States, into innumerable errors. After the Second World War, American policy seemed to be largely based on the belief that the people of Asia only wanted money. 'Give them a higher standard of living and they will be quite happy', was the idea. This prescription, which was drawn up without examining the patient, was based on an entirely wrong diagnosis.

Of course, money is useful but not in return for a loss of dignity. The Western Powers themselves decided (quite sincerely in many cases) what the peoples of Asia needed, but they did not take much trouble to consult them, because they were 'backward peoples'. But when the money came, together with instructions as to how it should be used, it was often rejected. The West then denounced the Asians as being ungrateful. It was a sad misunderstanding.

Their unwillingness to put money first is described in the West as 'oriental lethargy'. To most Western minds, making money is thought to be the basic human activity. They unconsciously assume that Asians hold the same view. The fact that they do not pursue this activity with all their energy is interpreted to be due to feebleness and lack of intelligence. No one in the West could visualize that there may be intelligent, strong and active people, who do not consider money-making as the purpose of human life.

Unfortunately our ideas are gaining ground. The many Asian students who graduate in Western universities carry home with them the news that the object of human life is to make money. They are partly persuaded to this view by the contempt of Western nations for poor countries. It is unpleasant to be treated as an inferior, and Arabs who mix for several years with the Western peoples, wish to introduce money-making, socialism, slack sexual morals and other Western customs of today, in order to escape from the slur of inferiority. Perhaps such influences will prove superficial and eventually fade.

When I first went to Jordan in 1930, there were no great differences in wealth, social classes or standards of living. Farmers and stockbreeders who borrowed money from merchants gave no receipts. Everyone trusted everyone else. I was interested in the indebtedness of the rural population and I often asked a nomad tribesman how much he owed to a merchant. As often as not the answer was, 'I don't know. Ask him'.

But all this has changed since Western laws and judicial

procedure have been introduced. Merchants will no longer lend to a farmer without a legal document and a mortgage on the farm. If the rains fail in two consecutive years, the merchant forecloses on the mortgage and the farm becomes his property. He does not take it over, he leaves the farmer there. But henceforward the farmer pays a crippling 'rent' to the merchant for what was his own farm. The merchant grows rich and sends his son to a university in the United States. The farmer becomes a wage-slave on his own land.

When the sons return from America, they are 'educated'. They now form a superior class which looks down with contempt on the serfs who work on the land, whereas the grandfathers of both had been equals.

Western society today bitterly criticises in its own countries, the gap in income between rich and poor and the separation between social classes. Yet the Arabs, before the West came to them, were largely a classless society, with only a small gap between rich and poor. As a result of the introduction of Western ideas, the rich have grown richer and the poor poorer, and class distinctions have divided the people.

It is, of course, true that in large cities, like Damascus, Aleppo and Baghdad there always were rich business men. But over the greater part of these countries there was far more social and financial equality than there is now.

Children

Under traditional Arab conditions, children grew up naturally in their families. In most cases, they continued in the family way of life, whether they were shepherds, farmers, merchants or whatever they might be. There was no caste system nor were there different social classes, but to follow on with the family occupation came naturally.

In towns, the boys went to day school and the girls learned domestic duties in their families. There were no clever people about, telling them that their parents were not handling them correctly and suggesting other ways of life. For all practical purposes, the boys served their apprenticeships in their families, it being understood that 'family' did not mean father and mother and the children, but a wide circle of aunts, uncles, grandparents, cousins and more distant connections and neighbours.

Living among such a cross-section of the community, amid people of every age from babies to grandmothers, no one had ever heard of a 'generation gap', a sickness gratuitously invented by us in the last thirty years.

We collect thousands of young people together in colleges or universities, cut off from family contacts. In the United States, there are universities of thirty-five thousand or more students. I taught for one term at such an institution. I was accommodated in a little house on the campus, but all the professors lived out, sometimes several miles away, and 'commuted' to the college every morning. At night, I was the only adult on the campus.

In the larger universities, the professors often did not know the names of their students, nor, in some cases, did the students know the names of the professors or the lecturers. There were few if any human relationships, and virtually no guidance, advice, consultation or personal contacts. Teaching became the cramming of 'facts' into the students' memories. This left no scope for influence, for character building, for absorbing the wisdom or the philosophy of the professor.

Governments at the same time, press the universities to increase their 'output' of students, just as they press factories to raise their output of cars, porcelain, electronics, lipstick or whatever it may be. University education becomes increasingly a production-line, mass-output problem. Students are fed in at one end, 'facts' are placed in their memories as they pass along the conveyor belts and, at the other end, they come out graduates.

Adolescents suffer from intense emotional problems, increased by the introduction of co-education. But their problems are by no means limited to sex. The object of life, the existence of God, the reform of society and a hundred other problems involve them in emotional and spiritual anxieties. For four or five years, at this most sensitive time of their lives, they are cut off from the natural, loving and essential advice and sympathy of mothers, fathers and relations. No wonder many become delinquents, drug-addicts, or suicides.

The other side of this tyrannical system is that academic degrees are considered the one essential to success. Character, honesty, experience, courage are never enquired of, or even thought necessary.

High academic qualifications are really necessary for only a small number of professions. A far greater number of occupations need precisely those qualities which are never thought of and which cannot be academically taught, but only absorbed from other persons with whom we live, or acquired in the rough apprenticeship of life.

None of these problems arises in Arab society, except in a few places where universities have been formed which slavishly imitate Western methods.

To those who have been fortunate enough to live intimately inside both Asian and Western communities, the situation seems ironical indeed. The three problems which today cause the most perplexity in the West seem to be the difference in incomes between the very rich and the very poor, the existence of social classes and the 'generation gap' between young and old. None of these problems existed in Arab society in general (excluding Egypt) before 1914. As the result of the spread of European ideas, all are now increasing in the Middle East.

Wisdom and Knowledge

One of the most striking peculiarities of life in this country, which has impressed me since my return to Britain, is the loss of our appreciation of the difference between Wisdom and Knowledge.

This development is doubtless due to the expansion of science in education, and to the general veering of the attitude of the general public towards what they believe to be science. In general, what we call science is the study of the material facts of this world. These facts can be ascertained and committed to memory. They are normally governed by laws, that is to say that certain processes may be trusted always to produce the same result.

Thus material science, like mathematics, is the result of cause and effect and can be mastered with accuracy. A vast amount of 'knowledge' of these material phenomena has been accumulated and can be known. More knowledge of material facts is constantly being acquired and added to the store.

Wisdom is as different from knowledge as chalk is from cheese. It is an activity of an entirely different nature. Wisdom cannot be taught to a class nor learned from a text book. It is the art of living and can only be acquired by experience gained in the process of living. While it is true, that it cannot be taught in a set lesson, it can to some extent be 'caught' by living with another person or other persons, who are wise. But, really, to know how to live can only be ascertained by living.

Wisdom is thus an art which deals with human beings, for the secret of happy and successful living lies in our relationship with other people. It is an atmosphere, an attitude, at times it almost seems like an aura.

Wisdom has no connection with acquired knowledge. An old peasant may be wiser than the world's greatest scientist. Sometimes, indeed, wisdom and knowledge seem to be incompatible. Great knowledge can often produce intellectual pride, and a contemptuous attitude towards 'uneducated' people. Humility is the essence of wisdom. Pride and arrogance are the very antithesis of wisdom.

I remember once calling on the Ameer Abdulla of Jordan. As I entered the ante-chamber, a number of politicians came out of the king's room. When I was shown in, he said to me,

'If I were to drive out into the desert, and stop and ask the first shepherd I met whether we should fight against the Jews in Palestine, he would ask me, "How many men have you got and how many have they?"'

'Even a shepherd knows that there is no use fighting if you cannot win. But these politicians all have university degrees, they despise all of us who have not. Yet if I prove to them that we shall lose by starting a war, they reply that Zionism is unjust, we must fight. I agree as much as they do that it is unjust, but it is not wise to fight when the enemy is stronger.'[i]

On one or two occasions I have remarked that I have known village headmen in Asia, who were wiser than the President of the United States. I am regarded as a lunatic, yet there is nothing absurd in such a statement.

Sometimes I wonder whether a technological age is compatible with wisdom. In theory, of course, a physicist or a mathematician can be as wise as anyone else. But our occupations produce impalpable effects on our minds, of which we ourselves are entirely unaware. Certainly living in a constant hustle is incompatible with wisdom, which requires not only humility but a measure of detachment from the wild rush of modern city life. There is much truth in the saying that we have learnt how to control matter, but have lost the art of controlling men.

Politics

We are rightly proud of the fact that we no longer persecute people for their religious beliefs. But, in politics, we are as narrow as our ancestors were in religion. We are as small-minded, perhaps more so than were our ancestors of several centuries ago.

Nobody, in any age or country, has found the ideal way of governing men. When we look around us today, with our strikes, our protests, our financial crises, our rising crime statistics, we can scarcely claim that we have found the perfect system. Yet we insist that everyone else in the world must adopt our methods.

Presumably the ideal of government is to find the correct balance between authority and freedom. The perfect method of achieving this end is for the people to love their rulers and, consequently, to obey their authority willingly without compulsion.

On one occasion during the Second World War, a foreign correspondent asked if he could tour Jordan. We gave him all the facilities he requested, but we did not give him an escort, who might have inhibited his conversations with the local people. He returned in a fortnight and the first thing he said was, 'This is the first country I have ever visited where everyone I have spoken to praises the government'.

Many years later, when I had left Jordan, I was being interviewed by a British journalist, who said to me, 'I assume you would agree that the government of Jordan in your time was entirely reactionary and feudalistic, and really an anachronism in the modern world?' A comparison between these two stories seems to me enlightening.

It may, perhaps, be admitted that Asian governments used to tend towards paternalism, a word rarely used in this country without a sneer. The relation of the government to the public was like that of a father to his children – one of affection and mutual understanding. Such systems were often extremely happy, as I know from experience. To be contented with the government is called, in the West, 'Asian lethargy'.

Living in England, we take our 'democracy' for granted without much thought, but coming to this country after thirty-six years in Asia, certain points impress one forcibly. One of those which I found most interesting was that our democracy always means strife. Europeans who came to Jordan, in the old happy days when everyone liked the government, would urge the people to form an opposition. A situation where everyone was happy was not democracy.

During the period of the Mandate in Palestine, the British

government gave orders that Trade Unions must be established. There were no industrial disputes, which was assumed to mean that somebody must be oppressing someone else. The Trade Unions remained in existence on paper until the British left, when no one ever heard of them again.

Presumably the Western assumption is that all men must seek their own interests, and consequently that the strong will always oppress and defraud the weak. The assumption is not correct. The most important thing about every organisation is not its laws or its constitution, but the spirit which inspires it. Spirit is not allowed for in a materialist system, which is chiefly interested in money.

In fact, however, under traditional paternalistic systems, a spirit of affection does often unite the ruler and the people thereby producing a happy country, until Western democracy arrives on the scene and sets every man against his neighbour.

This constant desire to provoke a quarrel is to me very curious. I was once giving a lecture in England, when somebody stood up and contradicted me. The chairman rubbed his hands with delight. 'This is fine,' he said. 'Now we can have a good row.'

In the United States, I have often been asked to engage in a public debate with someone thought to hold opposite views. The result of such public debates is usually that both sides go much further than they would otherwise have done. Moreover the audience gets angry also and both sides to the debate become much more violent and malevolent than before. We constantly lament the bitter hatreds with which we are surrounded, yet most of them have been introduced and stoked up to fever heat by ourselves.

Government

The Prophet Muhammad began life as a religious teacher, but gradually became the ruler of a community which depended solely on him. He found himself their judge, their administrator and their army commander. When he died, his successors sought only to imitate his example. Every successive Muslim regime was ruled by a single man, who was the religious, political and military head of the community.

In theory, the ruler must be the best available man for the post. In theory, also, the headship of the State was not hereditary, and quite often it was not so in fact. The ruler, when selected, was not supposed to surround himself with royal pomp and ritual. The early Arab Khalifs used to walk in the streets, rubbing shoulders with their fellow citizens.

Accessibility

The key to the traditional Arab form of government was accessibility. The ruler frequently, sometimes every day, sat in an open hall to which everybody was admitted. Anyone present could address him, explain his grievance and ask for redress. Sometimes a messenger was sent off immediately to bring the person against whom the complaint was made, and the affair was settled immediately. In any case, there were no lawyers, no legal fees and no avoidable delays. Everyone had direct access to the man who had the power to give a decision.

When the Arabs had conquered a great empire, it was, of course, no longer possible for the Khalif (Caliph) in person to hear every complaint. But the same system was reproduced on a smaller scale in every province, where the local governor would sit in public every day and hear complaints.

It may, of course, be admitted that so simple a system could no longer be applied in a complicated society like our own, with such immense numbers of laws which only professional lawyers can understand. Two points, however, are worth recording.

Firstly, that the Arabs did have a system of government, which was highly developed and produced and administered the largest empire the world had ever seen.

Secondly, that the basic principle of their system was that one man must be responsible for every job, and that he must be accessible to his public. If he proved unsatisfactory, he could be dismissed, or even murdered, and a better man appointed. But the Arab system made no allowance for government by assemblies, committees or other joint bodies.

By contrast, our own system today has completely lost the chief asset of the Arab system, namely accessibility. No single man is responsible for anything. Information conveyed to complainants always takes the form that the council, the committee, the department, or whoever it might be, decided this or that.

In addition to the fact that, with us, the individual is always concealed in a committee, the immense and increasing amount of paper work with which all officials are flooded, makes it difficult for them to see, and listen to, people. The result is a dehumanized and depersonalized machine. In the Middle East, human relationships are of supreme importance. They cannot understand a depersonalized system conducted in official memoranda, or loyalties to vague ideas like socialism, capitalism or communism.

Personally, I think that different nations need different systems, many of which are based on traditions thousands of years old. If I criticize at all, it is the arrogance with which we assume that our particular system is the only one which should be followed by the whole human race. 'Western Democracy' may or may not be the best system for us. But no one has discovered the ideal system of government and many other forms exist, some of them with traditions much older than ours, and which operate successfully in the various countries where they originated.

I feel that we are not justified in demanding that all these other nations abandon their traditions and institutions and adopt our own.

Chivalry

There is one other point to which I should like to refer, because it has always appealed to me, even if it may not be thought important in the modern world. It is the origin of Chivalry.

Before the preaching of Islam in the seventh century A.D., the Arabs consisted largely of nomadic tribes, which lived in the desert, where they carried on endless wars against one another. These wars, however, were governed by strict rules of honour, and had virtually no political object; that is to say, no tribe wished to conquer, subdue or exterminate another tribe. Perhaps their basic cause was the need felt by the tribesmen for some excitement and glamour in their otherwise monotonous lives.

The object of their wars, therefore, was to provide a means by which men could win honour, rather than wealth or power. Thus to fight honourably was more important than to win. When men compete for honour, it is natural that women should be the arbiters of honour, and it is for their favour that men compete. This factor gave women an honourable status among the bedouin tribes, which they did not enjoy in the cities or in the agricultural community.

It was these very nomads who formed the spearhead of the Arab conquests. The Romanized populations of Syria and Egypt rejected these nomad customs and the bedouins passed on with the wave of conquest, many of them finishing up in Spain or in Afghanistan.

In Spain and in the south of France they established their ideas of war for honour, and a chivalrous attitude towards women. It is not always remembered that the Arabs remained in Spain for nearly eight hundred years, a period as long as from Edward III to ourselves. During the early centuries, first Normandy and then Southern France, belonged to the King of England. Thus France, Spain and England, the homes of European chivalry were all in close touch with the Arabs of Spain.

Dr. Levi-Provencal, a great French scholar, is the best known expert in our times on the subject of the Arabs in Spain. Many English people are surprised to read one of his statements to the effect that 'the Arabs taught Europe respect and courtesy to women'.

NOTE

(i) This occurred in 1948, just before the end of the British Mandate and before the Proclamation of Israel.

2

Gond Society and Lore

Gondwana is the name that the Mughals gave to a large area of Central India, much of which is now Madhya Pradesh. Amongst the hills and within the thick forests, have traditionally lived a most extraordinary people: the tribe of the *Gonds*. It is not known how many Gonds there are, or indeed how many there ever were. Research and information has been hampered because of the inaccessibility of their territory.

This monograph looks at the history and social structure of the Gond tribe. It notes their developed use of symbols, their religious practices, as well as the ancient lore and use of sacred magic, that are unique to the Gonds.

The topographical nature of Gondwana has provided the Gond people with unparalleled isolation. The dense jungle and wooded areas were avoided for centuries by explorers, missionaries and conquering armies. The fact that Gondwana was avoided, as traders and adventurers usually passed down its western side, meant that the area is not mentioned in many accounts of Indian history. This isolation allowed the Gond, as well as other tribal societies, to evolve in completely different ways from those in more accessible areas in Central India. Gond beliefs, lore, magic, superstitions, and social structure are set very much apart from the dominantly Hindu areas of Central India. The Gonds were seen by all about them as heathen barbarians. Most of those writers who mentioned them, including many of the early British anthropologists, looked down upon them as a primitive aboriginal race. Comparatively recently, the surprising social cohesion and sensibility of the Gonds has begun to be understood. The tribal unit, with its extraordinarily effective systems of regulation, provided the Gonds with a strong sense of unity. Abu'l-Fazl Allami, the legendary Muslim chronicler at the time of Akbar, wrote a few damning words about the Gond people and their society:

> In the spacious territories of India there is a country called Gondwara, the country inhabited by the Gonds. They are a numerous race and mostly live in the wilds. Having chosen this as their abode, they devote themselves to eating and drinking and to venery. They are a low-caste tribe and the people of India despise them and regard them as outside the pale of their realm and religion. The east part of the country joins Ratanpur which belongs to Jharkhand, and the west is contiguous to Raisin which belongs to the province of Malwa. Its length [from east to west] may be 150 kos. On the north is the country of Pannah, and on the south the Deccan.[16]

History of Gondwana

It is thought that the Gonds are descended from the Dravidian race (of which the Tamils of Southern India are also members). Another thesis is that they came from Baluchistan: as their customs and language resemble the *Brahuis* tribe who live there. They are a stocky, dark-skinned people, distinguished in looks from the newcomers to Gondwana. Early Gond society was extremely nomadic, largely concerned with herding cattle and goats, or sometimes clearing a patch of land to cultivate before moving on. Their attitude towards land seems to have much in common with the aboriginal race of Australia: for whom also, ownership of the land was not traditionally a concept used by the society. It is not clear when the Gonds actually moved into the region which became Gondwana. Their legends assert that the tribe were created there, and never inhabited another place.

It seems that some five hundred years ago a number of Rajput adventurers started to explore the hilly jungle regions of Gondwana, which until that time had been left completely undisturbed. Some of these Rajput knights, who were of vague royal descent, married daughters of the Gond chiefs. As a result several small kingdoms were founded, and a basic trend of development was instigated within the Gond civilization.

These Gond Rajahs ruled in earnest for four centuries. Fortresses of some size were constructed on hilltops around Gondwana, such as the ones at Deogarth and Chauragarth. There were four main kingdoms, which were influenced to a certain extent by both Islam and Hinduism. Despite these influences, the Gond kings managed to keep hold of the reins of power, and the influx of new ideas and traditions were often assimilated into Gond culture as if they had always existed there. The fact that there never was any Gond literature, as the *Gondi* language was never written, meant that from one generation to the next, traditions and behaviour were able to change.

One of the last great Gond Rajahs was Hirde Shah. After his death his kingdom crumbled, and the fortunes he and his ancestors had amassed were spent buying off the enemies of subsequent generations. Hirde Shah built a substantial palace at Ramnagar near the town of Mandla. Artists from around the region were commissioned to decorate the rooms. The extremely elaborate pedigree of Hirde Shah was inscribed upon the walls of the Court. It ran to some fifty-two verses, and was completed in 1724. A sample follows:

Of this Lord of the earth the queen is Sundari Devi, the abode is prosperity, as being, in effect, the wealth of merit, embodied.

From whom are constantly obtained by Brahmans, elephants, beauteous as dusky clouds, with the copious ichor of their frontal exudations; given with water a donation ever at hand; precluding to the needy the cause of clustering miseries.

Who shines resplendent throughout the world with her fair fame earned unceasingly by endowments in succession as ordained; which endowments, finding, amongst the nations, straightened scope for encomium, reached to heaven; giving forth such effulgence as a hundred autumnal moons would realise.[17]

The kingdoms of the Gond Rajahs collapsed and fell into the hands of the Marathas. This disintegration came about not only because of a lack of further strong Gond rulers, but more particularly due to a completely unruly invasion by the Marathas. Akbar had forged a great highway linking Upper India with the Deccan. He had opened up certain areas, thus providing the Maratha invaders with an easy entrance into Gondwana. In the latter part of the eighteenth century, at the time of the Maratha invasion, many of the Gond people moved to the higher plateaux, where they lived by hunting and basic cultivation. The Marathas seem to have been very savage, to one other as well as to the tribes whose territories they had invaded. Their constant infighting and lack of a central governing body made it comparatively easy for the British to take over in about 1818.

Initial British interests in Gondwana were held by the East India Company, which was anxious to increase its trading links in Central India. By 1820, the British had increased their control in the central territories, first acquiring the northern parts and then, following the death of Raghuji III (the Maratha ruler of southern areas) they gained control of all Gondwana. The influx of Hindus carried on. It had begun during the time of the four Gond kingdoms when a few Hindu sages sought refuge in the jungle areas to contemplate life, and subject themselves to hardship. The British knew these Central Indian Highlands as the 'Central Provinces' – thus the term Gondwana was struck from the maps.

Gond Society

The Gond people no longer form a homogeneous tribe. Their society has been eroded as ever greater numbers of non-Gonds have moved into Gond territories, forcing the indigenous people to move away. The very nature of Gond society, which is in many ways nomadic, means that the Gonds frequently move to new areas, and are not in communication with all other Gonds. As Hindus have encroached into Gond lands, their culture has influenced Gond traditions. It is therefore erroneous to speak of the existence of one Gond people with a single heritage. We must take into account specific examples, and remember that what is done or believed in one Gond community may be quite foreign to another.

Since the rise of the Gond kingdoms, there have been many standards of living amongst the Gond people. The Gond Rajahs had a status equal to many Hindu princes of the time, while other Gonds were living in primitive conditions. However, Gond society is very egalitarian: all Gonds see themselves as equal. As we shall see, there is a head man in a Gond village, and various other people are held in respect, but essentially no one person has any more rights than another.

By tradition, Gonds have got up and left their villages every few years to build others nearby, so their villages are randomly ordered. The grouping of houses varies between the linear and clustered groups. The dwellings are generally thatched with grass, rectangular in shape, made of timber, with low roofs and windowless mud walls. A veranda, covered by the eaves of the roof, is the favourite place for men to lounge about and receive their guests.

It has been rare in past Gond generations for a person to stay in the village of his birth for life. A Gond has no obligation to stay in one village. The fact that, in the past, Gonds would often take off and all desert their village, made it difficult for Indian cartographers to keep up with the uninhabited villages. Until recent times, it was usual for a particular village to be composed of Gonds from the same Gond clan. But now, due to extensive intermingling, it is common for several clans to share the same village.

Gond Beliefs and Customs

The whole of Gond society revolves around omens and rituals, which touch everyday life. The setting up of a new village is no exception. Several families leave for the proposed site, watching carefully for omens that will foretell the prosperity or doom of a new community. For example, if a *Tine* bird crosses the path of the party from right to left, that is taken as a very good sign. But if the bird flies from left to right, the mission is aborted for the day and the group returns home. At the site eventually chosen, an area is cleared and rice is offered to the guardian gods of the village, *Aki Pen* and *Siwa Marke*. Tobacco may also be scattered about in their honour.

Before the full moon, the families who have decided to move take their possessions to the site, and the process of erecting buildings begins. The two people most important to the village are then appointed: the *Patla*, head of the community; and the *Devari*, the village priest. A teak tree is felled and made into a *Munda* post out of respect for Aki Pen. (The Munda post is erected in awe of a particular deity, or in memory of a deceased person – often it is square and pointed at the top.) A sheep is sacrificed to the Village Mother god, to whom the Gonds turn in times of hardship. A stone, known as *Kon Aki* is laid at each of the four corners of the compound, and a small chicken is sacrificed on each. A fifth stone, known as *Gabur Aki* is laid near the Munda post, guaranteeing the village's spiritual safety. The stones create a magical symmetry that is very important in Gond society.

An altar to *Sri Shambu Mahedeo* is constructed with a stone statue, which must not be removed unless the village is uninhabited. Each new settler is approved by the Patla, and gives offerings to the gods. Elaborate rituals regulate exactly what the Gonds can and cannot do. A failure to comply with the necessary ceremonies obligates one to take part in lengthy rites. It is thought that if the rituals are neglected, or something is done which is taboo, wild animals will be enabled to attack.

In some regions of Gondwana, such as Bastar, it is common for all young unmarried members of the village to live together in communal dormitories: known as *Ghotul*. The reason is supposedly for them to learn about civic responsibility. It is the youths' duty to run the Ghotul – adults are not permitted to interfere. Studies have shown that Gonds who have lived in Ghotuls for a time are less likely to have broken marriages: something that is otherwise very prevalent in most parts of Gondwana. It is quite usual for a wife to go and live with another man. Her husband initially tries to persuade her to come back. If this does not work, the couple can divorce – a very frequent occurrence. Contrary to custom in many societies, a woman who has remarried several times is of the same status as a woman who is bound by her first marriage. Men are allowed to have several wives at a time, but this is surprisingly rare. Sexual relations between Gonds are very relaxed, something that scandalises both Hindus and Muslims who have moved into the same areas as the Gonds.

The Patla, or headman, of a village is responsible for organizing social activities, making arrangements for feasts, as well as making sure that visitors to the village are entertained properly. His most important function is to keep morale and the communal spirit high, and to see that cooperation is fostered between the village members. Traditionally, the Patla is allowed one day's free ploughing a year by every adult. In some cases where the Patla has become too greedy or hungry for power, he is replaced by the villagers. If that is impossible, because he owns too much land or comes from a good lineage, the villagers all get up, leaving him, and build another village nearby.

The Patla is also usually the leader of the village council, or

Panch, as it is known. All sorts of disputes and problems are brought to its attention, for adjudication. Its prime function is to maintain a certain social equilibrium in the village, interpreting traditional laws and the wills of the gods. The Panch also decides in matters of excommunication.

There are three ways in which an offender can be ostracised:

(i) *Tapu* – occurs when a Gond mixes sexually or even eats with someone of much lower status than a Gond. It prohibits the offender from using communal pipes, and taking part in village activities. Most importantly, the condition is seen as contagious. Very lengthy and complicated purification rituals must be performed before the offending Gond can regain his standing in society.

(ii) *Jatil Habri Mandana* – much the same as Tapu, but not contagious, and so the offender's family is not affected. No rituals of purification are necessary, but he is cautioned by the Panch.

(iii) Excommunication from taking part in the worship of the clan gods: if, for example, someone has neglected their rituals. It is generally used to bring the offender back into line. Gond society does not seek to punish but to make sure that the offender does not harm or pollute the rest of the villagers.

It is very rare that someone is expelled from the village (except in cases of witchcraft: witches are seen as a grave danger to the village). Worse than expulsion is to treat a Gond as if they were not a Gond, for Gonds are proud to be Gond. The constant rituals and rites and purification ceremonies are used to ensure that diseases and malevolent thoughts are not spread. Pollution through carelessness is a grave matter. For example if a woman at time of menstruation draws water from a well, everyone is forbidden to drink the water until it has been purified. Perhaps the most important social idea upheld by Gonds, is that each Gond is responsible for his own actions. The Gonds have no use for prisons –

the Panch system makes sure that social harmony is achieved.

The village priest, or Devari as he is known, acts as a mediator between the members of the community and the gods. Often the position is handed down from father to son. There are few benefits, and the Devari has little influence outside religious affairs. He is sometimes called to give an explanation of a particular catastrophe. This is done by taking a sacred object that represents a certain deity. He places it on the ground, and recites the names of the gods. It is immovable until the correct name has been mentioned. Only then can the object (such as a clay horse) be picked up by the Devari. When the god responsible for the disaster is known, sacrifices are made to it. Once a year a ceremony is held in which the deceased from the preceding year are formally introduced to their ancestors. The Devari organises ceremonies such as these at the clan shrine, and at other significant places around the village.

The Gonds have seers, or *Bhaktal*, as they call them. When in a trance, they can relay messages and instructions from the gods, and also work as oracles. Like the Devari, the Bhaktal mediates between god and man. Gonds do not believe in a separate spiritual world. They maintain that the deities are all around them and are part of nature (i.e. they are not supernatural). Many Hindu gods have been borrowed by the Gonds and incorporated into Gond tradition. In different parts of Gondwana, various different deities are worshipped. The Gonds are always willing to take on a new god if it is likely to benefit them.

The Bhaktal is empowered to prepare medicines and certain concoctions on the advice of a particular deity. Snakes, bats, frogs as well as fruits and roots are used to cure the sick. The seer can judge which god has been offended. For example, if he says that the Tiger god is angry, a small hut is constructed at some distance from the village. It is built as a residence for the Tiger god, so he will not come and take revenge on the village. If a member of the village dies, the

Bhaktal tracks the ghost of the deceased by omens into a small creature such as a chicken. The animal, representing the ghost in a tangible form, is buried with the dead Gond.

The exorcism of evil spells is very popular. If something does not go according to plan, it either means that a god is upset or that a spell has been cast. It is thought that both witches and sorcerers exist. A sorcerer attacks in many ways: sometimes by transforming himself into a wild animal; or by getting help from a malevolent ghost. He can slip a charm or magical substance into the food of another; or send an animal to attack on his behalf. It is widely believed that no creature will attack a man unless black magic has been used against the victim. Elwin[9–12] cites numerous examples of baths of blood, thought to bestow supernatural powers. In some cases, it seems that the constant threat of black magic hanging over someone drives that person to suicide. In his book *The Story of Gondwana*[8], E. Chatterton wrote of human sacrifice amongst the Gonds. There have been many conflicting accounts concerning these sacrifices which apparently occurred in varying parts of Gondwana. Chatterton mentions the Rajah of Bastar who, he says, had twenty-five of his people put to death as a sacrifice preceding a prolonged excursion, to ensure a peaceful trip.

Symbolism and Myth in Gond Society

As mentioned before, the importance of symbolism in Gond society cannot be overestimated. The range of symbolic articles is highly developed and varies throughout Gondwana. Daily propitiation of numerous deities ensures that the guardians of the village, and the other invisible forces that control the lives of Gonds, are kept at bay. A symbol is usually a rough manifestation of a god, giving the worshipping Gonds something to pray towards, but Gond effigies are not usually as detailed and precise as those in the Hindu religion. They may take the form of, for example, an iron spear head. This represents the great god, *Mahadeva*, and is placed outside a village. Once a year great ceremonies take place to plead for good crops, during which numerous sacrifices are made. Small figures exist in abundance to give protection against wild animals and pests – such as iron forms of ant-eaters which guard against ant infestation. *Dhan Thakur*, a cone of iron which is cast in honour of the god of cattle, is thought to bring about an increase in the stock of cattle. It is believed in Gond society that luck and fortune, and relief from blights and pestilence do not come automatically. These things must be striven for and only the necessary ceremonial rituals can bring them about.

As well as symbols, amulets are worn by the Gonds to shield the wearer from specific dangers. A ring of white metal worn on the big toe protects one from the sting of a scorpion. Finger rings guard against bad spirits. A talisman fashioned from an ant-eater's scale threaded upon a string and tied around the legs or loins, is thought to deflect pain. Amulets with *Satab* leaves enclosed, avert the evil eye and ward off vicious animals.

The strangest relationship in Gond society is that between the Gonds and the *Pardhans*, or bards. It is these people who carry the Gond legends from one generation to the next. The curious thing is that Pardhans are not Gonds, and the Gonds look down on them as extremely inferior. They perform the essential task of reciting the epic Gond legends at rites and feasts, and they do so in Gondi, the Gond language. When speaking to each other they generally communicate in Marathi. They have always been the bards to the Gonds for as long as anyone can remember: and they alone can decide what is remembered, as there is no Gond literature. Pardhans are not permitted to enter Gond kitchens, and Gonds will not eat food prepared by these bards. Neither are they greeted with the usual '*Ram Ram*', or any other formal greetings.

The chief Pardhan plays upon a three-stringed instrument known as a *Kingri*, which is accompanied by wind instruments called *Pepre*. It is to this music that the tales of the Gonds are told. This head bard gives the recital, and his words are echoed by his apprentice bards: who slowly learn the epic myths that go to make up the legend of the Gonds. The Pardhans have traditionally been given an allowance by the community from childhood onwards to recite at village functions. But now that the Gonds are in such a poor financial state, they often cannot afford to pay the Pardhan. As society changes rapidly, the very history of the Gonds is now at stake.

The most developed, and in many ways the most fascinating feature of Gond culture is that of its mythology. Long detailed legends, sung by the Pardhan bards on all occasions, stipulate how the Gond people must behave. They show the ways of their ancestors. These myths are the guiding force which define both routine and etiquette. The very fact that until comparatively recent times, no Gond legends were written down, means that they vary drastically from one area to another. There are several reasons for the variations. Sometimes it is due to great exposure to Hinduism; or the development of a particular clan's own lore. Core legends do however appear throughout Gondwana, the most important of which is the *Tale of Lingo*.

Almost a thousand lines in length, it details the origin of the Gonds and how they were tamed from a barbaric people into the relatively docile group of today. The missionary, Stephen Hislop, first documented the tale in the 1860s and published his version with a transliteration of the original Gond text. Captain James Forsyth, in his book *The Highlands of Central India*[1] (1889), noted its resemblance to the Red Indian legend of Hiawatha. Consequently he presented the epic in Hiawathian metre. Although it has been pointed out that Forsyth's documentation of the legend omits key passages, it remains the most readable and enjoyable form. In this poetic format we can imagine more easily how the epic was traditionally sung by the Pardhans.

The Tale of Lingo

In the beginning there were no Gonds. Gondwana lay peaceful and uninhabited. But the gods were sad because other
tribes existed, but no *Koitor* (literally: men), the name the
Gonds give themselves:

> In the Glens of Seven Mountains,
> Of the Twelve Hills in the Valleys,
> Is the mountain Lingawangad,
> Is the flowering tree Pahindi,
> And the Gods were greatly troubled.
> In their heavenly courts and councils
> Sat no Gods of Gonds among them.
> Then the Strong God Karto Subal,
> The first born of Mahadeva,
> Pondered deeply in his bosom
> O'er a circumstance so curious;
> Pondered thus till on his left hand
> Rose a Portentous Tumour,
> Tumour boil-like, red, and growing
> Bigger daily, daily bigger,
> Till it burst, and from its centre
> Came the Koitor, came they trooping.
> Everywhere they filled the country;
> Killing, eating, every creature;
> Nothing knowing of distinction;
> Eating raw and eating rotten;
> Eating squirrels, eating jackals,
> Eating lizards, frogs and beetles,
> Eating cows and eating calves,
> Eating rats, and mice, and bandicoots;
> So the Gonds made no distinction.

The Gonds ran wild about Gondwana. They did not wash,
and their stench reached the Great God, Mahadeva. He was
furious and threw down *Warche*, the King of Squirrels,

amongst the Gonds. They pursued the squirrel, and followed
it into a cave, where Mahadeva trapped them:

> Some took sticks and some took stones,
> Some took clods and off they scurried
> After Wache, King of Squirrels,
> Hip-cloths streaming out behind them.
> But the Squirrel – Artful Dodger –
> Popped into a hole convenient
> In the mountain Dewalgiri.
> And the Gonds all ran after –
> All but four that stayed behind them.
> Then took a stone Mahadeva,
> Shut them up within the cavern
> Shut them up, and placed the demon –
> Monster horrid, fierce Basamasur –
> Placed him guardian o'er the entrance.

The four remaining Gonds ran off and hid deep in the forest.
Mahadeva's consort, *Parbuttee*, missed the Gond tribe and
their smell, both of which she liked. She pined and fasted for
six months, causing the King of Gods, *Bhagwantal* to worry.
When Parbuttee told of the loss of the Koitor, Bhagwantal
assured her that he would find them. In the forests he spotted
the four wretched Gonds, wandering in misery. He sat in
contemplation. Then making a rain-cloud, he cast a shower
of enchantment over the mountain Lingawangad, where the
four Gonds were. A flower on the tree *Pahindi* opened and
conceived the prophet. From the bud Lingo was born. As he
grew he became restless and pined for people:

> Purest water may be stained;
> Stainless all and pure was Lingo.
> Diamond sparkled on his navel;
> On his forehead beamed the Tika
> Nine years old became my Lingo,
> When his soul began to wonder
> Whether all alone his lot was
> In that forest shade primeval.

Lingo climbed a great mountain, and on its summit he climbed the tree *Mandita*. He peered out over the forest:

> Saw a little smoke ascending,
> Saw and very greatly marvelled
> At this circumstance portentous.
> Wandered on and soon discovered
> In that forest shade primeval,
> Manlike forms four discovered –
> Saw the four Gonds that remained
> Hiding fearful of the Great God.

The Gonds took Lingo on an expedition in the jungle to hunt. In the dense undergrowth Lingo told the Gonds to make a clearing. The Koitor chopped at one tree and got blisters. So Lingo took up an axe and in an hour had created a large field. The Gonds were impressed. He showed them how to sow rice. Rains came and the rice grew high. A herd of *Rohees*, deer, could not resist the temptation: they ate all the rice, leaving only stubble. Lingo was furious. He and the four Gonds set out to trap and kill the Rohees. They left three alive. Lingo told the Gonds to light a fire so the Rohees' livers could be cooked, but their tinder would not strike. He sent them to get fire from the giant *Rikad Gowree*:

> He the very dreadful monster,
> He the terrible Devourer.
> In his field a fire is smoking;
> Thither go and fetch a firebrand.

The Koitor reached the giant's enclosure, they sent the youngest, *Ahkeseral*, to take the fire. He crept up to where the giant was sleeping, but whilst rushing off, he dropped the burning torch on Rikad Gowree. A blister swelled and the giant chased the boy into the forest, but could not catch him. When Lingo heard the Gonds' report he set off to the giant's camp himself. On the way he made an instrument from a bottle-gourd. The giant was still sleeping; Lingo climbed a tree and began to play. When the giant awoke he danced to the music and was happy. He greeted Lingo and they became friends. He offered his seven daughters to wed the Gond men. Lingo refused a wife, but wed the brothers to the giant's daughters. The brothers headed into the forest to go hunting in honour of Lingo.

The daughters swung Lingo gently back and forth in his swing while their husbands hunted in the forest. Lingo slept soundly and when the girls pinched him, his sleep only deepened: and so they hugged him:

> Hugged that very virtuous Lingo,
> Till they woke him from his sleeping.
> Wrathful then was holy Lingo,
> At those wanton Giant's daughters
> Rose the flame of indignation
> From his boots up to his top-knot;
> Looked about him for a weapon,
> For a weapon to chastise them;
> Saw a pestle hard and heavy;
> With it thrashed those Giant's daughters;
> Thrashed them till they bellowed loudly.

When the brothers returned they found their wives all bruised and Lingo sleeping. The women told of how Lingo had tried to seduce them: the brothers in their rage lured Lingo into the jungle and slew him. They gouged his eyes from his face and took them back to play marbles with them:

> Called their wives, and lit some torches,
> Blazing torches made of flaxstalks;
> Played their horrid game of marbles
> With the bored out eyes of Lingo.
> So the brothers four of Lingo
> And those seven nice young women
> Chucked his eyes about like marbles
> For an hour's time by the torch light.

The King of Gods, Bhagwantal, wondered as he sat at

court, where the body of Lingo was. He sent *Kasesur*, the Lord of Ravens, to find the corpse. When the bird had found the remains, Bhagwantal sent *Amrit*, water of immortality, to revive the prophet Lingo. The water was sprinkled upon his wounds and he rose. It was then he sought to find the other sixteen scores of Gonds. He searched long and hard but could not find them. He asked the moon and stars, and then the sun, but they had not seen the tribe of Gonds. Lingo came upon a hermit, the greatest of all magicians, who told him that the sixteen scores of Gonds were shut up in a cave within a mountain. For twelve months Lingo fasted, sleeping on a bed of spikes.

The Great God, Mahadeva, could no longer stand Lingo's penance, and so he went to him and offered him riches to stop. Lingo refused and only pushed the spikes deeper against his flesh – asking for his sixteen scores of Gonds. Mahadeva agreed to provide the Gonds, asking a favour in return. The prophet was to bring the chicks of the *Bindo* bird as an offering to Mahadeva. It was an epic journey and, after many months of weary venture, Lingo returned with a nest of the birds. He offered them to the Great God, who had not expected the favour to be possible. At the cave, the mighty boulder was drawn back and the sixteen scores of Gonds ran out to follow Lingo, and he taught them:

> They travelled through the forest,
> Over mountain, over valley,
> To the Glens of Seven Mountains,
> To the Twelve Hills in the Valleys.
> There they remained with Holy Lingo.
> He the very wise and prudent,
> Taught to clear the forest thickets,
> Taught to rear the stately millet,
> Taught to yoke the sturdy oxen,
> Taught to build a roomy wagon.
> Raised a city, raised Narbumi;
> City fenced in from the forest.

When the sixteen score had prospered well, and had learnt all he had to teach them: Lingo gathered all around him and divided them into clans. He sent for the four wretched brothers and their wives, and they were mixed with the sixteen score. Then he showed them all how to build altars, offer sacrifices and worship the gods:

Thus he taught them, Holy Lingo;
And his last words then he uttered –
'Keep your promise to the Turtle,
To the River-Turtle Dame;
To the Gods I now am going.'
Then he melted from their vision;
And they strained their eyes to see him.
But he vanished, and was seen not.

Disintegration of Gond Society

In the early 1920s, there began a period of extremely rapid exposure which brought Gond society face to face with the outside world. It came about due to several sets of circumstances, one of which was the introduction of the formal British legal system. It encouraged Hindus to enter the areas which were once held exclusively by the Gonds. British policy at the time was, in part, to open up areas of the Central Provinces, to increase transportation and trade, thus generally augmenting the revenue gained from the land. Settlers from Southern and Western India flocked from the heavily urbanized areas, swamping Gondwana. The inception of a system where actually to *own* land, one had to hold the title deed, or *Patta* as it was known, placed the illiterate Gonds in an extremely disadvantageous position. Gond tribesmen had no understanding of how the bureaucracy worked. Very often Hindu and Muslim settlers would quietly go and apply for the Patta for a particular area of land. When the Gonds were about to harvest their crops, the settlers would arrive producing the title deeds. They would explain that they now owned that land and the Gonds would have to move out immediately. Gonds were thus forced to become tenant farmers, only allowed to live on and farm their tribal territories if they paid large amounts in rent to the unscrupulous settlers.

The complex administrative system forced many Gond groups away, to go and live in unwanted areas on rugged hillsides and almost inaccessible tracts. The Gonds quickly turned from a people who were used to moving from place to place, able to inhabit any new site at will, to a tribe of landless serfs. Their troubles only increased when the Gonds started to clear areas of forest at will: the Government's Hindu forest officials would not permit random plots of land to be cleared. The officials were corrupt and so the Gonds, who had no ready cash or knowledge of such ways had little chance of success.

Widespread educational programmes were initially very successful in the 1940s, but stagnated when instruction in the Gondi language was dropped. English and Hindi were adopted in most schools, languages foreign to the Gonds, who had no use for them anyway. Many of the Gond children could not even pass the entrance examinations because they had not had the right basic schooling. Their places were taken by non-Gond pupils. The children of the Pardhans who were traditionally instructed in the Gond myths, could adapt their sharp memories for education. They often excelled far beyond levels that the Gonds could ever dream of achieving. Although they had always been looked down upon by the Gonds, they now found themselves masters of pitiful Gond workers.

As the Gonds became more influenced by the Hindu and Muslim settlers, learning their languages and customs, the deep-rooted Gond sense of priorities was lost.

So in these and other ways, the Gonds began to lose their grasp upon a vast area, one which they and their ancestors had controlled for as long as anyone could recall. The premises of Gond society have been so eroded that the tribe has lost its identity; an identity previously kept intact by a very assertive social structure, which had always maintained a perfect equilibrium. The isolation of the Gonds had provided them with no preparation for the drastic changes that they have had to face in recent years.

With the liberation of the Pardhans, fuelled by education – the very foundations of Gond society became endangered.

The Gonds had no educated elite to lead them either militarily or academically.

As the swarms of settlers landed and chopped down the giant teak and sal trees, the Gonds were driven away, banished from their territories. They had no work, and in many cases were forced to fell their own sacred trees to earn a few rupees. At about this time, Hindu settlers introduced alcohol to their melancholy Gond workforce. Gonds had never tasted distilled liquor before, and droves of labourers were soon addicted to the spirits, on which they would spend all their earnings. The alcohol became an incentive to cut down the forests more quickly or to commit crime. Alcohol production was controlled by the Hindus, and so the Gonds not only lost their forests and their land, but gained nothing in return.

A Visit to Gondwana

Gondwana lends it name to the hypothetical supercontinent *Gondwanaland*, that was once supposed to have consisted of what is now India, North and South America, as well as Australia. The idea was that certain plant forms and geological conditions were to be found throughout all Gondwanaland.

Having read several books about the Gonds, I set off for what had been Gondwana. I headed for the small town of *Gondia* in Madhya Pradesh. It is situated almost centrally in Gondwana, some miles north-east of the former Gond capital of Nagpur. Eagerly, I looked out for signs of the famous teak and sal, for the dense undergrowth of forest land and for the rare flora and fauna that were to be found in this area.

Today the landscape has been stripped of its forest. Only

the most rudimentary vegetation clings to the baked earth. Replanting has become impossible as the topsoil is quickly eroded by the monsoons.

In Gondia, when I searched for the Gond people – I was greeted instead by Hindus from the far ends of India. Had anyone seen a Gond? Everyone shook their heads and laughed. Gonds are very different in physical characteristics from these people who had taken their lands. They are dark and stocky, similar in some ways to the Tamils of the South, who are also Dravidian in origin.

After arriving in Gondwana, it was some time before I came in contact with a small Gond settlement. A few haphazard buildings clung to the dusty earth of a steep slope. Some children played in the dirt, each held an infant smaller than itself. A boy, who spoke broken English, no older than about nine, who had adopted me in Gondia, acted as my guide, translator and companion. We found an old Gond lying under the shade on a tree, his eyes clouded with age, but his memories were clear.

He spoke of how his father had been the Patla in his native village. An outbreak of cholera had killed his parents, and many of the inhabitants. As outside settlers bought more and more land it was impossible to remain free. The village was destroyed when the Government decided to build a road through its land. The old Gond seemed tired of life and awkward in a situation in which he was not a native.

I asked questions about Gond lore. His eyes twitched as if for the first time in many years someone had shown interest in these tales. He recounted briefly some of the passages from the 'Tale of Lingo', but they were deeply admixed with Hindu mythology. I felt that I was witnessing Gond society in its last moments – as if the heart of the Gond race were about to stop. The ancient Gond was weak, and so we left him to sleep under the meagre shade of the thorn tree, and walked off towards Gondia.

Concluding Remarks

It is surprising that the Gond tribe managed to avoid complete assimilation into the Hindu and Muslim ways of existence for so long. Their strength came in part from their language; and in part from the nature of the extraordinary society that they had developed. The rigidity of the Gond way of living and the existence of their explanations about life, had made it quite unnecessary for the Gonds to seek out new solutions to ancient problems, as in many cultures. Their tremendous isolation in the past had enabled them to learn very well how to deal with anything in Gond life; but when exposed to new laws, new religions and new ways of existence, they had a hard time integrating the new with the old.

The gradual exposure of Gondwana and its people to the ways of Hinduism, and to modern laws of the ownership of land, changed the tribal society of the Gonds and has forced them from their hereditary lands. As Gond society crumbled, knowledge of its traditions and ancient lore has been lost. All that remains are a few watered-down traces of their heritage and a few, mostly colonial accounts, of how things used to be.

BIBLIOGRAPHY

1 *The Highlands of Central India*, Captain J. Forsyth, Chapman and Hall, London, 1919.
2 *The Gonds of Andhra Pradesh*, C. Von Furer-Haimendorf, George Allen and Unwin, London, 1979.
3 *Gond Kingdom of Chanda*, K.N. Thusu, Anthropological Survey of India (Government of India), Calcutta, 1980.
4 *Gonds of the Central Indian Highlands*, (Volumes I & II), B. H. Mehta, Concept Publishing Co., New Delhi, 1984.
5 *The Gonds of Central India*, Shelagh Weir, Trustees of the British Museum, London, 1973.
6 *Papers Relating to the Aboriginal Tribes of India*, S. Hislop (Edited by R.Temple), Nagpore, 1866.

7 *The Maria Gonds of Bastar*, W.V. Grigson, Oxford University Press, London, 1938.

8 *The Story of Gondwana*, E. Chatterton, Pitman, London, 1916.

9 *Phumlmat of the Hills*, H.V.H. Elwin, John Murray, London, 1937.

10 *Leaves from the Jungle: Life in a Gond Village*, H.V.H. Elwin, John Murray, London, 1936.

11 *The Maria and their Ghotul*, H.V.H. Elwin, Oxford University Press, Bombay, 1947.

12 *Maria Murder and Suicide*, H.V.H. Elwin, Oxford University Press, Bombay, 1943.

13 *Among the Gonds of Adilabad*, Rao Pagdi, Popular Book Depot, Bombay, 1952.

14 *Gondwana and the Gonds*, I. Singh, Universal Publishers, Bombay, 1944.

15 *Tribal Demography of the Gonds*, B.G. Banerjee, Gian Publishing House, New Delhi, 1988.

16 *The Akbarnama*, Abu 'l-Fazl Allami, translated by H. Beveridge, Asiatic Society of Bengal, (No. 940, in 3 Volumes), Calcutta, 1899. (See Vol. II, p. 323).

17 *Pedigree of Hirde Shah*, translated by Fitz-Edward Hall, American Oriental Society, 1860.

3

Secret Societies of Sierra Leone

AN HISTORICAL EXAMINATION

Sierra Leone, a former British Colony, gained independence in 1961. Its lack of hygiene and unsanitary conditions earned it the title 'The White Man's Grave', during the early years of colonial rule. Although the coastline is generally flat, the jungles of the interior proved exceedingly dangerous for the colonial adventurers. The hazards were both human and animal: for living within the densest of the jungles were certain 'Secret Societies', many of which revolved around cannibalism.

These Societies still exist. They provide for their members a vital education in etiquette, lore, remedies, but most of all they teach survival. The British colonists documented extensively their impressions and association with the Societies. Persecution drove the cannibalistic groups underground. As a result, their already elaborate secret procedures were made more secret to prevent infiltration. The vast majority of secret Societies in Sierra Leone benefit the society by instilling cultural and social values in their young members. Following Independence, the government attempted to reduce the power and size of many of the Societies. This proved very difficult. The clamp-down has made the study of contemporary Societies almost impossible, for the activities of the groups are now protected behind a wall of absolute secrecy. Many Societies still operate in Sierra Leone; but to identify particular groups in detail would be to put them in danger of persecution. For such reasons this monograph seeks to examine the secret Societies in an historical light.

44

We can divide most of the Societies into two main groups: those that are cannibalistic, and those which are not. The more extreme Societies, such as the *Human Leopard* and *Human Alligator Society* were outlawed by the British colonizers – an action that simply made them even more secretive. A few of the less extreme Societies have mild cannibalistic tendencies – but most were established for other reasons completely. They act as an educational system, and through complex initiation procedures seek to teach an initiate all that will be necessary for him, or her to survive in their environment.

This monograph will look at the different Societies that exist, their practices, use of magic, social structure, and their reasons for existence.

Animal Societies

We shall look first at perhaps the strangest of all the groups. They have been grouped collectively as the *Animal Societies*: but are usually known by their individual names. In English, they are called: the Human Leopard, Boa, Alligator, Panther and Baboon Societies. They exist for the purpose of killing people and eating them in sacrificial rites. The most common is thought to be the Human Leopard Society.

The Society's rituals revolve around the leopard. It is in the guise of this creature that its members venture forth from their encampment and stalk their prey. Wrapped in leopard skins, they crawl on all fours through the village. Then they pounce, striking the victim with their three-pronged iron claws, inflicting wounds similar to those of an actual leopard. The corpse is dragged off by the pack, back to the camp, where it is consumed. Those not in the brotherhood might see the animal running off, and think that a real leopard was the killer. But it is thought by many that members of this Society hold the power to transform themselves into leopards in order to slaughter, before turning back to men when the kill is successful.

The Human Leopard Society was recorded for perhaps the first time as late as 1894, when Bishop Ingham wrote this passage in his *Sierra Leone After A Hundred Years*:

The Temnes believe that by witchcraft a man may turn himself into an animal, and, that in that form, may injure an enemy. A man was burned at Port Lokkoh in 1854 for having turned himself into a leopard.[14]

In 1895, a huge increase in the deaths caused by Human Leopard killings was a great worry to the government of the colony and a Bill was passed to try to eradicate such cannibalistic practices. Numbered 15 of 1895, it was entitled *The Human Leopard Society Ordinance*. From that time on it was an offence to own a leopard skin 'shaped as to make a man wearing it resemble a leopard', as well as a three-pronged claw knife, and the 'native medicine known as *Borfima*'.

It is thought that the Human Leopard Society was not in existence until the 1850s, but the extraordinary levels of secrecy involved, prevented the colonizers from obtaining details on the subject. The expansion of the Leopard Society encouraged other such groups to start up. The Human Alligator Society was only discovered whilst investigations were taking place into the Leopard People. In 1901 the first Ordinance was amended to make it henceforth an offence 'to have in one's possession an alligator skin shaped or made as to make a man wearing it resemble an alligator'. The sentence of public execution was announced for anyone breaking the new laws.

Sightings of what appear to be alligators swimming away with corpses are not at all uncommon in West Africa. Anyone unaware that craft fashioned to resemble alligators were in existence, would immediately jump to the conclusion that a living alligator was responsible. Reports by various colonial administrators pointed out that quite often the bodies were not pulled underwater by the reptile, as is usual.

Instead, the replica of the creature would move slowly along just below the surface of the water.

Models of crocodiles were designed around dug-out canoes with which to stalk and consume unsuspecting victims. The Sherbro knew such craft as *kunkube*, and the Mende called them *ilendei*. They were often made from two canoes fixed together, and positioned to form a hollow hull, which could encase the Society's members. The front of the craft would be made up to look like a crocodile's head and mouth. The eyes, made from tiny pieces of glass, were used as spy-holes by the assassins.

Those who saw the animal moving through the water, were unlikely to realise its true nature. The backbone of the craft's upper surface was weighted, making it barely visible above the water-line. Those inside would propel it using paddles, fashioned as crocodile legs, which sprouted from the sides of the craft. Leather, beeswax and other resins ensured that the vessel was watertight.

Killings continued with such regularity that the government was forced to step in. People were disappearing every day – sometimes whole parties of people would just vanish. In 1907, just as things were really getting out of hand, some Human Leopard members confessed and 400 people were arrested. In the same year, the Attorney General issued another Ordinance making it illegal to possess a 'dress made of baboon skins, commonly used by members of an unlawful Society; a *kukoi*, or whistle, commonly used for calling together the members of an unlawful Society; or an iron needle commonly used for branding members of an unlawful Society'. The Human Baboon Society had begun to take off in the Karina district of Sierra Leone. Into a member clothed in the skin of a baboon, flowed the spirits of all at the meeting, or so it was believed. He lunged at the victim (usually a small child) biting off lumps of flesh for the brethren to devour.

Cannibalism

The question arises: 'Why do these people want to eat another human?' Several answers have been put forward. The best substantiated is that cannibalism is thought to increase a man's virility. This is particularly plausible since many of the men taking part in the ceremonies were past the prime of their lives. Another idea is that a certain bond is created between those who eat of the same man which goes to strengthen the brotherhood. Then again, the Leopard People, or the members of other Societies, were merely re-enacting what the wild creature would have done with the corpse.

However, there is yet another reason, which seems to have fuelled the launching of these strange Societies. It is known as *Borfima*, and is the sacred medicine of the *Poro* Society.

The Poro are exceedingly secretive, and amongst the most notorious secret Societies in West Africa. Many other groups have been derived from them. It is with the Poro that the Animal Societies, and in particular the Human Leopard Society, are associated.

One of the first accounts of the Poro was recorded by Major Laing in 1822, when he travelled deep into the jungles of central Sierra Leone. He found that anyone approaching the Poros' lair would be apprehended. An intruder might be given the chance to become a Poro, but would usually be sold as a slave, or simply killed. Major Laing wrote:

> The Purrahs do not confine themselves always to the seizure of those who approach their enclosures, but frequently carry off single travellers, and occasionally whole parties, who are imprudent enough to pass from one town to another in a certain district without applying for an escort from the body. To ensure safety, one Purrah man is sufficient, who, while leading the party, blows a small reed whistle suspended from his neck. At the advice of the *Ba Kooro*, I procured one of these persons as a guide from *Ma Bung* to *Ma Yasoo*, the intermediate country being thickly

inhabited by the Purrah. As we pressed along, they signified their vicinity to us, by howling and screaming in the woods, but although the sounds denoted their neighbourhood, no individual was seen.

As mentioned, the Borfima is sacred to the Poro. The word is thought to be a contraction of *Boreh* and *Fima* which mean 'medicine bag'. Its importance to the Society cannot be overestimated. It is the centre of all rituals, the ingredient needed for all spells and powerful magical activities. In his work *Human Leopards*, published in 1915, Beatty[2] mentions what the actual contents of a Borfima are:

This package contains, amongst other things, the white of an egg, the blood of a cock, and a few grains of rice, but to make it efficacious it must occasionally be anointed with human fat and smeared with human blood. So anointed and smeared, it is an all-powerful instrument in the hands of its owner. It will make people hold him in honour, it will help him in cases in the White Man's Court, it certainly has the effect of instilling in the native mind a great respect for its owner, and a terrible fear lest he use it hostilely.

The Borfima is the symbol on which oaths central to keeping the Society secret are sworn. When it was found that the Borfima was not as effective as it was supposed to be, it was decided that more victims were needed with which to feed the medicine bag. Thus the legend that the Borfima must be 'fed' with human fat, blood and organs came into being. It was with this purpose in mind that Human Animal Societies were created.

William Finch, who was one of the first intrepid adventurers to enter Sierra Leone, wrote in 1607:

To the South of the Bay, some fortie or fiftie leagues distant within the countrey, inhabiteth a very fierce people which are maneaters, which sometimes infest them.[i]

The rise of cannibalism by the end of the nineteenth century was becoming a major problem for tribal chiefs, whose villagers were disappearing at an alarming rate. In 1891, reports reached the Attorney General that a large number of cannibals had been burned to death. Gradually, what had actually happened became clear.

The people of the *Imperri* chiefdom had complained to their chief that members of their families were being taken almost daily and eaten. Their leader sent immediately for the *Tongo-Players* – itself a Secret Society famed for seeking out cannibals. They arrived and built a tremendous fire at the corner of two roads, to burn any cannibals found. Each wore a leopard skin cap with side flaps to cover the face, with a leopard's tail dangling from the back of the cap, with a bell on the end of it.

There were several tests to judge if a person were guilty of cannibalism. One method with an obviously high success rate was to make the suspect plunge his hand into a vat of boiling oil and pull out a lump of blistering iron. If the hand was burnt the man was guilty without a doubt: if not, he was innocent.

When the Tongo-Players were ready to perform, they got the villagers to line up in rows. *Buamor Neppor*, the chief Tongo man, and his two assistants *Akawa* (Big Thing), and *Bojuwa* (Great Thing), walked along the row and, if they saw someone who had all the looks of a cannibal, they would strike the individual over the head with the knob of a staff and thrust them into the fire.

Unfortunately, one of the first to be thus identified as a cannibal was the chief who had sent for the Tongo-Players. They said that he was definitely a man-eater. Between eighty and ninety others were also cast into the flames and burned to death. The colonial officer in charge of the resulting inquiry reported that a heap of charred bones and ash, four feet high was found at the spot where the Tongo-Players had performed. The outcome of the inquiry was that all Tongo-Players were ordered to leave Sierra Leone within twenty-one days or to cease all activities associated with the Society. They left – and cannibal feasts increased as never before.

As the killings continued, the courts documented in great detail the cases of suspected killers who were brought before them. From time to time, a group of Human Leopards, or members of other Societies, would confess. In April 1913, a court found six men guilty of murder and sentenced them to death. In this extraordinary case, one member informed on his brethren during the trial, and an insight into the workings of such Societies was obtained for the first time. The informant told how the Borfima was weak, or so the witch doctor had announced, and it was necessary to feed it up: a murder had to be committed. The chief of the Society chose a member to surrender his adopted son to be the victim. When the man protested, he was told that he too would be sacrificed unless the boy was provided. The man reluctantly agreed.

Two murderers arrived that night at the man's house, clothed in the skin of leopards. The boy was stabbed in the neck, but before he died, he cried out, wakening the village. The murderers ran off, leaving the corpse. In the confusion, the adoptive father of the lad said that the *Koribrah*, the 'Leopard Men', had murdered his son. Later the Society castigated the man for revealing that it had been responsible. Rumours that a wild leopard had killed the child were circulated by the Society. By chance, a District Commissioner heard of the incident while at a market, and went to the village. He looked at the corpse and noticed deep stab wounds in the neck, obviously something of which no leopard is capable. The father, prompted about his earlier 'error', owned up and gave the names of the guilty people. The six, all of whom were branded with a secret sign, maintained that they were just feeding the Borfima. All were condemned to death.

It is common for members of animal Societies to supply their own kin for sacrifice – thus illustrating their abiding allegiance to the brotherhood. Milan Kalous' book *Cannibals and Tongo-Players of Sierra Leone*[13], which is a compilation of court confessions and colonial officers' reports, emphasises testimonies in various cases. Statements made by two Baboon Society defendants follow:

> I am a baboon person. I gave my son Bai to the Society two years ago. Its thumb and one of its fingers were cut off and eaten.
>
> I am a baboon person. I was present when Bai's flesh was cooked. His toe cooked and part of his forehead . . . I ate some of the boy's flesh.[ii]

Poro members lurk deep in the densest undergrowth in the *Poro Bush*. The Human Leopard Society also meets there. The *Big Bush* is roughly constructed from palm leaves and matting which hangs down and hides the enclosure, shrouding the encampment from the outside world. Young males are taken for initiation into the bush when between seven and twenty years old. Usually though, all the Societies hold initiations for those around puberty. The initiation of the youth into the Society is an official mark of adulthood, a time for abandoning childish practices. The novices are taught to sing and dance; they learn the history of the cult; and they are educated in the secrets of the Poro peoples' power. Oaths are sworn, binding the novice to keep all deeds secret, on pain of death.

In the Poro brotherhood, the Borfima is the 'mother' of the Society; and as the mother she makes all its members brothers. It is not uncommon for older initiates to donate a piece of flesh to feed the Borfima so that an unbreakable bond with the Society shall be created. Usually a piece of buttock is removed by a witch doctor and put into the Borfima bag. Thus they believe, the Borfima is made happy.

Classification

In Sierra Leone there are about fifty major Secret Societies. Some are offshoots from the more established ones, other are amalgamations. Many of them exist also in other parts of West Africa, or have been influenced by those in other countries. Three main types have been noted in Sierra Leone:

(1) Mystic and religious;
(2) Democratic and patriotic;
(3) Subversive and criminal.

Societies such as *Bundu* have females only as permanent members, although men are allowed to watch them dance. There may be a male counterpart Society with which their Society is associated. Most of them are cross-tribal, accepting initiates from various tribal groups. The Islamic-based Societies are probably the oldest, amongst them the *Jamboi* and *Sembe*, whose membership, or more certainly whose influence, is to be found across the whole of North Africa.

The main Societies in Sierra Leone are as follows:

Agbaia, Aiyasa, Alligator, Ampora, Andonba, Ankoi, Ankumunko, Baboon, Banban, Baya-Gbunde, Boa, Boibente, Borro-Mia-Gundu, Bundu, Dubaia, Egungun, Gbangani, Humoi, Jamboi, Joosai, Kaloko, Kambonbonke, Kangar, Kemah, Kinki, Kofoo, Koliumbo, Kono, Kufong, Kure, Leopard, Manhammah-Jamboh, Mannekeh, Nanam, Nimm, Poro, Ramena, Raruba, Sande, Segere, Sembe, Tilang, Tongo-Players, Tuntu, Tormai, Wanka, Wunde, Yassi.

It must be noted that, although there are various extremely subversive groups amongst them, like the Human Leopards, most of the Societies perform very important functions for their members.

Their bases are usually at some distance from a village, but many have headquarters in Freetown and other towns. Devotees finance the construction and running of the establishments, often also funding the initiation of the novices which can sometimes take months. The uninitiated are never permitted to enter the enclosure or building which is the heart of the Society: there is often a paranoid fear that an intruder might see something of their closely guarded secrets. Most of the Societies have grades with varying levels of knowledge and secrets being confided to the different members. Originally, the Societies initiated only men, but associated groups taking only women are well established now, like the Bundu, which at first took members only from the *Temne* tribe.

Fees for Society membership, many of which are very high, reflect the Society's degree of exclusiveness. For the Bundus the fees include: a bushel of clean rice, a fowl, a gallon of palm oil, a new handkerchief and a bottle of rum. Poros surrender a particular fee at each fence in their enclosure. Eight leaves of tobacco are given at the outer gate, then twelve leaves at the first inner gate, sixteen at the third fence, and twenty-four at the innermost barrier. Extra gifts are also made to the officials. The more desperate an individual is to join, the higher the fees.

Witchcraft

The witch doctor commands the respect of all members of the Society. The position is often passed down from father to son, although only one may practise at a time. He acts as a skilled herbalist as well as a surgeon, using witchcraft to release his patient from the devil. A Poro doctor has the power to trap a devil in a bottle: the patient can decide whether it should be destroyed or turned into a friendly devil. As well as locating stolen property, witch doctors are capable of telling if a women is guilty of infidelity.

Magic is the central theme for many Societies. It is the reason for the Society's existence, while the Society provides the structure for the sacred and powerful magical knowledge. For the members, as well as for many Western observers, the magic actually works.

Charms and amulets contain the magic by which spells may be cast. A range of objects and materials is employed – some of which are actually used in potions.

Many of the items of great importance in the concoctions

and rites seem to us extraordinary. Others are common in nature, and have been revered by other civilizations. Tortoise shells, lion and leopard claws are used. Gourds, birds' bills and heads (such as that of the hoopoe) snakes' scales, and hairs from a horse's ear are also favoured. Certain body parts were thought especially effective: the underlip of an ass, or a certain piece of a chameleon for example.

Such things are used to give protection or lay harm on another, to prolong life, give strength, success, increase virility, help someone to bargain well, or to get good crops as well as to ensure that evil forces do not intrude at marriages and births.

Witch doctors also learn the remedies necessary to counteract the effects of their medicines. They can amaze their fellows by swallowing poison, thus illustrating their fantastic power. Many of the potions that they concoct have been found to have sound bases as remedial medicines.

As in most primitive Societies, there is a lot of hypochondria. Hypnotism is widely used to put an individual into a trance, and to lessen pain during surgery. A Bundu witch doctor, who had taken a St. John's Ambulance course in Freetown, was seen applying the certificate to the forehead of those suffering from headaches. It was said to work every time.

Rising through the hierarchy of a Society can take decades and in consequence the leader is held in great esteem. He is often seen as something of an oracle to the Guardian Deity, the one who knows all the secrets. The *Suekoi* branch of the *Ampora* Society have a head-dress for their chief. It is topped with the skull of his predecessor, and has feathers protruding above it. The Poro's *Tanga-Tanga* head-dress and mask has a very substantial frame. It is mounted high above the head and has a collection of the skulls of previous chiefs. As many as sixteen skulls have been seen attached to one mask.

Initiation

The candidates for initiation arrive at the front entrance of the bush house. They know that after entering the Society's encampment, their apprenticeship into the laws and secrets will begin. They are taught new ways of behaviour, lore and legends, how to hunt and act in society, as well as the methods by which the Society's secrets are to be kept safe. There are varying kinds of password to learn. Some Societies have straightforward words, others use riddles. The Poros have many riddles such as: 'Can a basket hold water?' or 'Could you pull up a palm tree with your hands?'

In some Societies, the guard or executioner on duty sings a song and the person who wishes to enter must supply the missing words. Sometimes a particular bunch of flowers must be brought. The Ampora sentry holds up some partially hidden sticks; the visitor must say how many sticks are short. The most elaborate form of entry procedure that has to be learned is the system of mazes that various Societies use. The mazes have secret doors, camouflaged pits, and hooks that tear the flesh of anyone who does not know the correct way to move through them.

The *Dubaia* smear the candidates with blood as if their hearts had been pulled out. They are often drugged, forced to take potions and magical herbs with their food, which signify that their past mind and body have died. *Kufong* youths are buried in sand for days at a time. When the drugging is stopped, the candidates are told that they have been reborn. Their bodies ache, they are in a strange place, frightened and disorientated, lethargic from the concoctions – it is easy for them to believe that they are now in another world.

Novices are taught to endure pain in silence, to learn to put up with hunger, thirst, going without sleep; all in an attempt to strengthen their minds and bodies. They are forced to eat inedible food, lapping at a bowl with bound hands. They learn to walk on red hot coals or to sit on a knife blade. Some

Societies force the novices to watch the adults feast, whilst they remain starving. Others are forced to consume a drink known as *chibolo*: made up of a host of ingredients, which may include crystal dust, the faeces of dogs, shavings from the feet of armadillos, scorpions, elephants and crocodiles, as well as specific herbs and creepers.

Boys learn to master weapons; how to maim and kill. Girls meanwhile are schooled in the details of child-birth and marriage. Often a girl will be sent to become initiated at a Secret Society at the expense of her prospective husband, so that she will learn to be a good wife.

The Poro teach that no individual may have ownership of the land. The area within the tribal barrier belongs to the tribe as a whole. If the land is sold, the revenue from the transaction is seen as blood money, gained by the betrayal of the tribe.

Similar to the practices of the Borfima, the *Butwa* Society of Angola used an extraordinary magical mixture. The initiate-to-be had to learn the properties of this concoction, and swear all oaths upon it. It is mentioned here because it is thought to be representative of the potions used by the most secretive Societies in Sierra Leone. It was said to contain human tissue, as well as organs and bone from the human victims of the Society. Also present were pieces from animals, such as the heart of a leopard, claws from a lion, parts of an elephant's foot, the eyes from a bird of prey (such as the osprey), the head of the *ngweshi* serpent, teeth from hyenas, a crocodile's nostrils, powder obtained from a crushed meteorite, the head of a newly-born baby, the eyebrow from a vulture and hairs from the head of a dead leader of the Society.

At last comes the end of initiation rites. Successful candidates are carried out of the huts on mats, their clothes burned and new garments given to them. *Yassi* girls are painted with spots, whilst Kufong boys have their eyes painted with *to-pirey*, a lotion made from cork bark. A special magical name

is usually chosen for each by the witch doctor, something
that reflects the character of the initiated.

Communication within the Societies

Many of the Societies have complete languages of their own,
known by the full members. In others, letters of words in
the tribal tongue are transposed to create an unrecogniz-
able variant. Plays on words are used in the epic songs –
knowledge of such word-play can identify one as a member.
Through the songs, which are sung at rites and celebrations,
a general feeling of solidarity is achieved. Each Society has a
distinctive cry. The Bundu women shriek whilst raising their
hands into the air, before pressing them onto the earth. The
Tongo-Players call ahead like owls; the Ampora summon
their members by using a tortoise shell as a gong.

Drum language is widespread, since beats made by a large
drum can carry messages many miles across the jungle. The
Kufong's *fange*, a war drum, is said to be fashioned from the
thigh bone of an enemy chief. The Yassi use a hollowed-out
tree trunk with a hide spread tightly across it, and played by
up to three men. Other instruments, such as roughly made
rattles, xylophones and flutes are used. The Dubaia send
messages by means of a selection of small items. Each signifies a particular topic or idea. For example, a pebble sent to a
friend signifies that the sender is hard, strong, and therefore
well. The Kufong are experts with knots. One man will make
a series of knots in a piece of twine; another will identify
himself by making the necessary knot to complete the sequence. Or messages are sent through knotted codes, unbreakable by an enemy Society.

Signs and Symbols

The number 'three' is thought to be sacred and very powerful in many Societies. Pora and Ampora rites are repeated
three times; Bundu songs are sung thrice, in groups of three.

Witch doctors commonly give medicaments in threes, such as in the *Banban* Society where three leaves of a certain plant will be prescribed.

Symbols of invincibility are used, many of them mathematically strong, symmetrical and simple. They are placed outside the entrance to the base and tattooed or painted onto the members during ceremonies, as well as being etched on stones and other objects to be used in ceremonies, thus asserting the magical presence. Some are drawn in a particular way, such as the Kufong's pyramid, which must be constructed in the dirt using a stick held between the palms of both hands.

Variations

Attempts to document a Society's age were not undertaken until the colonizers had arrived. The legends and epic tales that each Society retells have no recognised dating systems, but one of the first established Societies is thought to be the *Manhammah-Jamboh*. It is an Islamic Society, termed by early colonial explorers as *Mumbo-Jumbo*. Groups of the Society have been found as far north as Fez and as far south as Luanda, the capital of Angola. The Mahammah-Jamboh and other ancient Societies have extremely rigid structures. They are usually set up by men for men, but at times offer honorary membership to women. Some Societies offer membership to all those belonging to another Society. *Na-nam* for instance invites Poro, Bundu and Yassi members to join their ranks. Societies such as Poro take initiates from a wide spectrum of tribal groups, such as Fula, Kafu-Bullom, Koya, Mende, Sherbro, Susu and Temne. Poro, which is thought to have originated in French Guinea, is heavily influenced by the powerful West African *Si'mo* Society.

Nimm, which exists throughout West Africa, and has religious beliefs, was taken by slaves to St. Domingo, as well as to other parts of the West Indies. It was in this way that the Nimm's *Voodoo* practices travelled west.

Ankoi and *Sande*, both of which are women's Societies, are break-away groups from the Bundu, but rival the Bundu in power. The *Kofoo* is the female branch of the Kufong, the latter being the greatest rival to the Ampora. They maintain that they have the ability to enable a member to levitate. *Koliumbo* is mainly for farming people, with secret rituals and rites for harvest. Societies such as the *Borro-Mia-Gundu*, although having passwords and secret emblems, are benevolent, and act as co-operatives for the benefit of their members.

Kaloko and *Aiyasa* are primarily dance Societies. Elaborate masks and costumes are used in ritualistic dances dedicated to the ancestors of the cult. Magical movements are taught to pupils from the age of five and upwards.

Politically motivated Societies, such as the *Kinki*, were heavily restricted by the colonial administrations, having at one time been extremely powerful. The activities of such Societies are by their nature well-concealed, but their existence is still thought to be widespread.

Indeed, in April 1992, a man was convicted in central Sierra Leone for dressing in a Baboon costume, and trying to make off with a baby. The report (carried by the Reuters News Agency) illustrates that the 'Animal Societies' are certainly not near extinction. The account follows:

FREETOWN, April 5, – Reuter – A Sierra Leone man who donned a Baboon outfit and tried to snatch a baby away from its sister has been jailed for 10 years for trying to perform a ritual murder, a local newspaper reported Sunday.

The newspaper, *Vision*, said hundreds of onlookers packed the high court in Makeni, in the centre of the West African country, for the trial of the man known as 'the human baboon'.

His suit – made of raffia and palm thatch with a convincing baboon mask – was among the evidence displayed in court.

James Kargbo was found guilty of attempted murder and third-degree assault and given three 10-year sentences to run concurrently.[iii]

NOTES

i From: William Finch's *Observations in Sierra Leone in 1607. A New Collection*. Printed in 1745. See Bibliography[18] below.

ii From: Sierra Leone Government Archives; Minute papers 1913. See Bibliography [13] below.

iii By kind courtesy of The Reuters News Service, 5 April 1992. 'HUMAN BABOON' FOUND GUILTY IN RITUAL MURDER CASE.

SELECT BIBLIOGRAPHY

1 *The Sherbro and its Hinterland*, T.J. Alldridge, Macmillan & Co., London, 1901.

2 *Human Leopards*, K.J. Beatty, Hugh Rees Ltd., London, 1915.

3 *West African Secret Societies*, F.W. Butt-Thompson, H.F. & G. Witherby, London, 1929.

4 *Secret Societies of all Ages and Countries*, C.W. Heckethorn, G. Redway Ltd., 1897.

5 *Leopard Men*, G.U.B. Lindskog, Uppsala University, Sweden, 1954.

6 *Bibliography of Sierra Leone*, H.C. Lukach, Humphrey Milford, London, 1925 (2nd Edition).

7 *Mande Blacksmiths*, P.R. McNaughton, Bloomington: Indian University Press, 1988.

8 *In Witchbound Africa*, Frank Melland, Sealey, Service & Co., London, 1923.

9 *Be Stronger Than Black Magic*, Isaac Oben, Gottingen: Edition Herodot, 1983.

10 *Seven Years in Sierra Leone*, A.T. Pierson, J. Nisbit & Co., London, 1897.

11 *Life, Scenery, & Customs in Sierra Leone and the Gambia*, (Volumes I & II), T.E. Poole, London, 1850.

12 *Primitive Secret Societies*, H. Webster, Macmillan & Co., New York, 1908.

13 *Cannibals and Tongo Players*, Milan Kalous, University of Auckland, Auckland, 1974.

14 *Sierra Leone After One Hundred Years*, Bishop E.G Ingham, Seeley & Co., London, 1894

15 *Sierra Leone: Its Peoples, Products and Secret Societies*, H.O. Newland, John Bale & Sons & Danielson, London, 1916.

16 *The Human Leopard Society in Sierra Leone*, Dr. D. Burrows, Journal of the African Society, (Volume XIII, pp.143–151), Macmillan and Co., London, 1913.

17 *A Bibliography of Sierra Leone*, H.C. Luke, Negro Universities Press, New York, 1969.

18 *Observations in Sierra Leone in 1607. A New Collection.* William Finch, Printed in 1745.

4

The Sokodae: A West African Dance

DRID WILLIAMS

Preliminaries

The complexity, richness and diversity of the world, plus an unprecedented fund of available information in all fields of study produces fascinating subjects in the social sciences. Study of **the** dance, dance**s** and danc**ing**, one small, sub-field of research in social anthropology has unique attractions, advantages and disadvantages. One of the latter pertains to the fact that in Western societies, dances have been classified, not as objects of research, but primarily as entertainments or vehicles through which people might savour the delights of aesthetic enjoyment. These classifications don't always reflect the attitudes of specialists. Over sixty years ago, Evans-Pritchard pointed out that:

> In ethnological accounts the dance is usually given a place quite unworthy of its social importance. It is often viewed as an independent activity and is described without reference to its contextual setting in native life. Such treatment leaves out many problems as to the composition and organisation of the dance and hides from view its sociological function (1928:446).

Evans-Pritchard issued a challenge with regard to future research, specifically regarding 'problems as to the composition and organisation of the dance' which have since been powerfully developed (see Williams 1991) into a field of human movement studies which has cracked several old chestnuts with regard to long-standing misconceptions about human behaviour. Current writers in the field have developed new theoretical insights, not only into the socio-linguistic functions of dances and dancing, but sign-languages, martial arts, rituals and ceremonies as well (see, for example, Farnell [in press], Page (1990), Puri and Hart-Johnson (1982), Williams (1986) and Fairbank (1985 and 1986). The dance, however, not only provided the original inspiration for explorations into the nature and meaning of all kinds of human systems of non-vocalised communication, it provided the initial thinking out of which *semasiology* emerged (see, for full definition, Williams 1991:363–364, Note 11).

The Director and members of the Institute for Cultural Research – always, I believe, at the cutting edge of in-tellectual developments and creative innovations in the human sciences – took an enlightened interest in these ideas 22 years ago when they were still in the process of development. A lecture was presented at I.C.R. on 31 October, 1970. The lecture subsequently became a written paper, based on research carried out in Ghana, during the years 1967–70. The paper dealt with two questions which are still valid in spite of the passage of time:

1. *What* does one study: movements, 'emotional ex-pression' or what?
2. *Why* does anyone study this sort of thing at all?

The Paper

When people ask these kinds of questions, I wish they would formulate them in somewhat plainer terms; terms which would, I think, state what is really on their minds. What seems to puzzle them is what *use* does the study of an African dance have for them, or for anyone in a highly organised, technological society?

The Sokodae, a Ghanaian dance around which this dis-cussion will turn, belongs to the Ntwumuru people – a small group of approximately 9,000 human beings who live in the north-eastern section of central Ghana. They are part of a larger group of Guang-speaking peoples, including the Kra-chi, whose history and social organisation in 1970 was intimately involved with this dance. As far as I know, that condition has not changed. We may well ask, however, 'Are these people and this dance not completely remote from the interests of members of developed societies?' The answer I would give is, 'Not so much as we might think'.

Study of the Sokodae (and of other similar genres of African dances) can be of use to them simply because they are from different environments, different traditions and ways of life. This may seem a rather obvious point, but it is one which can hardly be overstressed. From a perspective of these differences, the majority of Westerners are ill-equipped to judge or to criticise these dances, or to try to do anything at the outset, except to understand them. It has been my experience that many people are willing to try to understand, even if the process involves some loss of cherished notions about 'primitives' and/or stereotypes about the evolutionary process, but it is at this very point, no matter how positive the attitude or how sympathetic we try to be, that we are in difficulties about which we are frequently unaware.

These difficulties lie in habits of thought, culturally conditioned; basically learned ways of seeing and responding which can actively prevent (or at least obstruct) our understanding of traditional African art forms in the ways their practitioners understand and practise them, or for that matter, the traditional arts of India, China, Islam or the South Pacific Islands – any 'foreign' or 'alien' art forms.

For example, I have known many people to look at an African mask and the first thought that comes to them is, 'That was made before these people understood anything about perspective or anatomical drawing'. In a like manner, many people look at an African dance as a rather disordered and chaotic affair. If not that, they think the dance is totally spontaneous, improvised or 'free expression' which lacks form, coherence or intelligibility.

Apart from anything else, most Westerners are used to seeing a dance, first, with a picture frame around it – the familiar proscenium stage opening which is as appropriate to Western danced forms as a cleared space in the village is to the Ntwumuru, or the terrace of a *pueblo* to the Hopi. Second, because of the extraordinary abundance of extremely poor literature that is available on the subject of African dances, it is likely that the novice Western observer will want to believe that at least in the dances of Africa, they might find some untrammelled, uninhibited expression of primitive human beings – an attitude which involves two stereotypes. These are (1) the image of the emotionally and sexually uninhibited African and (2) the naive belief that all danced behaviour is somehow *symptomatic of* the participants' individual or collective feelings. Unknowingly, they are in danger of classifying these dances as the first 'simple' ('childish', 'undisciplined') beginnings of what they imagine is a 'world history' of the dance, which culminates in classical ballet or in some other contemporary Western theatrical dance-form.

To be quite blunt about it, these points of view are just dead wrong. They assume that a people like the Ntwumuru are, or were, trying to do the same things with their dances, sculptures, and other artifacts that we try to do. It assumes that their dances have the same reasons for existing that ours do, and that they (poor dears!) just missed the point somehow. Research into any of the traditional art forms of the world demonstrate beyond reasonable doubt that other societies are (and were) not trying to do the same things with their 'arts' that we have done with ours – at least for the last two hundred years, and that their criteria for what we call 'art' is different from ours. Needless to say, perhaps, such attitudes and beliefs are blatantly ethnocentric and condescending.

Four major differences in cultural expression that can be discerned in the Sokodae dance are as follows:

(1) The Ntwumuru and Krachi peoples, like people in most pre-industrialised societies, are not expressing *themselves* in their dances so much as they are expressing a set of ideas which are meaningful to them. The truth of this assertion becomes apparent when we examine the oral tradition for the Sokodae and the seven sections of it. This apparent lack of the Western concept of 'personality' or 'individuality' means that –

(2) their art is not an end in itself in the same way that many Western dances are. Their dances are not 'products' in the same sense that art is a product in the contexts of producer/consumer, industrialised societies.

(3) We should not forget, too, that the kind of traditional African art of which Sokodae is representative was, on the whole, anonymous, as indeed, much of pre-Renaissance Western art was anonymous. That doesn't mean that *people* didn't initially create these dances. It simply means that their names are probably not remembered after one or two generations, or that, like many traditional Australian Aboriginal dances, they were given to the people as coming from culture-heroes or Creator Beings, and were not, therefore, of human origin. Neo-African arts, including dances, have acquired many of the same conventions as present-day Western art forms, together with personality cults and all the rest.

(4) Finally, traditional African art *is not* relevant, in the plastic and graphic areas, because it is 'like' Picasso or Modigliani or, in the dance field, because it is 'like' the works of Pearl Primus, Alvin Ailey or Martha Graham or any other contemporary dancer. That is really putting the cart before the horse! Nor are these arts relevant primarily because of their design, aesthetic surfaces, or any of their surface characteristics, elegant and beautiful though they may be.

Traditional African dances are relevant because of their content, because of the vital functions they perform in the societies to which they belong. In those contexts, they are considered to be 'successful' in traditional terms, if they 'work'; that is, if they accomplish the purpose for which they were performed.[1] [*See footnote*]

It is important to try to understand the Sokodae in terms of *its* content and *its* criteria; an attempt much more akin to an anthropological, rather than an aesthetic point of view. Anthropologists are committed to try to understand how people outside their own native socio-linguistic contexts think. They are committed to try to understand the meanings and substance of cultural acts and actions in any society, including their own. Anthropologists of human movement bring the same kinds of attitudes to bear upon dances, rituals and art forms wherever they may be found.

The results of an anthropological commitment with reference to human artifacts are too numerous to list here, but two points immediately spring to mind: 1) research of the kind I carried out in Ghana can produce fresh, interesting points of departure for re-evaluations of art and artistic behaviour in our own society, and 2) we might begin to share in an impulse toward a category of mutual, albeit secularised, *metanoia*[2]; a process of developing awareness which is a result of a search for global understanding and which constitutes a basic human need to recognise, rationalise[3] and re-rationalise the significance of things and events.

The Sokodae Dance

In what follows, I shall tell you what the dance, Sokodae, *is about*, in contrast to telling you *about the Sokodae* dance, for in maintaining the previous line of thought, we will get nearer the mark[4].

---

* In this monograph, superscript Arabic numerals refer to *END NOTES*. References to the *BIBLIOGRAPHY* are not numbered.

Ee--------eee------------eeee---
Akyemba, agyanka bedi agoro,
Agoro, agoro
Agoro a eye me de nono
Agoro
Ee---------ee-------------eee--
Akyemba, agyanka
Agoro, agoro

Ee--------eee------------eeee---
The weaver bird's child, the orphan, comes to
dance,
Dance, dance
This dance belongs to me (which I own)
Dance
Ee---------ee-------------eee--
The child of the weaver bird, the orphan, comes
[to] Dance, dance.

This song in the Twi language is one of those sung in the
first section of the Sokodae. It is reproduced here because it
contains the three key ideas which the dance is about:
1. Ownership, 2. Orphan, and 3. Birds in general and the
weaver-bird in particular.

Ownership

In order to establish their ownership of the dance and to give
some idea of its age, the Ntwumurus tell the following story
from their oral tradition[5]: In 1750–1800, the Ntwumurus
crossed the Volta River (see map at end of monograph) from
the western to the eastern side with the intention of settling
in the new location. They had to abandon their homes on the
western side of the river because of infringement by the
Juabens. Some of the Ntwumuru clans sought the protection
of Dente[6] in the Krachi area and some of the kings of the
Ntwumuru and the Basa fled to the Republic of Dahomey
where they settled at Safé, Gbede. The Bejamso Ntwumurus
did not go to Dahomey, but to the place where they established the present village which bears their name.

It was through conquest, therefore, that the chief (Juaben-hene) of the Twi-speaking Juabens became the overlord of these areas and over many of the other Guang peoples as well[7]. The Krachis, for example, had already crossed the Volta some time before and were permanently settled in their present area south of the Ntwumurus. They simply submitted without any warfare to the Juabenhene's rule. Dente became more and more important to the Juabens, who appropriated all of the customs and traditions related to Dente because their own Obosom (gods) did not have the power of prophecy, of seeing into the future. Dente did.

When the Guang-speaking peoples became subjects of the Juabenhene, they had to pay homage to him. These annual homage payments took place at the Juaben festivals of Apa-fram – a yearly affair which the Ashantehene holds for the whole Ashanti State, of which the Juabens are a part. At this time, the Krachis and all of the subservient peoples presented gifts of slaves, sheep, elephant tusks, fresh fish, meat, honey and salt to the Juabenhene. Besides this, the Ntwu-murus of Bejamso came to honour the Juabenhene with the drumming and dancing of the Sokodae. Usually, after paying tribute, the Krachis and Ntwumurus would go back to their homes across the river.

One year, they were not granted permission by the Jua-benhene to return to their homes. They were kept at the town and used to labour on the farms of the Juaben chief and his elders. The visitors greatly resented this imposition but were afraid to act. They were sorely outnumbered and, of course, completely unarmed. The result was that they stayed for some time before they finally decided to ask for the help of Dente in their plight. They invoked the powers of Dente by calling his special names and by playing the drums and horns of the Sokodae.

The story emphasises that Dente reacted strongly to the appeals of his troubled people, for several things began to happen to the Juabens; heavy storms destroyed part of the town, elephants destroyed crops and many of the towns-people were caught and mangled or killed by leopards and lions. The Juabenhene consulted many oracles to try to find out what was behind all of the trouble. The oracles told him that he was keeping the Krachi and Ntwumuru in Juaben against their wills and more important, against the will of Dente. The Juaben chief was ordered by Dente to let his people return to their homes across the river.

Not wishing any further ills and misfortunes to fall upon his people and lands, the Juabenhene ordered that the former prisoners should go. He sent special messengers along with them who were accompanied by slaves in order to ensure that Dente would know of his obedience to his wishes. The slaves were given as gifts to Dente, who subsequently ordered them to be distributed among several nearby villages.

After this, the Juaben chief sent his drummers and dancers who were adept at the Kete (an Ashanti dance done only for chiefs) to dance in honour of Dente in Krachi. The Krachis didn't want these visitors to be in Krachikrom proper, so they assigned them a place to stay which was near to the old Krachikrom, now inundated by the waters of the Volta Lake. People used to say, 'I am going to where they are playing Kete'. Gradually, this developed into 'I am going to Kete-Krachi', the two words which compose the present name 'Ketekrachi'.

It is in this way that the Sokodae is intimately connected with the known oral history of the Ntwumuru people. We are told that the dance was already done many years before this event took place. The fact that the Ntwumurus had this connection with a Twi-speaking people for so long accounts for the fact that some songs like the weaver bird's song were translated into Twi from Ntwumuru. The song quoted was especially important, because the Ntwumurus wanted to be sure that the Juabens clearly understood the origins, meaning and ownership of the dance.

Orphan

The other two ideas connected with the weaver bird's song are somewhat different both in character and in kind, i.e.

the notion of 'orphan' and that of 'birds'. The word 'orphan', as it is used here, has no literal meaning as we would understand it. The dance is not about someone who has lost his or her parents. It has what might be called a figurative meaning stemming from the fact that the Sokodae dance belongs to everyone. This dance has no 'parents'; that is, it is not restricted in any way to persons of a particular cult or class. It does not require any special knowledge nor does it have any priests, or other ritual specialists attached to it. All Ntwumuru may participate in it regardless of status, economic standing or other considerations.

Birds

Another kind of ownership of this dance is expressed in connection with ideas about birds. In that part of the song (see *supra* p. 69) which says, '. . . which belongs to me' or 'which I own', the 'I' is used in a generic sense; it means 'I, an Ntwumuru'. The idea is expressed symbolically through metaphorical associations with the weaver-bird. As everyone knows, this bird builds one of the most complex and distinctive nests to be found among all birds. No other bird can reproduce it. The Ntwumurus see themselves as the weaver-birds and the Sokodae as the nest. May I hasten to point out that by no means is there any confusion in their minds as to whether they are really weaver-birds or not, any more than there is a confusion in an English ballet dancer's mind as to whether she is really a swan while performing Swan Lake. The weaver-bird in Sokodae is used as a metaphorical concept which these people find good to think with.

I. Kowurobenye

The major motif of the Sokodae is that of the courting and mating of birds. In the first section of the dance, called *Kowurobenye* (Kowurobe = orphan, nye = has got it), the men dance in clockwise and counter-clockwise circles simultaneously. They present a striking spectacle with their brilliantly coloured cloths streaming out behind them. The cloths in motion extend the male dancers' bodies like the bright tail plumage of peacocks, cockatoos and parrots. The movements all suggest the bowing, strutting and ecstatic rushing movements of a courting male bird. My informants pointed out that in the Kowurobenye, the males rival each other for the attention of the watching women. Within the step pattern, they even try to bump against one another in an attempt to knock each other off balance so that they will make their rivals appear clumsy and unaccomplished to their female audience.

II. Kenemoe

The second section of the dance is the female counterpart of the first male section, although the movements are quite different. Men, if they wish, can change the positioning of their cloths to simulate how women wear them, and dance in this part as well. In decided contrast to the vigorous use of space and running moves in the first section, the steps in *Kenemoe* are subtle and delicate, both in terms of footwork and movements of the torso. The whole of the torso is involved in a kind of light rippling movement from front to back, having no lateral overtones at all. Sometimes, this move is carried into the head and neck, reminding one of fowls walking or pecking softly at grains of food. The word, 'kenemoe', means 'a movement'.

III. Kumumuwuru

The third section, *Kumumuwuru* (spinning), is probably the most spectacular from a Western point of view. It involves whirling, spinning turns done by the men in solo sequences. They practise the rather difficult manipulation of their cloths privately – part of the skill required to perform the turns properly – for the cloth must be made to rise up in such a way that the upper part of the body is invisible. While turning, the total shape of the man and his cloth should resemble a

tulip blossom and stem. The men do this to 'make themselves look beautiful' – and it does. Kumumuwuru is done
for the same reason that the peacock spreads his tail or that
the male *legen* vibrates in the sunlight making his beautifully
coloured wings bedazzle the female.

IV. Kikyen

Two women will usually dance the fourth section (another
women's section) together. The kind of step involved in this
section makes a track in the earth and the way the footwork is
accented is closely related to the name of the section, *kikyen*
(pronounced key-CHEN). The track made in the earth is of
special importance: the evenness of the steps and the
straightness of the track are the desired results of the performance. It is perhaps interesting to know that this type of
step may be seen in many parts of Ghana, always in women's
dances and usually in dances involving puberty and marriage. There seems to be a strong association between women
and the earth among the Ntwumurus and throughout
Ghana. The essential meaning of this step is that it is important that a woman makes her mark firmly in the earth, for it
symbolizes her passage through life.

V. Kedenkenkyew

The fifth section is danced by men and women together. The
name *kedenkenkyew* is taken from the drum beats. This
whole passage of the dance is freely, strongly and boldly
erotic. Contrary to uninformed (or ill-informed) opinion,
this is one of the comparatively few dances or sections of
dances among many hundreds in Ghana which has the theme
of eroticism as its content. The movement patterns are quite
consistent with the overall theme of courting and mating
birds already established in previous sections. Kedenkenkyew's movements are unselfconscious, direct and unmis-
takable in their meaning. The atmosphere is one of

heightened awareness, joy and ease; a genuine zest for living seems to pervade the whole dancing community. As far as I could see, there was a complete absence of fear, hatred, shame or frustration, in contrast to much of what currently passed for eroticism on the Western theatre dance stage in 1970.

VI. Kyenkyenbrika

The word is translated as 'step-step-turn-around', and the section is also danced by men and women. They do not necessarily dance together in *kyenkyenbrika* however, as in the previous section. If someone wishes to dance solo, he or she may do so. One of the most interesting gestures for women occurs chiefly here. The woman points to her forehead with her right hand and to the small of her back with her left. This means that the woman follows the man with her mind and supports him with the strength of her back. The image given by my informants to explain this gesture was, 'all during the day from the morning, the woman follows the man in her mind when he is hunting or in the fields. At night, when he comes home, he rests and she tends to his needs, feeding him and serving him – all this because of the strength of her back'. Women use this characteristic gesture whether dancing alone, with each other, or with men.

VII. Kedenkyenkprofe

Also a name taken from the drums, this section contains the greatest variety of step patterns. It is danced mainly by men, with the women occasionally forming complementary patterns, either with the kikyen or the kenemoe steps. There is one gesture which means, 'I am a true son of the land'; another which means that the dancer's great-grandfather killed a man in battle. A complex series of jumps, changing from one leg to another, means, 'My father was an Ojya', (a priest of one of the state gods or divinities).

Cloth and Music

I was told that in the old days, only older men would dance
Sokodae with cloths. All cloth was handwoven then and
younger men would not have acquired sufficient wealth or
status to have them. The young men wore waistbands and a
loin-cloth and danced with their arms lifted to simulate the
outspread wings and breast of a courting male bird. Now,
everyone wears an imported Java-print cloth, or a cotton
cloth made in Ghana, or an Adinkira cloth[8]. The art of
weaving has, to my knowledge, disappeared among the
Ntwumuru.

The musical ensemble which accompanies Sokodae is of
special interest. It includes both drums and (animal tusk or
head) horns. There are six drums in all: the master drums,
called *Kitinmpene*, which are pitched 'talking drums', supported by one *Kakwedji* and two *Prentren*, all accompanied
by a *Dondo*, the familiar 'squeeze drum' of West Africa. The
tusk horns, called *Ntahera* in Twi are seven in number.[9]
They are led by the master horn, named *Kabretense*, which
plays melodies somewhat reminiscent of plainsong. Ac-
companying this horn are two *Kajesolo*, two *Namu* and two
Brekye. A gong accompanies the horns, for they are often
played by themselves with no drum accompaniment. Originally, there were three of each type of horn, totalling twelve
horns in all. It is not known why there are only seven horns in
use now. These horns are now made from the head horns of
the buffalo, but in the past, they were made from elephant
tusks.

Occasions for Sokodae

Once a year, the drummers, horn-players and a group of
dancers come to Ketekrachi from Bejamso to dance the
complete Sokodae to honour Dente, thereby taking active
part in the Dente festival. This annual observance commem-
orates the occasion upon which Dente freed his people from
the Juabens. One of the results of this is that parts of the

Sokodae – the Kowurobenye and the Kumumuwuru, are done in the Krachi area and have come to be known as the 'Krachi Flying Dance'.

The Sokodae is considered to be 'in the hands of the chief' who can command it for special occasions for the gods or whenever else he chooses. It is performed at special funeral occasions. For example, when the present Asafohene[10] of Bejamso dies, this dance will be drummed and danced for seven days. Once a year, Sokodae is danced and played for Sonko, one of the traditional war gods of the Ntwumuru. Sonko's shrine is situated outside Bejamso in the bush and is visited by most of the people during April. Great amounts of guinea corn are provided for the ceremonies, prepared three days in advance by the old women of Bejamso into *pito*, a kind of fermented wine made from the corn. Six or eight male goats are obtained as sacrifices for Sonko. On the eve of the ceremony, the Sokodae is danced. There is a contest between the two divisions of the town, Lentai and Chambai, in clearing the path to the shrine. It is a time of high celebration. These kinds of occasions and any others which are of great import are the occasions which belong to Sokodae.

Reflections

Dancing, one of the ancient art forms of humanity, has many sources, many impulses and many uses. Considered casually and superficially, we may only see in the Sokodae the leisure activities of a group of adult people who are imitating the movements of birds. We may well wonder why people do this sort of thing. Is it not a childish, simplistic (even if pretty and pleasurable) activity? I think not.

In an attempt to classify, categorise and explain their impressions and experiences – in attempts to formulate in non-vocalised symbolic terms their knowledge about their particular universes, human beings have used the movements, colours, shapes and sounds metonymically derived from other creatures and from nature to convey their ideas about phenomena and themselves. In the Sokodae, the weaver-bird is used as an extended metaphor to communicate ideas about social relationships and divisions of labour between men and women. The propensity to conceptualise in these ways is, according to Levi-Strauss, a fundamental characteristic of the human mind.[11]

We might profitably reflect on the fact that although a dance like Swan Lake carries some rather profound notions about psychological transformations instead of social roles or divisions of labour, groups of adult Western dancers have for the last century been imitating the movements of swans. In saying this, I do not mean to imply that Swan Lake and Sokodae are *the same*. Nor do I mean to suggest that the forms, gestures, muscular co-ordinations, costumes, musical accompaniment etc., are the same. However, I would want to say that on *a certain level of conceptualisation*, the use of weaver-birds and swans as metaphorical vehicles for whole constellations of ideas about the nature of humanity, is in fact *similar*. I feel constrained to add, because of the intellectual level of my audience, that neither Swan Lake nor Sokodae discloses the highest levels of conceptualisation or function which it is possible to attain *via* the medium of movement or through dances. This fact is abundantly clear even if one reads the available extant literature about various forms of dancing in the Far and Near Eastern countries of, say, Ceylon and India (e.g. de Zoete 1953, 1957 and 1963). The existence of Bharata Natyam, the dances of Bali, or even the Gisaro ceremony of the Bosavi people in New Guinea (see Schieffelin 1978), however, in no way lessens the importance of Swan Lake or Sokodae, or numerous more humble examples of the world's danced traditions. All genuine traditional dances are important to the people whose ethnic identities are tied up with them, including our own. It is to be hoped that this brief examination of the Ntwumuru people's Sokodae has contributed in some measure to an enlargement of understanding about the potential depth and complexity of 'a dance'.

The Sokodae was (and I hope still is) a living expression of the social identity of at least 9,000 people. The dance offers many insights into human relationships and behaviour that are important to the Ntwumuru themselves. Like any serious danced artifact, the Sokodae represents an attempt to order experience into intelligibility through a kind of reasoning by analogy.

Dances, regardless of where they are found in the world, are highly organized, highly structured human systems of actions and symbolic expression. They reflect, as we can see from the example I have given, an interesting and fairly broad range of ideas, associations, cultural mores, value systems and symbols belonging to the societies in which they originated.

> ... rituals reveal values at their deepest level ... men express in ritual what moves them most, and since the form of expression is conventionalised and obligatory, it is the values of the group that are revealed. I see in the study of rituals the key to an understanding of the essential constitution of human societies (Wilson 1968:166).

Research

The remaining problem to be dealt with in this discussion was stated in the first question asked at the beginning of the essay, '*What* does one study?' From the ethnographic account you have read of the Sokodae, some of the necessary components of information needed for this kind of research emerge:

(a) The oral traditions, myths and historical evidence (if there are any);

(b) The material culture, i.e. cloths, weapons, pots and dishes and such. Sokodae, unlike some dances, e.g. those using masks, perhaps statuary and other paraphernalia, was not problematic in this regard. The

cloths worn by the dancers were the only item of this
kind involved.
(c) The musical accompaniment and the songs. This area
of study alone has generated the field of ethnomusicology. An excellent example of research in this discipline, carried out in Ghana, will be found in
Chernoff (1979).

Often, research into dances is looked at as a sub-field of
ethnomusicology, and given the history of the discipline,
especially in the United States, it was both reasonable and
generous of ethnomusicologists to adopt the comparatively
few dance researchers there were in the beginning and
middle of this century. However, modern trends indicate
that the young, but vigorous field of the anthropology of
human movement studies may well establish itself as an
autonomous discipline, in which case, research into dances
would come into its own, along with sign languages, drama,
rituals, martial arts – all of the human structured systems of
meaning which have movement and non-vocalised human
action as their primary mode of expression.

Practically speaking, from an anthropological standpoint,
research into a dance involves the analysis of an event (see
Ardener 1973, for apposite discussion). The analysis of a
danced event details at least six features of space/time organisation, i.e.

(1) the physical space
(2) the lived time
(3) the social space
(4) the social time
(5) the conceptual space
(6) the mythological time.

'A dance' is a complex, self-contained finite event which
takes place according to certain specifications. It possesses a
'context' (the environment in which it takes place) and an
'internal space' or shape, which semasiologists call the 'form

space' of a dance. A dance has a beginning, a middle and an end, and while each danced event will have a different configuration of elements within the structures outlined above, each can be profitably studied using the elements indicated above as a plan to commence work.

The physical space of a dance is the easiest to define, because it is empirically observable, unlike the conceptual space of the dance, which is generally invisible. For example, physical spaces for dances might include (a) the proscenium stage, which might be 40 feet wide and 25 feet deep, with a 19 foot vertical opening, or perhaps it is larger or smaller than that. On the other hand, the physical space may be a forest clearing 100 feet wide and 200 feet long, filled with people who leave only a small open space (or spaces) in the centre, the physical dimensions of which are marked off by an arrangement of drummers and singers, seats for prestigious ritual leaders, honoured guests and such. In Sokodae, the physical space was the 'village square' or meeting place in Bejamso, near the chief's house, partly shaded by an enormous mango tree by which the people gathered, creating a circle or 'dance space' approximately 40 feet in diameter. The physical space of a dance might be a semi-circular arrangement of people seated upon cushions and divans on a raised platform or series of steps, with a solo dancer being the focal point at a place on the marble floor which is equidistant from either end of the semi-circle, if it were a performance of Kathak dancing in the north of India. The physical space might be a longhouse in Papua New Guinea. The list of examples is nearly infinitely extendable, but these should give some idea of what is meant by the physical space of a dance.

The 'lived time' of a dance means the actual time required for the observed and observable performance. Is it one or two hours; a half hour, 15 minutes, or, as in the case of some Australian Aboriginal 'dances', are the units so short that they are often only 10, 16, 18, 24 or 36 beats long? The notion of 'lived time' is important to the researcher because he or

she must make distinctions between this 'time' and the se-
mantics of the 'time' of the mythological, historical, or conceptual time (which may be past, present or future) of the
dance. A Western example is relevant: Antony Tudor's ballet, *Jardin aux Lilas* (The Garden of Lilacs) took up about a
half hour of 'lived time' on the part of the dancers and the
audience, but the ballet itself was the expansion of the instant
of recognition on the part of the bride and groom at their
wedding, in which many events took place 'in another dimension' as it were. In the Sokodae, the lived time of the
dance on the occasion I saw it was approximately two hours,
but during that time, I was projected into a kind of 'timeless'
dimension of Ntwumuru ethnic identity, into a definitional
time which, because of the content of the dance, revealed
matters which, for the Ntwumuru, 'were', 'are', and 'always
would continue' as long as they continue to exist.

The 'social space' and 'social time' of a dance are not so
easy to define, because with them, the researcher begins to
enter the domains of those elements of a dance which are *not*
empirically observable. Let us examine the notion of social
space first: here, before us are two women dancing the
Kenemoe section of Sokodae. They are in close physical
proximity to one another with regard to the physical space of
that section of the dance. One is old and one is younger,
'middle-aged' we will say. I cannot see what social relationship lies between them; are they mother and daughter, are
they aunt and niece, are they age-group mates, are they just
good friends, are they dancing together because they are
deemed to be 'the best dancers' for that section, meaning that
they could be from different clans, or are they from the same
clan? The step patterns of the dance *tell us nothing about any
of this*, which is why semasiologists say there is much about a
dance that is 'invisible'.

We discovered, however, that Sokodae (see *supra* p. 71,
section: 'orphan') 'has no parents', meaning that:

   ... it is not restricted in any way to persons of a particular cult or class. It does not require any special knowledge nor does it have any priests, or other ritual specialists attached to it. All Ntwumuru may participate . . .

As it happened, the two women I have in mind for this example were simply 'good friends' and they enjoyed dancing Kenemoe together, because it was a context in which they could. Contrary to the stereotype of 'unfettered spontaneity', that is supposed to be a *sine qua non* of Africa's traditional dances, I suggest that unfettered spontaneity (and its many derivatives) is a characteristic of a contemporary disco dance, but will not be found in traditional dances, where 'spontaneity' is certainly not 'unfettered', but exists, as indeed it does in the ballet, in the context of complex sets of rules, not only with regard to the acceptable performances of steps and gestures, but with regard to the permissible social space/times of any given dance.

I have seen dances in Aboriginal Australia which my informants told me were 'not really the "X" dance', because a whole section could not be performed because relevant family members who performed it were not present; therefore, it was simply left out.[12] But these kinds of considerations lead to the notion of the social roles/rules which directly influence the semantic content of a dance. There are dances from the Krachi-Ntwumuru area which are exclusive to members of a certain cult, e.g. Tigari. There are dances which cannot be performed by anyone except an Ojya because they are possession dances (e.g. Yentumi) and anyone who is not an Ojya cannot perform the actions of the divinity whose dance it is, for that would amount to something like sacrilege, and severe penalties would be exacted. An old man in Pokwasi (a village close to Accra) told me, 'I have come to watch the gods dance'. He didn't mean by that statement that he had come to watch some god-like dancer dance. He meant literally what he said; he was coming to that part of the festival to enter the socially prepared space/time (the festival) of the divinities (the next level, i.e. mythological time) – to see *them* dance, not the dancers.

Research into danced events is to me somewhat like playing with a beautifully constructed set of Russian dolls – the nested dolls, where there is one big doll visible on the outside containing successively smaller and smaller dolls inside, until one has reached the last, tiniest doll, whereupon the researcher retreats into silence, for the limit of explanation, of verbalisation, analysis and all the rest has been reached. With regard to the kind of research I advocate, the investigator is getting nearer the last doll when grappling with the notion of the conceptual space/time of a dance.

Some of the main features of the conceptual space of a dance are linguistic. That is, although the dimensions of physical space (up/down, right/left, front/back, outside/inside) are universal in the sense that no human movement, danced or not danced, takes place outside them, different cultures, different ethnicities within the same culture, even, assign different meanings to them. In Ghana, for example, the left/right dimension is specifically weighted, particularly with regard to the values placed on right hands and left hands.

Spatial restrictions prevent enumerating many examples, but suffice to say that the values of left and right with reference to eating, shaking hands, giving objects, whether food, books, pots or whatever, to another person: The right side of the body and the right hand are 'good'. The left side of the body and the left hand are not 'bad', but the left hand cannot perform the same functions as the right (say handing someone an object) unless the right hand touches the arm or wrist at the same time. One carries a spear, eats, shakes hands, swears oaths, gives objects to others with the right hand. One does not clean oneself after using the toilet with the right hand, nor does one swear oaths, eat, and so forth with the left hand. Left-handed people were, on the whole, considered 'special', and the condition was recognised among the peoples with whom I was familiar, but the condition meant special ceremonies, pouring of libations, etc. in order to make the condition 'right' in terms of the whole society.

I noticed these facts in dances because right-handed people are generally more comfortable dancing in, say, a clockwise circle, with their right sides toward the centre of the circle. Left-handed people found this difficult so, often, one of my teachers would explain why he or she was moving 'upstream', so to speak; why they preferred the left sides of their bodies towards the centre of the circle. They explained to me that they had had to sacrifice goats, pour libations and have many prayers said before they could go against the mainstream. The general point is that *orientational metaphors* (see Lakoff and Johnson 1980: 14–21) are essential to adequate understanding of danced events, because they are the first steps in the process of understanding the conceptual space of the dance.

With regard to conceptual, or mythological, time: we have touched on the subject by mentioning possession dances above, and a 'created time', as in *Jardin aux Lilas*, where the choreographer stretched an instant to cover a half hour of 'lived time'. At the risk of doing the subject a disservice, I can do no more than mention some aspects of this area of research here, hoping to enlist the judicious sympathy of readers for tackling an impossible task in a short essay.

As I never cease to wonder at the different spatial universes that are created by different peoples, I am no less astonished at the variety of concepts of time to be found in danced spaces. The most recent encounter occurred through the Maasai student, Makiya, to whom I refer in Endnote 1 (q.v.). In a class discussion of orientational metaphors, we talked about 'front/back', and I had explained how English-speaking people generally associate the future with 'front' and the space directly ahead of them. 'Past' to an English-speaker is 'back' or 'behind'. 'Now' is 'here', where I stand, where my axis of gravity happens to be. As I talked, I noticed that Makiya had a withdrawn, puzzled look on his face. I asked him what was the matter. He replied, 'I don't think that way,' to which I replied, 'That's all right. Can you explain how you do think about all this?' There was a long silence. Then he said, 'You go towards the future. I don't. My future comes to me. Death comes to me. I stand. Time moves past, around, over and through me. I don't go into it.'

Needless to say perhaps, I haven't even begun to work out the implications of this. Having seen Makiya perform the actions of his war dance, I know it contains keys, for I have never seen moves like those the *ilmurran* make – fantastically high leaps, for a start, without bending their knees. They seem propelled a foot or two off the ground by virtue of invisible springs. But, interesting as that is, it isn't the most

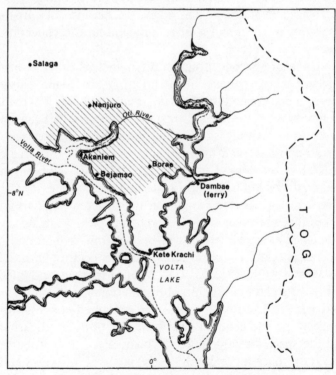

Map of North-Eastern Section of Central Ghana
(Shading indicates Ntwumuru Territory)

important thing. 'How?' I ask myself, 'can I understand what he says? Can I conceive of a universe where I (and everyone) stands still – a universe where it isn't time that stands still, but *us*?'

At the end of the original lecture/paper I gave for the I.C.R. in 1970, I concluded by evoking an extended metaphor of buildings and bridges. I attempted in a somewhat clumsy manner, to finish by drawing attention to levels, which I described in terms of physical bridges, social bridges and mythological bridges, tying this to the notion of a physically observable dance and the social meanings elaborated in the dance through discovery of its role/rule structures. This led to 'the conceptual and mythological aspects of a dance' – a pompous, pedantic phrase, if I ever heard one!

Today, I prefer to leave you with the Maasai *ilmurran*:

> 'My future comes to me. Death comes to me. I stand . . .'

END NOTES

1 Relevant to the present situation in north eastern Kenya are the circumstances in which one of my students – Makiya Le Sarge, a Maasai 'moran' (Warrior) – finds himself. His family grazes their cattle in an area 62 miles north of Isiolo, Kenya, where Somali bandits regularly raid. Maasai war-dances are without doubt spectacular, and they would be classified by Westerners as 'art', but in their context they are not so considered. The dances prepare the *ilmurran* for war, thus they perform these dances because they are in deadly earnest. They might be killed, but if the dance is effective, it is not Makiya who will die, but his Somali enemy.

2 Briefly, a 'change of mind'. For thorough discussion in a religious context, see Williams (1975).

3 This word is not used in the narrow, psychological sense of 'falsifying'. It is to be construed in its broader definition, which means 'rendering something to the rational processes of thought' or 'creating a rationale for'.

4 The orthography of the Twi language uses phonetic symbols which are not available in this publication, therefore the following signs have

been used as substitutions. Approximate English pronunciations are given: 'o' is the sound 'awe' in English; 'e' is the sound 'eh' as in 'bet'; 'ky' always has the sound of 'ch' as in 'church'; 'N' at the beginning of a word, i.e. Ntwumuru, is not 'en', but n-n-n (the sound). In this particular word, the 'tw' is pronounced 'ch', and 'n' has the sound 'ng', as in 'sing'.

5 The Krachis, Yejis and Ntwumurus all tell this story and they are all positive about it. The story is to some extent 'historically valid' in a Western sense, because the event it recounts marked the beginning of the independence of the Krachi State as it existed in 1970; that is, its independence from Juaben domination, not from the nation of Ghana. The story also agrees with accounts from the Ashanti-Juaben history according to Dr. Adu-Boahene (Dept. of History, University of Ghaha, Legon). There are obvious mythological elements in the story as well, so that we might also think of the story as a mythological *charter* for the dance. Malinowski (1948), whose theoretical work is outdated in many ways, nevertheless stressed the importance of myth as *charter*; thereby focussing on the living relationship of myth to society, and removing such stigmas from the notion as 'falsified history' or 'phantasy'. Whether or not the story is true or false history from an European point of view is really irrelevant. The fact that the story has a role in connection with the dance and that it validates the dance in Ntwumuru and Krachi society is sufficient to justify its existence.

6 Dente (noun), also Lente, also Konkom, although the latter name is never used in speaking. Dente is the highest of the Ikisi [gods] of the Krachi, except for Nana Brukun, who is older. The Krachis brought Dente with them to their present location when they moved there during the 19th century. Dente resides in a cave a short distance from Krachikrom. When the capital had to be moved to a different location (the present location on the map) because of the flooding of the Volta Lake, Dente moved as well and took up his abode in another cave about a mile or so from Ketekrachi.

7 Krachis and Ntwumurus, together with Nkonyas, Gonjas, Nawures, Atwodes, Anums, Kyrepongs, Efutus and Yejis form the large linguistic group known as the Guang (also spelled Guan) people. Guang means 'run-aways' in Twi.

8 Adinkira, or Adinkra, is a name given to cloth which is hand-block-printed with very old symbolic patterns, usually black on a brilliantly coloured background.

9 There was some controversy over the original ownership of these horns. Some people claim that they were originally Akan, actually Ashanti horns which the Ntwumurus copied. A set of *ntahere* were used as state horns by the Ashantehene. They are carved elephant tusks. However, according to the Ntwumuru, these very horns were

originally owned by one of their chiefs, Atere Firam. Evidence to support this claim, hence original Ntwumuru ownership, is to be found in The Ashanti Court Records: in the Asantehene's 'A' Court in Kumasi, in the matter of Kumawuhene vs. Dwanhene, 1951, pp. 53, 55, 59, 61 and 75. The Ntwumuru chief, Atere Firam, lost a war to the Ashanti, and the horns were a part of the *dwira* (booty) that the Ashanti took from him.

10 'Asafo' is a noun in the Fanti language, which translates roughly as 'group', 'body' or 'company'. The French word 'corps' is more accurate. An Asafohene is simply a leader of a group.

11 See Levi-Strauss (1962). Although the English edition of this book bears the title *The Savage Mind*, the French word 'sauvage' bears none of the usual connotations that the English word 'savage' implies. The book should have been entitled *The Untamed Mind*.

12 I refer to versions of the Wallaby Dance, owned by the Wanam people of Edward River and Aurukun, Cape York Peninsula, which required the presence of cross-cousins to execute a particular move in the dance where men dancing 'wallabies' were meant to pass between the 'hunter's' legs.

BIBLIOGRAPHY – References cited:

Ardener, E.W. 1973/1989. *Problems in the Analysis of Events*. Paper for the Decenial Conference of the A.S.A., Oxford, July. Reprinted in 1989. *Edwin Ardener: The Voice of Prophecy* (Ed. M. Chapman), Blackwell, Oxford.

Chernoff, J.M. 1979. *African Rhythm and African Sensibility*. University of Chicago Press, Chicago.

Evans-Pritchard, E.E. 1928. *The Dance (Azande)*. Africa, 1(4):446.

Fairbank, H. 1985. *Chinese Minority Dances: Processors and Preservationists* Part I. Jour. for the Anthrop. Study of Human Movement. [JASHM], 3(4):235-250.

Fairbank, H. 1986. *Chinese Minority Dances: Processors and Preservationists* Part II. [JASHM], 4(1):36-55.

Farnell, B. (Ed.) [in press]. *The Visible and the Invisible: Human Movement Systems in Cultural Context*. Scarecrow Press Metuchen, N.J.

Lakoff, G. and Johnson, M. 1980. *Metaphors We Live By*. University of Chicago Press.

Levi-Strauss, C. 1962. *La pensée sauvage*. Plon, Paris.

Page, J. 1990. *A Comparison Between Two Movement-Writing Systems: Laban and Benesh*. M.A. Thesis, University of Sydney.

Puri, R. and Hart-Johnson, D. 1982. *Thinking With Movement: Improvising vs. Composing?* [JASHM], 2(2):99-111.

Schieffelin, E.L. 1976. *The Sorrow of the Lonely and the Burning of the Dancers.* St. Martin's Press, New York.

Williams D.

1975. '*The Brides of Christ*'. *Perceiving Women.* (Ed. S. Ardener), Malaby Press, London, or Halsted Press, New York.

1986. '*(Non) Anthropologists, the Dance and Human Movement*'. *Theatrical Movement: A Bibliographic Anthology.* (Ed. B. Fleshman), Scarecrow Press, Metuchen, New Jersey. [Chapter 9].

1988. *Homo Nullius: The Status of Aboriginal Dancing in Northern Queensland.* Paper for the 5th International Conference on Hunters and Gatherers, Darwin, Northern Territory, August 31. (Available from the AIATSIS Library, GPO Box 553, Canberra, A.C.T. 2601, Australia.)

1991. *Ten Lectures on Theories of the Dance.* Scarecrow Press, Metuchen, New Jersey.

Wilson, M. 1967. '*Nyakyusa Ritual and Symbolism*'. *Myth and Cosmos. Readings in Mythology and Symbolism.* (Ed. J. Middleton), University of Texas Press, Austin and London, pp. 149–166.

Zoete, Beryl de:

1953. *The Other Mind. A Study of Dance in South India.* V. Gollancz, London.

1957. *Dance and Magic Drama in Ceylon.* Faber & Faber, London.

1963. *The Thunder and the Freshness.* Spearman Ltd., London. (Preface by Arthur Waley).

5

The Moriscos and the Demise of the Arab Empire in Spain

The Arab Empire lasted for over seven hundred years. It extended across Asia and Africa, and at its height, parts of Europe. With the spread of Islam came the development of science and technology. Great cities rose throughout the Middle East making use of, and housing the new learning. The Iberian peninsula was transformed by the Arab and Berber conquest of the eighth century. The Arab name for the greater part of Spain was *al-Andalus*, from which we get its present name *Andalucia*.

The events that brought the end of the Islamic domination of Spain, after seven hundred years, are fascinating. This monograph looks at how the Arab Empire's Iberian front rose and fell. It considers the unrivalled architecture that the *Moors* (the name given to the Arab-Berber people who had come from North Africa), left in their wake, then focuses upon the *Moriscos*, the Muslims who remained in Spain following the Spanish re-conquest, and their subsequent persecution and expulsion from the peninsula.

History is full of examples where one society has oppressed another: but the study of the Moriscos is unlike most other situations. It shows the resilience, endurance and powers of adaptation of a people faced with extraordinary persecution, yet committed devoutly to their faith.

The Spread and Demise of the Arab Empire

With an unprecedented dynamism, the Arab Empire of the seventh century swept eastwards and westwards. From

91

China to the Atlantic, Islam was embraced by new converts. It had taken ground that even the Roman Empire had failed to secure; converting those under it and introducing new moral codes to its people.

Initial clashes with the Berbers of the North African hinterland brought disaster. The great Arab commander, Oqba Ben Nafi, was slaughtered along with many of his warriors. It became evident that if these Berber tribesmen could be persuaded to follow Islam, they would prove a powerful force with which to convert others. So the Arabs battled again with the Berbers, finally gaining their support and allegiance. Ironically Oqba Ben Nafi became a hero to the Berbers. The coalition of Moroccan Berbers with the Arab armies had, by 710 A.D., produced a formidable fighting force: for whom the most feasible route for expansion lay northwards – into Europe.

Most of the Iberian peninsula still lay in the hands of the Visigoths; descendents of those who had overrun the crumbling Roman Empire some two hundred years before. But the predominantly Christian Visigoth Empire was fragile and set to break apart. It was in 711 that the first major Moorish invasion of Iberia was undertaken. The North African Arab Governor, Musa, instructed his Berber ally, Tariq and his twelve thousand men to cross into Spanish territory. Tariq made a base on the rock of Gibraltar (which still bears his name – *Jabal Tariq*). His campaign met with little resistance and, having destroyed the weak defences of the Visigoths, he moved on to take Cordova and Toledo.

On hearing of Tariq's success, Musa left for Spain with a force of some ten thousand well-equipped Arab soldiers. He was eager to ensure that the conquest was seen to be the work of the Arabs. Musa publicly humiliated Tariq, before he himself was recalled to Damascus and later dismissed. Although the Moorish army pushed onwards to France, they were dealt a heavy blow. Their most crushing defeat came at the Battle of Poitiers in 732, where the Moorish expansion into mainland Europe was halted.

However on other fronts, the Moorish incursions brought further victories. The conquest of Sicily was achieved in 902 after a long and bloody onslaught. Several Italian cities were raided from time to time and overrun. Moorish invaders managed to gain control of Naples and Rome, forcing the Pope to pay them off. Although the Moors even took ground as far north as Switzerland, their most substantial and long-term European conquests were those in Spain and Sicily.

At its peak, the Arab Empire stretched from Central Asia to the Atlantic and was governed from Damascus. In 750, the ruling Umayyed family was wiped out by the Abbasids, who moved the central government to Baghdad. There the capital of the empire remained until Hulagu Khan, the grandson of Genghis Khan, sacked the city with his Mongol forces in the second half of the thirteenth century. Meanwhile one of the Umayyeds, the erstwhile rulers, having survived the Abbasid insurgency, headed for Spain. Known as Abd ar-Rahman, he realised that supporters of his family still lived in the Iberian peninsula and he hoped for the chance to gain command of the peninsula. In battle, Abd ar-Rahman fought from the back of a mule, showing thereby that, with such a beast, he could never flee and desert his troops. A worthy soldier and a popular commander, he took control of al-Andalus, founding a dynasty at Cordova which lasted until the eleventh century.

By the tenth century, the Cordovan caliphate was beginning to fall apart, breaking into small and politically weaker kingdoms. Although they lacked real power, under them there came a period of unrivalled artistic expression and development.

Northern Spain began to grow in strength under the leadership of a line of Christian Kings and, with the decline in Moorish power, the Christian forces pushed southwards to drive the enemy from the peninsula. Toledo was recaptured in 1085, a landmark in the waning of Moorish supremacy.

Fearing invasion, one Berber kingdom called for assistance from the *Almoravid* Berbers in North Africa. They arrived and defeated the Christian army at the Battle of al-Zallaga. Indeed they proved so bellicose that they also overran several of the Moorish kingdoms, and in consequence combined much of Andalucia under their own banners. But, as they moved on through Spain, taking Moorish lands not yet recaptured by the Christians, they were met and defeated by them at the battle of Las Navas de Tolosa, and driven from the peninsula. A power vacuum was left, thereby allowing the Christians to retake the remaining Moorish territories. Cordova fell in 1236, and Seville in 1248, leaving only Granada as the last Moorish stronghold, under the Nasrid dynasty. The union of two Catholic monarchies was achieved with the marriage of Ferdinand to Isabella of Castile. This alliance established a united front which finally won total supremacy with the fall of Granada, the final bastion of Moorish strength, in 1492.

The Rise and Fall of Granada

The first to establish its capital at Granada, the Berber Zirid dynasty, ruled there throughout the eleventh century. It was under Zirid rule that the first significant fortifications and buildings were constructed since the fall of the Roman Empire. Then, for two hundred years, Granada was captured and recaptured, becoming in turn part of several small kingdoms. Each decade brought further improvement and expansion to the buildings and institutions that went to earn the city such fame throughout the Arab World. But it was under the rule of Abu Abd Allah Mohammed Banu 'l-Ahmar that Granada achieved the unprecedented and magnificent architecture for which it is still renowned today. He built a fortified palace, the *al-Hamra* palace, the 'Alhambra' as we know it (meaning the 'Red Palace'). It was said to be capable of holding forty thousand soldiers. In his work *A Short History of the Saracens*[1], Ameer Ali gives a detailed description of the Alhambra:

It is impossible within the space at my command to do

justice to 'this fabric of the genii'. The towers, citadels, and palaces, with their light and elegant architecture, the graceful porticos and colonnades, the domes and ceilings still glowing with tints which have lost none of their original brilliancy; the airy halls, constructed to admit the perfume of surrounding gardens; the numberless fountains over which the owners had such perfect control, that the water could be made high or low, visible or invisible at pleasure, sometimes allowed to spout in the air, at other times to spread out in large, oblong sheets, in which were reflected buildings, fountains, and serene azure sky; the lovely arabesques, paintings and mosaics finished with such care and accuracy as to make even the smallest apartments fascinating, and illuminated in varied shades of gold, pink, light blue, and dusky purple; the lovely dados of porcelain mosaic of various figures and colours; the beautiful Hall of Lions with its cloister of a hundred and twenty-eight slender and graceful columns, its blue-and-white pavement, its harmony of scarlet, azure and gold; the arabesques glowing with colour like the pattern on a cashmere shawl, its lovely marble filigree filling in the arches, its beautiful cupolas, its famous alabaster cup in the centre; the enchanting Hall of Music, where the Court sat and listened to the music of the performers in the tribunes above; the beautiful seraglio with its delicate and graceful brass lattice work and exquisite ceilings; the lovely colouring of the stalactites in the larger halls and of the conical linings in the smaller chambers – all these require a master's pen to describe.

Granada was home to the sciences: it was where scholars came to meet and discuss their ideas. After centuries of Moorish warfare, came several lines of kings, under whom learning and art flourished. The development of Moorish arts and the movement away from previous belligerent tendencies, left the strengthening forces of the Catholic kings to go unchallenged. By the fifteenth century the Castilian armies managed to cause a rift between rival Muslim groups, who in turn began to wage a bloody civil war.

It was not until 1491 that the Catholic kings began to lay siege to Granada itself. With all food and supplies used up, the weak king Boabdil was forced to surrender. In doing so Boabdil ceded to Ferdinand and Isabella his prize: the Alhambra. Boabdil was the last Moorish king to rule in Spain.

S.P. Scott in his *The Moorish Empire in Europe*[10], wrote of him:

> There are few royal personages in history so impotent and contemptible as Boabdil, and who at the same time have been endowed with such a capacity for mischief. With singular propriety was he termed by his countrymen Al-Zogoibi, The Unfortunate. Born in the purple, he fought and negotiated for a throne which he eventually lost under circumstances of the deepest humiliation.

Boabdil's pleas to the sultans of Turkey and Egypt had gone unheeded. In November 1491, he called upon Ferdinand to come and take possession of Granada. He was allowed to go into exile to North Africa. It is said that, as he looked back one last time on his kingdom, Boabdil cried *'Allahu Akbar'* – 'God is Greater', and burst into tears. Legend has it that his mother, who was standing by his side said: 'You may well weep like a woman for what you could not defend like a man.' The spot on which they stood is still called *El Ultimo Sospiro del Moro*, (the Last Sigh of the Moor).

Mudejar Society

Following the passing of Moorish Spain, the Spanish Muslims living under Christian rule, were known as *Mudejar*. Literally it means: 'The one allowed to remain'. Although they lived in communities separate from the Spanish Christians, they mixed in all areas of life. They lived in *Morerias*, ghetto-type areas, with their own jurisdiction over each of the settlements. Mudejars followed Moorish law, adhering to Islamic customs and faith. When many of them converted to Christianity, under pressure from their conquerors, they began to influence Christian society with their Moorish ways.

Catholic conversions began on a large scale with the appointment of two men to take charge: Salazar de Mendoza and Hernando de Talavera. Both sought to convert through re-education and attempted to employ, where possible, priests of mixed Moorish-Christian ancestry who spoke Arabic. The procedure was slow although not unsuccessful. Then the Catholic Kings called upon Francisco Ximenez de Cisneros, Archbishop of Toledo, to aid Talavera. After some initial success, he began to stage mass conversions which angered the staunch Muslims. The situation was exacerbated when he began to turn mosques into churches (including the great mosque of Albaicin). The resulting revolt at Albaicin was quashed in 1501, and gave the king a reason to introduce a severe clamp-down on the Moriscos – those who followed Islam. Royal Ordinances followed, which officially gave them the choice between baptism and exile. '

With the Christian re-conquest successfully completed in 1492, Mudejar history is said to have come to an end, the Mudejars being followed by their descendants: the Moriscos.

Mudejar society was one gateway through which a plethora of Moorish and Arab traditions filtered into Spanish and, in consequence, into European society. European language, custom, belief, cuisine and ways of thought were heavily influenced by the more advanced Moorish culture.

As Moorish discoveries and knowledge passed into the hands of the Spanish, the Spanish language became enriched with specific terminology. Words such as 'alcove' (meaning in Arabic, 'a dome'), 'alkaline', 'alcohol' and 'zenith', seeped from Spanish into other European languages, including our own. New foodstuffs and materials too, came in from the Arab world and beyond. Cotton, sugar, oranges, lemons and rice were all first taken to Europe by the Arabs. Improved methods of farming, irrigation as an instance, were first introduced by them too. A complex Moorish cuisine thought to have existed on the Iberian peninsula, but long since disappeared, has influenced what we eat. Syrup and sherbet (both Arab delicacies) as well as mint sauce (which we put on lamb), came to us through Moorish Spain.

Recreational activities which played an important part in Moorish life, filtered into European culture, and became so completely assimilated as to be thought originally native to the societies in which they now exist. Morris Dancing came from Moorish Dancing, and has become traditionally English.

Mass Conversions and the Spanish Inquisition

The forced baptisms of Muslims began on a large scale about 1501. They were called *Moriscos*, meaning 'Little Moors', and persecution of Morisco culture and society became absolute. Those who followed Islam were treated as inferior citizens, to an inordinate degree. They were brought to trial over the most trivial points. Some were forced to eat pork or drink alcohol: refusing to do so brought imprisonment, torture and even death.

Morisco customs and traditions were eradicated one by one, as the persecution continued. They were written of in Spanish literature as fools and idiots; whose presence prevented the formation of a truly national Spanish identity. Morisco sympathy for the strengthening Turkish Empire only heightened the Spanish perception that the Moriscos were now a malignant foreign body.

The rise and expansion of Protestantism in Spain in the first half of the sixteenth century was seen as a grave threat by the Catholics. They foresaw a possible coalition being created between the two minority groups. During the reign of Charles V, such questions arose as, 'If a Morisco was forcibly converted to Catholicism, would he become a true

Catholic?'. It was decided that he would. With prompting from the Pope, Charles V began another harsh campaign of conversion, leaving exile as the only choice for those who would not convert. The long Arab robes, talismans and practices such as circumcision and killing animals according to Islamic custom, were outlawed.

The Spanish Inquisition's ruling body held supreme power. It suppressed the development of new ideas and education. Employing the most horrific tortures, it is said to have shocked even those called upon to carry through its demands. The Inquisition must be seen not only as a religious apparatus, but also as secular and political in its activities – the acceptance of large fees in return for suspending the sentences on heretics succeeded in enabling the Spanish Crown to regain its financial stability. In 1559, with another turn of the screw, numerous Moriscos were charged with taking the Catholic faith too light-heartedly; as well as for practicing Islamic beliefs covertly. A subsequent Ordinance of 1566 nullified all contracts written in the Arabic language, prohibited the speaking of Arabic and the use of Arab names within a period of thirty days. Bloody revolts resulted as Moriscos were forced to unveil their women, give up their native dress and traditions and hand in all books in Arabic.

In 1574, the fall of Tunis to the Turks, followed by the defeat of the Spanish Armada by the English in 1588, made the Spanish very uneasy. The French, English and the Dutch had united and in so doing, presented an external danger to the weakening Spanish monarchy, while, at home, there were constant problems with the Moriscos. As the Turks gained in strength and influence, the Moriscos ardently hoped that they would prove able to deliver them from the clutches of the Catholics, enabling Islam once again to hold Iberia.

Lack of Morisco participation and respect for the Catholic faith angered members of that church. Constant blasphemy and the disruption of church services, the ignoring of religious holidays and the Moriscos' failure to give up their often polygamous lifestyles only served to enhance the Catholics' fury.

A general sentiment that the conversions had failed gained ground. The Bishop of Segorbe, in his famous proclamation of 1587, demanded that the Morisco people should immediately be expelled from the Iberian peninsula. He maintained that they could and would never become truly Catholic. Even after baptism they used Moorish names, refrained from eating pork – and, when asked why their children were circumcised, replied that they had been born that way.

The Morisco Expulsion

The Royal Notice of Expulsion was granted following Phillip III's ascension to the throne. Details of the deportations were a closely guarded secret. The decree was officially announced by Padre Guadalajara in his *Memorabile Expulsion y Instissimo Destierro de los Moriscos de Espana* and just three days' notice was given to those to be expelled. Morisco wives of Christians were allowed to remain, but Morisco husbands of Christian women were banished. Morisco children under four who wished to stay on the Iberian peninsula were permitted to do so. Moriscos who were found hiding to escape expulsion, risked execution. Between 1609 and 1614, hundreds of thousands of Moriscos were taken to North Africa with no more than a few personal belongings. Many fled into hiding, or escaped into France. As they dispersed throughout North Africa, the Moriscos influenced those with whom they came in contact. They continued to be the objects of prejudice – being seen by those around them as Spanish Catholics. In Morocco, large communities of expatriate Moriscos formed; but more usually they would disperse in their new surroundings, remaining perhaps in small groups.

The Catholic Church had got what it wanted: no Moriscos. But the price had to be paid. The economy stagnated as industry and agriculture declined as a result of the reduced work force. Spain's position as an international power was gradually lost.

Morisco Society

The Moriscos had an enormous pride in all that they and their ancestors had created. This was coupled with their strong devotion to Islam and the sense of unity gained through persecution. A feeling that the future held greatness in store abounded. The Moriscos believed fervently that their Muslim brothers would come to their rescue.

Often they were forced to live in isolated, scattered groups. Stripped of their possessions, customs and traditions, and obstructed in their religion, the Moriscos were put in an impossible situation. Many of their academics and leaders fled to escape execution, thereby leaving a weakened and less united Morisco people behind.

The Mufti of Oran's *fatwa* – religious opinion, of 1563 had provided a guideline for the persecuted Moriscos. It spoke of a superficial observance of Christian practice – 'speaking with your tongue but not believing the words in your heart'. Complex annulling of Christian ceremonies developed, as the Moriscos learned to observe two religions: one forcibly, and the other by choice. Needless to say, the North Africa Muslims were horrified that their Muslim brothers would even contemplate adhering to the laws of Christianity as well as those of Islam.

There were never any major Morisco academic institutions. The scarcity of scholars and learned men who remained in Spain, brought the development of science to a halt. The majority of Moriscos were overworked and partly – or completely – uneducated. With the cessation of formal education in Arabic and only the most elementary Christian teaching given as a substitute, there was a general deterioration in the culture. The Christian re-conquest had brought to an abrupt end, the outstanding Moorish achievements in all literary and scientific fields. Science, which under the Moors had been held in the highest esteem, was seen by the new regime as sorcery.

The main body of Morisco literature that developed is known as *Aljamiado* and appeared in Spanish. Most of it dates from the fifteenth and sixteenth centuries. Initially, Arabic script was placed alongside that of the Aljamiado, but gradually the understanding of Arabic faltered and then was lost. Scholars translated Islamic works so that they might be accessible to the larger audience. Most Aljamiado works are anonymous since its authors feared persecution. It kept alive Islamic stories, themes and information, and in doing so illustrates so well the frustration of the Moriscos in their time of persecution. Unlike much of the heavy and flowery Arab works, Aljamiado is essentially very simple – having been written in an attempt to gain the greatest audience possible. The material, completed at a time of extreme oppression, was a substantial achievement and went to show the dedication of the Moriscos in preserving their vanishing culture and tradition. Aljamiado proved to be a means whereby the Latin and Arab cultures could meet and mix in words. It was there that, at a time of dire conflict, ideas, words and idioms were traded from one society to the other.

Strangely enough, many of the Morisco writers who sought refuge in North Africa set their works down in the Latin script (writing in the Romance dialects). Factors such as these laid them open to persecution by the North African societies in which they settled.

Morisco Magic and Occultism

The restrictions on the Morisco study of science in university and at other levels led to the development of magical practices. Sorcery and the production of talismans had been emphasized by the Moors. Under the Moriscos, the magical systems that evolved compensated for the lack of medical and other scientific knowledge and information. An obsessive adoption of superstition emerged – each occasion, event, day and moment was associated with, or influenced by, a particular superstitious occurrence. A gargantuan number of solutions were set down for situations in all areas of life. One work in this area is *El Libro de Dichos Maravillosos*, the Book of Marvellous Sayings. Among other things, it instructs the reader on how to cure medical afflictions, and in the rudiments of exorcism.

Seals etched with inscriptions and mathematical symbols would be hung around the necks of the sick – or those needing special guidance. Mystical reverence for Quranic texts endowed them with the power of curing medical disorders. Couplets inscribed on a bowl would create a spell affecting all that was poured into it. Here are three such spells:

(1) Invisibility is achieved by wrapping a black cat's heart in a wolf's skin and attaching the package to the right thigh;

(2) The future may be seen by one who pulls the heart from a hoopoe's breast;

(3) He who covets his friend's possessions, or he who wants what his neighbour has, can be cured by feeding him a black dog's heart, recently killed.

'Ain el Kabeeh, the Evil Eye, as it is known to us, was thought by the Moors and Moriscos to be at the centre of all ailments and misfortune. It is still considered a very powerful force across North Africa today and one is never far from an evil eye averter. The most powerful charm against the evil eye is the 'Hand of Fatima', which takes the form of an outstretched palm.

Although many Catholics would not allow themselves to be treated by those Moriscos with medical knowledge, a number of Arab medical and scientific texts were translated into Latin by the Catholics. Cisneros placed a quantity of such works in the university at Henares. Sadly the Moriscos

lost the understanding and relevant background information
to use the material in such texts.

The Catholics used Morisco magic as an excuse for their
persecution. They attributed what they did not understand
to the magic of the Moriscos – even believing that Arabic,
with its harsh sounds and strange letters, had a basis in
magic.

The avid Morisco interest in occult sciences frightened the
Spanish Catholics. They thought that the charms and spells
would summon demons to avenge them. Books containing
spells and talismanic magic that professed great powers were
circulating. Armador Velasco, who had written a tome on
sorcery, was brought before the Inquisition. In his writings
were formulae through which wondrous things might be
achieved. By them, buried treasure could be sought, one
might understand the talk of birds, or destroy evil spells
which had been cast.

Much of the superstition and magic revolved around devils and the potential havoc that they might create if certain
procedures were not followed with rigorous accuracy. For
example, devils had to be left food, otherwise they would
gobble up children and livestock. From this resulted the
custom of leaving dishes of food out each night. When the
plates were found to be empty the next day, the superstition
was simply reinforced: the devils had indeed been hungry.

In Conclusion

With the collapse of the Moorish civilization on the Iberian
peninsula came, as we have seen, the Catholic persecution of
the Moriscos. Their subjugation and consequent expulsion
from Spain proved to be one of the most oppressive tyrannies
perpetrated by one people upon another, in all history. It is
impossible to say whether, using alternative means, the
Catholic conversion squads might have succeeded.
However, their curbs on the Moriscos created animosity
and enmity. The Moriscos lost basic human rights and the

privilege to practise their beliefs – and even speak their own language. Finally, they were driven from Spain to become a minority people again in the lands in which they sought refuge.

In the hands of the Inquisition, the Moriscos were helpless: they were a people with no rights, with no one to help them. They could trust nobody, and were persecuted by all. It is a wonder that any Morisco literature and culture managed to develop at all. The works which still exist show something of the ordeal of those oppressive times – with no faltering from the hope that God would deliver their people from such persecution. The saddest consideration is that a people descended from those famed throughout the civilized world for their achievements and sophistication, were driven to repudiate all that they had accomplished. One wonders what marvels might have been achieved if the Moorish Empire had continued.

SELECT BIBLIOGRAPHY

1 *A Short History of the Saracens*, Ameer Ali, Macmillan & Co, London, 1949.
2 *The Moors*, Michael Brett, Orbis Books Ltd., London, 1980.
3 *Islam & The West: The Moriscos*, Anwar G. Ckhejne, State University of New York, 1983.
4 *Spanish Islam*, R.P.A. Dozy, Chatto & Windus Ltd., London, 1913.
5 *History of the Arabs*, Philip K. Hitti, Macmillan & Co., London, 1951 (5th Edition).
6 *The Moriscos of Spain*, Henry Charles, Bernard Quaritch Ltd., London, 1901.
7 *The Moors*, J.E.B. Meakin, Swan Sonneschein & Co., London, 1902.
8 *The Moorish Empire*, J.E.B. Meakin, Swan Sonneschein & Co., London, 1899.
9 *Footprints of the Moors*, J.E.B. Meakin, From: The Times of Morocco, 1890.
10 *The Moorish Empire in Europe*, S.P. Scott, J.B. Lippincott Company, London, 1904.

11 *The Moors in Spain and Portugal*, Jan Read, Faber and Faber, London 1974.

12 *The Alhambra: a Series of Tales & Sketches of the Moors & Spaniards*, Washington Irving, Lea & Blanchard, Philadelphia, 1837.

13 *A Chronicle of the Conquest of Granada*, Washington Irving, Blackie's School and Home, Library, London, 1894.

14 *The Alhambra; or a New Sketchbook*, Washington Irving, B. Cormon & Blanc, Paris, 1832.

15 *Encyclopaedia of Islam*, Edited by H.A.R. Gibb & E. Lévi-Provençal, Luzac & Co., London, 1960.

6

Macumba: The Evolving Faith

AFRICAN-BASED BELIEFS IN BRAZIL

The colonizers transported hundreds of thousands of Africans to the Americas to work as slaves. However, their overcrowded vessels conveyed more than mere labourers to toil on the plantations: they brought experts in the magical and medicinal sciences to the New World. The African beliefs and their complex systems of worship flourished in Brazil and other American nations. They adapted their form and evolved, absorbing symbols and ideas from many religions, and in doing so ensured for themselves a mass following. The main Brazilian African-based belief-system is known as *Macumba*.

It has many names and many offspring, and, although it was originally only deeply embedded in the lower classes, Macumba has now permeated all levels of the middle, and even upper classes of Brazilian society. Macumba, which is known in other parts of the Americas as *Santeria*, is hard to classify. Some label it as a cult, others as a faith or belief: but its enormous following – about ten million Brazilians alone, not to mention its growing respectability, perhaps makes it worthy of being termed a religion.

In this monograph we shall consider what Macumba is and reflect upon the way it has absorbed the ideas and propaganda of those who have sought to influence it. We will look at its origins and the reasons why it first managed to gain such a firm hold over colonial Brazil: as well as discussing the symbols, ceremonies and ideas that it promotes. Then in conclusion we will note the expansion of Macumba, and its

107

sister Santeria, through South, Central and North America: from the southern tip of Brazil to the northern-most parts of Canada.

The Origins and Components of Macumba

To understand from where Macumba really came, we must consider the ancient tribal societies of West Africa, in particular the Yoruba people. Their kingdom, which was thought to have been founded in the twelfth century, held enormous power and wealth until the turn of the last century. Their rulers encouraged the production of metalwork and jewellery fashioned from precious metals and ivory. They governed according to the wishes of the *Orishas*: the tribal gods.

Yoruba society, based in southern Nigeria and Benin, was weakened by an invasion by the Ewe tribe, some three hundred years ago. Many of the Yoruba sought refuge from the barbarous attack, away from their native area of Daho-mey, along the Nigerian coast. As their society was just managing to regroup and to adjust to the new location, a new threat arrived: slave traders.

The traders took advantage of the settlements on the shore, carrying off all they could to their ships for transpor-tation to the Americas. For those subjected to an Atlantic crossing in the hold of a slave ship, there was little comfort. They clung onto their tribal beliefs, onto their gods, wor-shipping them more vigorously than ever. Inevitably, their convictions about these deities were reinforced.

The Yoruba tribespeople, like all others transported as slaves from Africa, were dispersed into small groups, often in the most remote parts of Brazil (as well as in other parts of the Americas). At times, they would work alongside enslaved American Indians, and they began to learn too about their captors: the Portuguese. They prayed to their gods, hoping for salvation. As they worked and worshipped in their new lands they began to be influenced by the Indians and by the

Catholic Portuguese. It was then that the pure Yoruba rites and ways absorbed something from all those around them. Symbols and ideas crept across the racial boundaries and, as this happened, the new system of Macumba was formed.

Symbols such as the Cross, which is so central to Catholicism, were simply digested and respected. Unlike many other religions, Macumba characteristically understands the 'power' of symbolism. It tends not to fight an idea or attribute, but absorbs it and gains through its strength. Numerous ideas have come across from Indian lore, as well as articles and medicinal herbs used in ceremonies and spells: such as feathers from Amazonian birds. From Catholicism, Macumba adopted the use of 'holy' water but, more importantly, it embraced the saints of Catholicism.

The traders and Brazilian authorities in whose custody the slaves remained, were keen that the slaves should not continue with their 'pagan' ceremonies. To cure them of these heathen beliefs, mass baptisms were carried out and each slave was taught to recite elementary Catholic prayers. Indeed, legislation was passed that all slaves were to be initiated in the ways of Catholicism as soon as they set foot in the Americas.

For some, following the ardours of the transatlantic crossing aboard a slave ship, the gentle words of a pastor will have been welcome. Perhaps this was the point at which Macumba began to listen to the other faiths and learn from them. In his acclaimed book *The Moon And Two Mountains*[1], Pedro McGregor notes that a superficial observance of the Catholic saints would have ensured the slaves less castigation and therefore more time to follow their own beliefs.

The Catholic system of worship of saints fitted in very well with the Yoruba ceremonies and faiths, for the Yoruba also had heroes whom they invoked; each in their large pantheon of deities representing a particular value. The main difference is that what the Catholics worship as a person with holy status, Macumba sees as an *Orisha*, a god. The leaders of the Yoruba realised that, as long as they seemed to be paying homage to the Catholic saints, they could do just about anything they liked.

Gradually, each of the Catholic saints became equated with a Yoruba god. As we shall see later, the Yoruba deities, which are known in Macumba by their Yoruba titles, are generally worshipped in the form of the Catholic saints. For example *Xango*, the Yoruba god of thunder and lightning, is equated with St. Barbara. Macumba relies on deeply primitive African magical systems and is not dependent on the Catholicism it has absorbed. It merely makes use of the structured framework that the Catholic religion provides so well, and onto that it imposes the traditional Yoruba beliefs.

Uprisings within the slave communities tended to fail, because the different groups of slaves were usually not from the same tribe. Two tribes, formerly hostile to each other, might now have been mixed together: they could therefore never completely trust one another. The authorities were so apprehensive that those whom they had enslaved would unite, that they even went to the length of allowing a few tribal activities to continue, so that tribal barriers should be kept alive.

Groups of Muslim slaves refused adamantly to have anything to do with Catholicism. Their famous 1835 uprising in Bahia Province was rigorously suppressed, with numerous casualties. The Muslim faith all but vanished, as it would not conform or adapt. Meanwhile Macumba carried on its coexistence with Catholicism, allowing it to form a secure base and to grow in size and strength.

As Macumba was frequently forced to develop within isolated groups, there came about a wide divergence in its activities. For example, proceedings are still very different in Rio de Janeiro, from their counterparts in Salvador. It is impossible to state what is the norm, but this makes Macumba all the more interesting and allows it constantly to surprise.

Macumba's infiltration of the white classes of Brazilian

society has been most widespread in recent times. Some writers have mentioned the important role the slave women-folk had in initially promoting Macumba in the white classes. As domestics, they came into close contact with the white colonizers, and as nannies to the white children, they could instil in them their powerful African beliefs.

The middle class of today has proved responsive to the ways of unorthodox religions and beliefs through the past experiences of the Portuguese and Spanish colonizers. Both, having lived under the rule of the North African Moorish peoples, were used to mixing racially and learning from other faiths.

The Moorish occupation of the Iberian peninsula left its mark on the people who lived under it. Their descendents, as colonizers in their turn, transferred these Moorish particularities onto the African and Indian slaves whom they oppressed. As a result, various Berber and North African symbols and ideas have been incorporated into Macumba. In particular, the North African expertise in the making of talismans, and the Arab methods of divination through numerical combinations, are to be found in Macumba.

The development of technology and modern methods of communication have had relatively little effect on the spread of Macumba. As one might have expected, a single uniform philosophy for the belief has not come about – such as the broad-based appreciations that major religions such as Catholicism, Christianity or Islam enjoy. Brazil still has a locally orientated society and, being such a vast country, there is often little integration between the more isolated parts. The ceremonial songs, offerings, spirits and activities are always varied, giving Macumba extra strength through this diversity.

The Shamanistic thread that has influenced some of Macumba's rites and ideals has come from an Amazon Indian faith known as *Pajelança*. It uses animals as a spiritual force and depends on the Amazon Indian knowledge of nature.

It seems that Hinduism as well as Christianity has now met this African-based faith. In San Paulo, the Hindu community has been exposed to the workings of Macumba. I have heard from several people of the new confluence of the two faiths. One man told me:

I have been participating in Yoruba ceremonies for several years. My interest came about when my father died . . . I wanted to find out what my future would be, it was emotionally a very hard time. Eighteen months ago I moved from Salvador down to San Paulo, I mixed with many groups of people. All the time I wanted to find a new Yoruba group with which I could carry on my faith. I asked many people in the city – finally the landlady of my apartment building suggested that I try a particular gathering, that always came together on Saturday nights.

I was introduced to the medium who presided over the assembly, and she said it would be fine for me to join in. I was very surprised when I went to the altar to pay my respects to the Orishas. Usually we give small offerings to figures of the Catholic saints. Alongside the saints there were some other statues. I did not recognize them. The medium explained that the group appealed to various Orishas, by praying to Hindu gods. Since I have been with these people, I have heard of other groups who pray to the Buddha.

Influences from all peoples represented in Brazilian society have filtered into Macumba. Like the Hindus, San Paulo's large Japanese community has entered its ranks. So new traits, with the attributes of West and North Africa, Amazonia, Berber and Catholic, are woven into one cohesive religious unit. And, as Macumba comes into contact with the minority groups in Brazil, a knowledge of it inevitably seeps back to the home countries of these minorities.

The Orishas

The Yoruba tribe traditionally invoked hundreds of gods. Their belief that the Orishas (gods) control every event and circumstance has entered Macumba as a central theme. One of the fundamental objectives of the followers of Macumba is to strive to keep their deities happy. This is done in several ways.

Corners of houses are set aside for offerings to, and images of, the Orishas. Each Orisha is linked to one or more specific 'strength', and each has his own favourite colour, food, stone and way of doing things. It is very important to bear these preferences in mind when requesting help or advice. Some Orishas hold more power than others, and the ones who are reputed to have performed the most astonishing miracles are considered to be superior.

However, the most significant way to please the Orishas is to allow them to descend and possess one's body. Followers believe that it pleases the Orishas so greatly to be inside a human form, that they will grant the wishes of the possessed person, and of those around him. It is believed that, whilst possession is taking place, the one possessed has no control over his or her own body. At a feast, the possessed one may eat huge amounts of food, drink bottles of alcohol, yet, following the possession, they will feel fine. This only goes to prove to those who embrace Macumba, that it is the Orisha who has been gorging himself, and it is he who has benefited.

The practice of referring to Orishas by different names makes matters very confusing. It is especially hard to determine which Orisha is possessing a person when it enters a body. A name unknown to the Macumba group may be used by the god. Those around the possessed try to ascertain which deity has descended, so that they can treat it in the appropriate manner. It is of the utmost importance not to trouble the Orisha with matters on which it is not an expert, since one would not want to embarrass a deity.

The general term for Macumba in other parts of the

Americas, especially Central and North America, is *Santeria*. It comes from the Spanish word *Santos*, a saint, and means the Way of the Saints. This title seems inappropriate as the faith to which it refers often worships the Yoruba Orishas, who are not seen merely as saints, but as deities.

Some of the main saint-Orisha combinations are as follows. *Yemanja* is the Virgin Mary, and is seen as the mother of the main Orishas. *Olofi* is the deity associated with Christ; *Xango* (also known as *Chango*), the god of lightning and thunder, is affiliated with St. Barbara. *Oba* is connected with St. Catherine, and *Oxun* with St. Anne. *Ogun*, the god linked to hunting and war is equated with the Catholic St. Peter, and *Oshossi* is the Yoruba equivalent of St. Sebastian. *Aganyu* is associated with St. Joseph, *Bacosco* with St. Christopher, and *Oddudua* with St. Claire. These correspondences vary enormously, as do the actual Yoruba names by which they are known.

Brazilian Macumba differs greatly from the practices of its sister Santeria faiths which occur throughout the Americas. With the migration of Brazilians to other parts of the Americas, specific elements found only in Macumba have been transported to, and been assimilated into, many Santeria groups. Similarly, Orisha-saint associations usually only found in Spanish-speaking American nations have crept into Brazilian society.

The Yoruba tribe did not necessarily give structured images to their deities; the use of classical Catholic icons became widespread for this purpose. It seemed however, that the Yoruba pantheon could be represented by other means alongside man-made forms, such as by a smoothly rounded stone or some other object fashioned by nature. But Catholic saints are now firmly entrenched in the religion of Macumba, and their forms can be found on the altars of Macumba shrines across Brazil.

Items known to be favoured by the particular Orisha being invoked, are kept around their image. These can range from anything made in their favourite colour, to a food they are known to be fond of. Even things of little value, such as a pebble, the kind that might catch one's attention for a moment whilst strolling on a beach, may be seen as having some special significance.

In Macumba ceremonies and rites, offerings are made to an Orisha, usually in the hope of persuading him to grant a wish. Sacrifices of animals are widespread, and include just about any creature one could mention. What is offered depends largely on the importance of the ceremony and the Orisha to whom it is addressed. Chickens and other birds such as ducks are very commonly used. Other animals that may be chosen for sacrifice are monkeys, rabbits, goats, pigs, turtles, mice, coloured tropical birds, and even bulls. The priest may specify that the creature must be black or have certain markings.

The procedure for the sacrifice is very important and it is vital that the one performing it understands the method preferred by the Orisha for whom it is intended.

Simple supplications to the Orisha and a sacrifice, may well not be enough to coax him into responding to a request. Often standard incantations must be repeated in front of the Orisha's image. Tobacco and sweetmeats are left to urge him to respond to the pleas. These things must be replaced once a week, and in that time the deity absorbs the spiritual essence of the oblation.

The Orisha *Elegua* is particularly powerful: great care must be taken not only in what is provided for him, but also to make sure that the offering is fresh and frequently replaced. In general, to sacrifice a single animal, or to offer one object for the pleasure of two deities, would be seen by them as extremely insulting and their anger at such an action would be incalculable.

The Yoruba legends concerning how the Orishas came into being were always passed down by word of mouth. The Yorubas who remained in West Africa still narrate the same ancient legends as they have always told them. However, the slaves brought to the New World had gaps in their knowledge of the stories, as the result of being wrenched from their native society. They filled the gaps with fresh ideas and tales, inspired by their new surroundings. These stories were influenced by the ordeal of the Atlantic crossing and the unimaginable traumas of the journey. American Indian myths and Catholic parables have also influenced Macumba's picture of its own origins. These new 'legends', if we can call them that, are scarcely recognisable when compared to their African counterparts.

The Yoruba deities and the saints with which they are equated, are seen as so sacred that one should not trouble them with minor problems and requests. A huge number of other spirits with a less prestigious status exist who can be consulted on a much more informal basis. They are known as *Encantados*, and are believed to live under the crust of the Earth in their *encantarias*, dwellings. They are not holy enough to reside in heaven with the regular saints but their very existence provides an additional division, thus raising still further the status of the deities. Their powers are weaker than those of the deities, but like them, they too can look into the future and assist people with their problems.

They are capable of inflicting pain and causing harm if only to demonstrate their strength. Like the Yoruba deities, the Encantados can also possess human beings, and in doing so they force the human soul out of its body into limbo. It is believed that the Earth and all within it belong to the Encantados.

These lesser spirits tend to stand for moral Christian principles, such as generosity and thoughtfulness towards others. They are well-known for reprimanding and punishing those of whom they are in possession. This is generally achieved by making the body strike the ground and bones are frequently broken. The Encantados have the power to prevent the possessed's soul from re-entering his body, so that he remains unconscious in a comatose state. They are known for fits of anger, if their wishes are not carried out with due respect and diligence.

Portugal's sixteenth century monarch Sebastian was killed in the battle of Alcazar-Kabir, whilst fighting in Morocco at the age of twenty-four. He is now seen as an Encantado, and is referred to by the title *Xapanan*. The Portuguese were so shocked that their young ruler had died that a legend developed, which said he would come back to life one day.

The Amazon Indians' veneration of nature's creatures is reflected in the range of Encantados who may ascend to possess a human being. If one's body is taken over by an Encantado in the form of a tropical animal, it may be necessary to seek advice from a specialist in such spirits. Until information about the particular Encantado in possession is obtained, those around must act with great caution and diplomacy, lest they upset it. The range of these spirits is a measure of the diversity of elements that have inspired the development of Macumba.

The fashion in which Macumba, and those beliefs related to it, absorb new Encantados and other material from diverse areas, acts almost as an incentive to new followers. Once these fresh elements have been absorbed, they are modified to fit in with the existing material practised by the group.

The Spiritual Guides, Priests and Magic

The Yoruba traditions dictate that only those who have passed through rigorous ceremonies of initiation may undertake its most solemn responsibilities. The 'priests' held in the highest esteem are known as *Babalawos*. The term has come directly from West Africa, and is thought to have originated from the words *Baba* (father) and *Li-Awo* (he who guards the secret). They preside at rites and ceremonial proceedings, and are capable of 'reading' signs obtained from various divinations. Neophytes are instructed by them in the ways of the cult and taught how to formulate the concoctions used in spells and magical charms. Babalawos working with Macumba are similar to their counterparts (also known as Babalawos) found in the Secret Societies of West Africa.

In the days of slavery, the men were put to work on the plantations and in the mines of Brazil. The exhausting labour prevented them from taking part even in the attenuated initiation procedures necessary to become a Babalawo. As a result there was, in many instances, a change whereby female slaves entered the ranks of priesthood. They carried on and developed the magical traditions and knowledge of Macumba. In Africa, these positions of high responsibility are very often closed to women.

Both those initiated into Macumba, and people with little knowledge of the faith come to the Babalawo seeking answers and information. No problem is thought to be too great for his wisdom and experience. He will respond by reading the signs given by cowrie shells and other forms of divination: only then does the will of the Orishas become clear.

One of the most appealing aspects of Macumba is that it allows spells to be cast, using both natural and supernatural means. Those brought up with staunch Catholic values have turned increasingly to Macumba, as they can approach a Babalawo to concoct a potion to heal an ailment or cast a spell. Babalawos are willing to take on cases even when a medical doctor might say there was no chance of recovery. Many in the lower ranges of society cannot afford the fees to see a physician, let alone pay for the medication he might prescribe. Although a Babalawo's remedies too are sometimes expensive, that will usually be due to the cost of the materials needed for the treatment. An understanding of South American natural herbs and extracts has come primarily from the Amazonian and other Indians.

The extent to which 'magical' practices may be used is unlimited: they are thought to be able to bring joy, anger, make a husband return, see into the future, or look into the mind. In Macumba, when magic is used to inflict punishment, it is usually done so as to bring justice where a wrong has been done. Macumba is by its nature set against such despicable activities as the Cuban *Mayomberos*, as we shall see later. The Yoruba Orishas concern themselves only with good: they abhor evil.

In her authoritative work *Santeria: African Magic in Latin America*[5], Migene Gonzalez-Wippler mentions what she terms as 'contagious magic'. That is, the idea that anything which has at one time been in contact with something, will always have contact with it, and will always be able to affect it in one way or another. So, hair pulled from a brush or some threads from the victim's shirt can be incorporated in a spell. The only prerequisite for a spell to work, seems to be one's absolute faith that it will be successful. If one is convinced that the desired effect is going to happen and one believes in the Yoruba pantheon, the required outcome is inevitable.

Each plant is thought by those initiated in the activities of Macumba, to have a part to play in one spell or another. Each Orisha has his own favourite plant and herb, and the relevant one must be invoked before the plant is picked. Many of the medicinal plants employed in Macumba have a known medical basis in the West. Garlic, for example, has traditionally been used in concoctions to reduce blood pressure.

Amulets and talismans (known sometimes as *resguardo*, protector), are made by Babalawos in dedication to a particular saint related to a particular illness. They may be tied to the afflicted part of the body, or placed near an image of the saint.

Santeros are also respected operators in the art of African-based magic (especially Santeria). Their techniques can differ from those of the Babalawos; for example they tend to divine by using coconut rinds rather than with cowrie shells and a Santero will have more contact with the uninitiated than will a Babalawo. They are seen as intermediaries between the world of mortals and that of the Orishas.

Babalowos and Santeros have perhaps their most important responsibilities during ceremonial rites. They have the correct understanding to carry out the sacrifice of animals, using the appropriate prayers and invocations. They are expert at determining which Orisha has descended to possess and, more importantly, exactly how to treat that particular deity. Inappropriate etiquette and procedure could bring disaster.

In Brazil, there have been a series of 'natural' healers who have claimed to work with the power of Macumba. Through using these natural forces they have done remarkable things. Although such healings may seem delusional to those who have not witnessed them first hand, and baffling to those who have, much has been written on such treatments. It would seem that, in those cases where orthodox medicine has no explanation for the miraculous healing, a great deal of strong-willed positive thought can have some effect. Some of Brazil's most acclaimed natural healers have been reprimanded by the authorities for using unlicensed methods to treat the sick. Many of them perform complex medical procedures, such as eye operations, using no anaesthetic and with the aid of nothing more than a pair of nail scissors.

One young educated Brazilian woman told me:

I had a teacher at school who would take the class to ceremonies in which she was participating. Children are not so sceptical about this sort of thing, and they tend to find it easier to believe in supernatural events. One of my classmates had broken her collarbone the previous summer and it had never healed properly. It was causing her a great deal of pain, and you could easily see the bone sticking out at the joint. One time, our teacher took us to her apartment. One third of the main living room was curtained off. She asked us to come in and sit down. When we were seated she said a prayer and spoke to one of the plaster statues of the saints, I think it was St. Barbara. For an hour we sat as she coaxed the saint to descend. When she did come down we were terrified and intrigued: our teacher spoke with a different voice and her eyes were wide open. Her movements were disjointed and uncoordinated; it was very strange.

She went over to where my friend sat, the girl with the

wrongly set collarbone. She placed her hands on the girl's head and moved them down her neck, until they were placed actually on the collarbone. Then she rubbed very gently. As we watched, the lump that had been there for a year or so went away. The girl's pain vanished. I never would have believed it if I hadn't seen it for myself.

Healers are at one extreme of traditional Macumba. They tend to use other names for the faith in which they work. This area is more popular than ever and it is expanding: appealing to the wealthy upper classes as it grows.

Ceremonies and Rites

The main activities encompassed by Macumba take place when a group of believers come together and invoke the Orishas. In such assemblies the disciples can benefit from the wisdom of their deities. Most of the rites are based on Yoruba liturgies which, having been brought to the New World, were fundamental in keeping the traditional beliefs alive. Macumba is essentially a group activity. It flourished by allowing the slaves a form of escape, and by providing an intense religious support through which they could endure the hardship of their lives. Human nature seems to require some means whereby unbearable circumstances can be made bearable. Macumba developed as a faith robust enough to give the slaves hope in the most dire situations. Many of the rituals have changed little since the slaves practised them while they were being persecuted.

The ceremonies performed in Brazil differ enormously, and many more varieties can be found throughout the Americas. Although the basic principles are usually the same, it is impossible to generalize as to the exact events of each gathering. Some groups are most secretive in their affairs, permitting only those initiated into the sect to attend. The initiation ceremonies can be lengthy, arduous and, more often than not, extremely costly for the neophyte. Other sects invite all to attend, even to the point of encouraging members of the public to watch. Spectators are frequently absorbed into the ranks of the faithful. Those supervising such large gatherings believe that it increases the power of the ritual to have as many as possible praying to the Orishas.

There is one principal ceremony of initiation used by the Yoruba-based faiths: it is known as *Asiento*, Making the Saint. The ritual entails the seating of the saint on the head of the neophyte. A bond is achieved by this, and the saint becomes a patron to the pupil.

First it is essential that the novice is cleansed, and his body is purged, so that it will be ready to accept the spirit of the saint. The head is thoroughly cleaned and made ready for the initiation rites. The initiate must wear a necklace of beads that has been specially strung for him by his sponsor, the *Yubbona*. The numerical pattern created by the beads, or shells is of great significance, as is their colour, for such details must correspond exactly to the preferences of the Orisha who is to be invoked. For instance, a necklace strung and worn in dedication to the deity *Orunla* would be constructed from a sequence of green and yellow beads.

A mixture of substances is sprinkled over the candidate's head, including coconut, butter and ground eggshell. Only when this mixture has been removed can the initiation begin. The Babalawo's part is very important in the ceremony. He is responsible for consulting the neophyte to make sure that he is ready to enter into a relationship with the Orisha. Through complex and lengthy processes of divination, the Babalawo will decide which deity the initiate must induce to descend into him. Sacrifices in abundance are made by the Babalawo: only through such offerings will the Orisha be persuaded to patronize the novice. Consequently such rituals can be extremely costly.

Those allowed to be present at an Asiento ceremony are restricted in number. In some cases only the Babalawo, the initiate and his sponsor may attend. However, other groups permit those who have been through the ceremony themselves to witness the event. The place where the ritual is carried out is of great importance. It is often special to such Macumba practices and is known as the *Terreiro*.

The procedure of the initiation ceremony differs widely from one place to another. In the remote areas of Amazonas when such ceremonies take place, comparatively traditional practices are used. In the big cities such as Rio de Janeiro, Belem, or San Paulo, the process is less formal.

The initiate, known in Macumba as the *Yaguo*, is brought forward into the Terreiro. His head is shaved and coloured circles of dye are painted onto his scalp. The hair and what is left of the dye is of great consequence. It must be kept and buried with the initiate when he dies. Animals are sacrificed according to the divination of the priest. He decides not only what to sacrifice, but the order in which the offerings are to be made. Only after the correct combination of offerings, prayers and observation of appropriate etiquette, does the desired Orisha descend and enter the body of the neophyte.

The pupil falls to the ground and goes into paroxysms, convulsing as the saint takes hold of his body. The Babalawo takes a chicken, pulls off its head, and passes the bird to the neophyte, bidding him to sip the blood. Blood is of the utmost significance to Macumba ceremonies.

Whilst in possession of a human body an Orisha will often drink animal blood. After the ceremony, the sacrificed animals usually will be eaten in a feast; their flesh being the food of man, while their blood is seen as the food of the gods.

The Yaguo must go into seclusion for a period of about a week, during which time his body is constantly washed in herbal mixtures (*Omiero*). One course of rites follows another, and only after several months is the initiate deemed to be a full member of Macumba. He is given a number of stones (*Otanes*), which are kept in sacred bowls known as *Soperas*. He is also given some shells which conceal within them divine secrets. It is through these shells that one can know the wishes and prophecies of the deities. Usually cowrie shells, these shells are fundamental in divination and are known as *Dilogun*. They can only reveal the fate of the initiated one, and others, if there are the correct number of observers (which is commonly 16 or 18). Their user must learn to read their signs accurately. The shells are rubbed and cast down on a mat. The order in which they fall each time, and the pattern which they make, determines how they are to be interpreted. Only after years of experience can one claim to be an expert in divination.

Minas Gerais, a member of a Macumba sect operating in a very fashionable part of Belo Horizonte, told me of the experience that he had had:

I had heard about Macumba, but so has everybody. Those of us who were brought up in a nice part of town always looked down on it. We would laugh when we saw its symbols, when we heard its chants and the beating of the drums. I might always have been that way, like many of my friends still are. Then one night I had a nightmare that I was going to be killed. It seemed crazy, as I had no enemies. My dream was that I would die the next day in a car crash, as the brake lines in my car had been cut. The next morning, before driving to work, I checked the brakes and just as I had dreamt – they didn't work. I was very confused, and in this state I confided what had happened in a colleague at work. He suggested that I go see the friend of a friend of his.

It was quite a shock when I met with the man to whom I had been recommended. He didn't conform to the usual idea of a Macumba priest. He was white, dressed in a hand-tailored suit, and lived in one of San Paulo's most prestigious residential areas. In one large room of his apartment, crammed with images of Catholic saints, he revealed the identity of the man trying to kill me.

This priest told me to go to a special shop and buy a particular statue of one of the saints. I was to take it home and say prayers to it every night. He made me an amulet which I was to have with me at all times. But the most important thing for me to do, he said, was to place my faith in him. He requested me to bring him a piece of clothing from my would-be killer; all that he asked was that it be freshly worn and not washed since. This man worked in the next office to me. While he was in the toilet I went into his office and took the silk scarf off the coat stand. It was that scarf that I presented to the Macumba priest.

He was pleased as there were hairs on the scarf: he said that they would give his spell extra force. I was instructed to appeal to the particular saint every day of two weeks, and the man said that his spell would relieve me of the killer.

For fourteen days I left offerings at the base of the image, and looked towards it in prayer. Then at the end of the second week I turned up to work as usual. The office next to mine was empty, and the man who had wished me harm had left. The word was that he had moved to the north of Brazil, but no one was quite sure of the details.

In the north-eastern Brazilian city of Belem, large Macumba ceremonies are held known as *Batuques*. Even those who are sceptical of the proceedings are permitted as spectators. People tend to gather before ten in the evening at the Terreiro. They pay their respects to the images of the Catholic saints, and other honoured figures who have been absorbed into the religion. They leave fresh offerings of food, tobacco and rum at the feet of the saints.

The form of Macumba in Belem is particularly absorbent in its nature. It will readily adopt new methods and notions in order to attract as many followers as it can. A strong group identity is created, by the donning of uniform robes: the preferred colours of certain Orishas. Mediums and the initiated wear their strings of beads, crucifixes, and medallions that bring good luck to those around them.

The ceremony begins with a short prayer; songs are sung to a rhythmic beat banged out on a *cheque-cheque* drum. One of the Orishas is called upon to descend. A spirit will enter one of those present, and each will greet it in turn with appropriate politeness. It is invited to eat and drink and move as it likes in the borrowed body. At times, the Orisha gorges itself, through the body of the possessed person. He may drink bottles of alcohol, devour plate after plate of food. Only after he has satisfied his appetite do those present begin to ask for favours. Some want solutions to their problems, others desire healing cures, or seek advice on what course of action to take. The Orisha may talk with a deep voice, distorting that of the possessed person. Whilst the deity is present, the experienced mediums stay close around him to interpret his wishes and prophecies.

Special feasts, sometimes called *Guemileres*, are held out of respect for a specific Orisha. The deity's favourite dishes and meals are produced and laid out for him to enjoy. Such banquets are prepared in gratitude for work that he has done, or in celebration of his birthday.

Mayombero and the Black Arts

Those who do not follow Macumba often assume that the faith concerns itself with sorcery and illegal activities. As mentioned above, Macumba usually seeks to cause injury to another, only if, by doing so, it will cause justice to prevail. However, the slaves who came from Africa did bring with them techniques of sorcery and witchcraft. Such matters have long been practised on African soil and were held to be of great importance. Small diverse groups work across the Americas in complete secrecy: each is prepared to cast spells by which life will be lost. Although we have been looking specifically at Brazilian Macumba, one of the more interesting African-based demonic sects is that of *Mayombero*.

Many of the techniques adopted by these cults have African origins. Some are similar in their initiations and the magic they use, to the practices of the West African Secret Societies.

The Mayomberos have something similar to a *Borfima* (used by the Human Leopard Society of Sierra Leone). It is the repository of all power, central to the society, and exists generally in the form of a bag – in which certain articles must regularly be placed so that the Borfima can preserve its strength. The outside of the bag must be anointed with human fat and fed human blood on occasion. The Mayomberos special source of power, similar to the Borfima, is called a *Gurunfinda*. It is more like an amulet than an actual bag of any significant size. Like the African Borfima, it contains parts of a human corpse (often someone is specially killed for the purpose); the eyes, tongues and hearts of various mammals, as well as items such as earth from the grave of one who has taken his own life.

Babalawos faithful to Macumba will be called upon from time to time to perform exorcisms. Some such rituals are necessary to put an end to a jealous spirit tormenting a person (known as *Despojos*). Passages from the Bible, particularly the Psalms, will be read aloud to pacify the demented spirit. In other instances, such as when the Mayomberos 'hire' a spirit to haunt a certain person, a Babalawo of sufficient power and magical knowledge must be sent for. Two of the more serious types of evil phantoms are the *Espiritu Intranquillo*, the Restless Spirit; and the *Espiritu Traviesos*, the poltergeist type, who haunts a material object.

The Mayomberos have an extensive knowledge of the natural powers of herbs and plants. They claim to be able to weave spells of great magical strength that can bring devastation and harm to those at whom they are directed. They make use of powders such as *Precipitado Rojo* to destroy and cause damage. Migene Gonzalez-Wippler mentions in her book *Santeria: African Magic in Latin America*[5], a number of Mayombero spells.

For example, in one which is aimed at doing away with someone, a lemon is sliced down the middle, and a scrap of paper inscribed with the name of the victim is pressed onto the surface of one of the halves. A little of the Precipitado Rojo powder is shaken onto the scrap of paper, before the lemon halves are rejoined. In the shape of a cross, fifty pins are stuck into the lemon, so that they join the lemon back together. The fruit is put into a black jar, which is then filled with vinegar, black coffee and urine. It is thrown into a river. As soon as the jar hits the surface of the water the spell is activated. The strength is achieved in part by the extreme power of Precipitado Rojo: so immense is its force that few are even prepared to use it.

The Mayomberos have been traced back to the African tribe of the Bantus. Their chief home in the Americas is in Cuba, where many Bantu slaves were sent. Mayombero activities are on many occasions alleged to have been involved in matters of political concern. It is a well-known fact that many Central and South American governments look towards the African-based religious systems for guidance and support. Following the 1959 Cuban revolution, a very large number of Cubans fled to the United States, where they made new homes. Miami and the extensive Cuban areas of New York (especially in the Bronx), are home to the practices of the Mayombero. The evil reasons for using such magic have changed from matters of tribal rivalry to conflict in the world of multinational corporations.

The Expansion of Macumba and Santeria

Macumba developed as a result of people from one continent being transferred to a new land many thousands of miles from their own. Unlike those who sought futures for themselves in the freedom of North America, the slaves arrived in the New World as captive labourers, who had been transported against their will. Through the decades of persecution they clung to their faith, as it alone could provide an escape from the tortured conditions of normal life. This utter dependence on Macumba developed it into a strong and resolute network. More was required of Macumba (or Santeria) than of its Catholic and Christian counterparts. It needed to be a faith that could respond to its followers: it has remained effective and streamlined. But more important than anything else, Macumba has kept its ability to adapt.

More than one hundred years have passed since slavery was finally abolished in Brazil, but still the Yoruba-based gods are all around. There are cries in the Yoruba tongue throughout the villages and the cities, and the faith continues to expand. It is firmly entrenched in Brazil. Each community has a group that looks towards the Orishas for guidance, and its observances spread as the slaves were moved from one area to another. It seems as if Macumba's very nature is that of a fully mobile religion.

Wherever the slaves went, their belief in Macumba went with them. The Portuguese, who have continued to keep strong economic and cultural ties with Brazil, absorbed Macumba. It can be found in Lisbon, being practised by the descendents of those who learnt its ways from slaves. When slavery was at its height, Cuba worked tens of thousands of Africans in its sugar mills. They were forced to harvest what was known as the 'White Gold'. As mentioned above, following the Cuban revolution in 1959, a large number of Cubans emigrated to the United States of America. Many of them were experienced in the ways of Santeria, or *Lucumi* as it is called in Cuba. Macumba has also filtered into the United States through the Brazilian communities, as have other forms of Santeria through their respective cultures.

In many cities in the United States, there are shops, sometimes even on the main street with giant plaster casts of Catholic saints in the windows. These shops, known as *Botanicas*, might at first sight seem to be preaching Catholic ways. But on closer examination of the window, or the shop itself, there are hundreds of items foreign to Catholicism: jars of beads, graded into their various colours and shapes; *Soperas* stacked in one corner and the stones of the Orishas nearby. There are rows of images of the saints in plaster and plastic lining one wall and books in Portuguese, Spanish and English stored on shelves. There are also amulets and talismans, strung on leather thongs; the bones of a small mammal in one box; the feathers of some tropical bird displayed neatly in a glass case; pouches of herbs and mixtures of dried leaves are all around. There is the smell of burnt brown sugar and garlic, to ward off evil spirits. But this is not San Paulo or some small town in Brazil – this is a shop on New York's fashionable Park Avenue.

Over one hundred million people in the Americas are now said to be looking towards African-based faiths for power and guidance. In the United States, the spread is occurring at a furious rate, as minority groups have come into contact with the Latin American ways of Macumba and Santeria. These groups have learnt, influenced, and been influenced. As Macumba increases in size and respectability one can only speculate on its future. Its existence however, seems to be very firmly established in the Western world. It offers primary ideas, activities and solutions, nonexistent in other faiths: which seem to satisfy a primitive core still lingering in peoples of even the most developed of nations.

SELECT BIBLIOGRAPHY

1 *The Moon and Two Mountains*, Pedro McGregor, Souvenir Press, London, 1966.
2 *Santeria: An African Religion in America*, J.M. Murphy, Original Publications, New York, 1989.
3 *The Golden Bough*, J.G. Frazer, MacMillan & Co., London, 1929 (Abridged Edition).
4 *Yoruba Beliefs and Sacrificial Rites*, J.O. Awolalu, Longman, London, 1979.
5 *Santeria: African Magic in Latin America*, Migene Gonzalez-Wippler, Original Publications, New York, 1981.
6 *Spirits of the Deep*, Seth and Ruth Leacock, New York, 1972.
7 *Afro-Brazilian Cults*, Frances O'Gorman, Livraria Francisco Alves Editoria, Rio de Janeiro, 1977.
8 *African Religions in Brazil*, R. Bastide, John Hopkins University (translated by Helen Shebba), 1978.

9 *Macumba: Cultos Afro-Brasileiros*, Crilo Folch, Ediçoes Paulinas, San Paulo, 1976.
10 *Candomble E Umbanda*, Raimundo Cintra, Paulinas, San Paulo, 1985.

7

The Fascination of Arabia

PETER BRENT

I must begin by confessing that I know very little about
Arabia. Yet there is a sense in which all of us know something
about Arabia, that is about 'an' Arabia. What interests me is
the way in which this Arabia, that we all carry as part of our
imaginative equipment, has been created. In other words, I
want to talk about the way in which we have been fascinated,
over many centuries, by this arid oblong of mountain and
desert which lies between the Red Sea and the Persian Gulf
and the ways in which that fascination has been expressed
and created again and again by the travellers who went there,
and took the risk of going there, on our behalf. Because there
'is' a fascination for us in that curiously potent wilderness
and in the people whose invisible trails criss-cross its aridities
and desert. If one says desert, nomad, bedouin, oasis, if one
says Arabia then the words drop into our understanding with
a very curious resonance, which is not to be found in other
parts of the world. And the echoes that they give us are very
complicated, the message that these echoes offer is a curious
one because it hints at something that no other part of the
world does, a sort of unobtainable nobility, freedom, an
ancient honour, a grandeur of simplicity and the great clean-
liness of distance.

Of course, this went to some people's heads; I have a
quotation from the obligatory countess who writes in the
mid-twenties of her travels there, 'How simple all their life
is, what clean-living men they are, proud and strong as their
faces are their actions and yet they have the faith and heart of

a child'. How did we get to see the Bedouins of Arabia like that? – not that the authoress herself did not have a certain child-like quality; she writes a bit later on 'They all called me Emira, though I never pretended to be anything but a simple countess'. Simple countess or not, she expressed the kind of admiration for the nomads of the Arabian desert which was then, and still remains to an extent, very widespread.

For modern Europe, that is the Europe that grew up after the collapse of the Roman Empire, I suppose the fascination of Arabia began in the years after the teachings of the Prophet had harnessed the necessary egalitarianism of the desert to a sort of aggressive cupidity, which was another factor in nomad survival. This was a combination which gave a tremendous energy to this new religion, so that the zeal of those who had discovered a great truth was channelled into the strategies of conquest. Over the centuries, Christianity and Islam faced each other with the dogged ferocity of those who know themselves to be the guardians of absolute truth. So it was through conflict initially that Europe knew the Moors of Spain and of North Africa, the Saracens of the Middle East, the Saracens against whom the Crusaders fought. In an odd way the Crusaders remind one of that eminent German-American rocket expert, Werner von Braun; in an earlier incarnation that nobody likes to remember, he helped to invent the V-2 and he wrote an autobiography which was called *We Aim for the Stars* to which somebody added the subtitle 'But Sometimes We Hit London'. The Crusaders were a bit like that; sometimes they aimed for Jerusalem, but sometimes they hit Constantinople.

From these Crusades, these wars, the Crusaders brought back the elements of the developing civilisation which they both envied and admired, though they pretended that they despised it, believing in European supremacy and so on. But in a curious way the area of Islam itself, because it was impenetrable to the travellers, became oddly mysterious; it was very close and yet mysterious. The Mongol conquest opened up the land bridge to the East, that lasted a hundred

years and stretched all the way to China; the Ottoman
Empire closed it and Europe went south and then round the
tip of South Africa to discover the sea route to the Indies, so
that the Ottoman Empire and the Middle East were left, as it
were, to lumber down the centuries towards inevitable
dissolution.

So behind the bureaucracy, this corroded bureaucracy
that it created and behind the screen of pashas and gover-
nors, behind the barriers of the ferocious prohibitions of the
orthodox, the heartlands of Islam, those deserts which had
seen the root of that matter, that Arabian peninsula became a
sort of legendary land, a place of rumour and speculation and
not of discovery. Of course Arab travellers went there and
wrote about their travels, but they were not translated, at
least for a very long time, and in the West no one read them.
Thus arose this frustrated curiosity, this enormous baffle-
ment in the face of a great mystery, and that was one of the
foundations of the abiding fascination of Arabia. What on
earth could be there, what incredible holy of holies could it
be that daily drew the attentive prayer of millions from Delhi
to Sarajevo, from Granada to Delhi?

Clearly for the spirit of the Renaissance particularly, this
was a challenge which really had to be met. So it is not
surprising that the first traveller into the field was an Italian,
a young Bolognese called Ludovico di Vatima, and he set off
from Damascus in April 1503. He attached himself to the
Mameluke escort which attended the pilgrim caravan,
having perfectly happily repeated the basic formulations of
Islam and been accepted; people did not really believe him
but they accepted him, as one must, and he did not care; he
was a child of the Italian Renaissance, in the time of the
Borgia popes and the Medici princes; he was relaxed, he was
a free-thinker and he yearned, as he said, 'after new things as
a thirsty man doth after fresh water'. He describes the caravan winding on, twenty hours at a time, resting a day and a
night and then going on and, if they found no water, then
they stopped every eighth day and dug a well, he tells us.

This meant a two-day halt and the two-day halt meant that descending upon them came the marauding tribesmen of the desert for whom the caravan has always been a fine source of booty. He describes the battle in which 24,000 Arabs demanded payment for the water that the caravan had taken. There was a fight and the escort killed six hundred of the Arabs and lost only two people, one of whom was a woman, he tells us; there was a French commentator who says how unfortunate those two were, given the odds.

He talks about the desert, he talks about the rocky hills. Today we know what to expect for we have seen films and so on, but for him it was a fascinating confirmation of what he read in the Bible. He did not, he says, care much for Medina; it was a small place, little more than a large village and he did not like its inhabitants; Mecca impressed him; he describes the pilgrimage and the buildings and so forth. But he says very little about the people who have since come to fascinate us so much, about the nomads, about the Bedouins, those travellers of the desert, except when he talks about the scene where the six hundred of them died. Incidentally, Richard Burton said later that it was possible that the Arabs did not wear very much in the way of armour and so firearms could effect such slaughter.

But what intrigued di Vatima was what intrigued the Europe of his day and that was the place, the mysterious place and not the people. Eventually he had a curious sort of Hollywood-type experience; he was captured in the Yemen and the queen of the place fell in love with him and he managed to escape, an adventure which might be written up by somebody and made into a vast movie. He went to Jeddah and sailed off to India; his journey was really extraordinarily interesting, but not our immediate concern. He wrote a book when he got back to Italy which, after all, is the only reason why decent people travel; it came out in 1510 and was very popular; it was soon reprinted and it was translated.

Next into Arabia was the first Englishman; people think this was Burton, but the first Englishman into this part of the world was actually a young chap called Joseph Pitts. His was in many ways an interesting life; he was born in Devon in the 1660s; he was captured by the Corsairs in his mid-teens, and became a slave. He had a very unpleasant master who over-reached himself by plotting against the Bey of Tunis and had his head cut off; he had a second master who was much kinder and who took him to Mecca. He went to Mecca, of course, as a reluctant but official Moslem; he did not have to pretend. He describes the Cairo of his day: 'People,' he says, 'call for an ass here as they do for a carriage in London; as for the plenty which abounds here, it is wonderful'. There was a certain ambivalence in his attitude towards the pilgrims, at least when he wrote it down; he wrote after all for a Christian readership. He records in a slightly apologetic way his respect for the thousands of people who travel to Mecca and he tells us that he 'could not choose but admire to see those poor creatures so extraordinarily devout and affectionate when they were about these superstitions in so much that I could scarce forbear the shedding of tears to see their zeal although blind and idolatrous'.

But what of the place and the people who lived in it? 'Mecca,' he wrote, 'was situated in a barren place, in a valley, or rather in the midst of many little hills; 'tis a place of no force, wanting both walls and gates. It would be a place of no tolerable entertainment were it not for the anniversary resort of so many thousand pilgrims. The people here, I observe, are a poor sort of people, very thin, lean and swarthy.' And he mentions dervishes 'most commonly such as live an ere-metic life (hermits), travelling up and down the country like mendicants, wearing white woollen garments and a long white woollen cap much like some of the orders of friars in the Roman Church; with a sheep or goatskin on their back to lie on and a long staff in their hand, when they read they commonly sit down putting their legs across and keeping their knees above the ground'. He describes in detail the devotions of the pilgrims which have altered very little, if at all, since his day. And he talks of the caravan journey back to

Egypt; he did not like Medina and mentions, only in passing, the tribesmen living in this part of the world, whom he calls the 'skulking, thievish Arabs'. Joseph Pitts was freed at Mecca as is the custom, and he made his way back to England after a lot of trouble and difficulty; he was a gunner at Smyrna and one thing and another. He arrived at Harwich in paroxysms of gratified home-sickness and he was immediately caught by the press-gang and flung into the navy. However, he had influential friends and did eventually get out; he settled down in Devon and wrote his memoirs and they too were very popular.

What these two early travellers had concentrated on was the description of the place, of Mecca and of Medina, places whose mystery in the eyes of Europeans overshadowed anything else which might be said of them, because in the 16th and 17th centuries the people of Europe did not really feel that there was very much they could learn from the races of other places. There was neither the respect nor that curious nostalgia with which we now regard, or perhaps a few years ago would have regarded, that area and the people who lived there. But a change was on the way.

In 1792 there was published in Edinburgh the English translation of an account by a Danish traveller, Niebuhr. He was perhaps the first great traveller there. He had travelled through Arabia thirty years earlier, so that takes us to the 1760s.

And suddenly the Arab, until now this 'skulking' sort of fellow and 'thievish', is seen through the quite different lenses supplied by the enlightenment and by the theories of men such as Rousseau about the 'noble savage' and so forth, the perfection of early man. 'And man,' says Niebuhr, following this line, 'even in society where civilisation has been carried perhaps to excess, where art extinguishes or disguises the sentiments of nature, never forgets his original destination; he is still fond even of the very shadow of that liberty, independence and simplicity which he has lost by refinement.' 'If any people in the world,' he says, 'afford in their history an instance of high antiquity and of great simplicity of manners, the Arabs surely do. Coming among them one, can hardly help fancying oneself suddenly carried backwards to the ages which succeeded immediately after the flood.' So for Niebuhr the Arab was a sort of noble savage, the relic of an ancient and an ethical age. But was this all? 'The spirit of liberty,' he writes, 'with which this warlike nation is animated, renders them incapable of servitude. And,' he says, 'the poverty of the wandering Arab is plainly voluntary; they prefer liberty to wealth, pastoral simplicity to a life of constraint and toil which might procure them a greater variety of gratification.'

Now sixty years on and little has altered in the desert but certain changes have come about in European sensibilities. We are in the era of Shelley, Schiller is alive; it is the year of Byron's slightly frantic involvement with Greek independence. Personal liberty has become everything, together with its mode of expression which is the free self-sustaining nation.

And so we come to Burkhardt, a Swiss; he was the first European to see the temples at Abu Simbel. He disguised himself as a Turk named Ibrahim Ibn Abdullah and made the pilgrimage to Mecca. He drove himself very hard, and was actually very nervous; he got very scared in Mecca and eventually died when he was only thirty-three. That did tend to happen to the early explorers; they did die a great deal. He was not entirely over the notion of the noble savage; in his notes on the Bedouins and Wahabis, he wrote of the Bedouins, 'With all their faults they are one of the noblest nations with which I ever had the opportunity of becoming acquainted. Whoever prefers the disorderly state of Bedouin freedom to the apathy of Turkish despotism must allow that it is better to be an uncivilised Arab of the desert, endowed with rude virtues, than a comparatively polished slave like the Turk with less fierce vices but few if any virtues.' It was not a time when Turkey was in favour with Europeans, of course, and Niebuhr had himself written that 'a comparison of the manners of the Turks with those of the Arabians will best prove the superior politeness of the latter nation'; politeness in the 18th century was more important than it is today.

And then Burkhardt talks of the Arabs and writes of their 'public spirit and their patriotism'; this is very much the spirit of his age based on 'that sentiment of liberty which has driven them, still keeps them in the desert,' (he insists that it is voluntary) 'and makes them look down with contempt upon slaves that dwell about them.' And so the desert too has changed its character; from having been a terrible wilderness, it has become this curious, vast, waterless paradox, the desirability of which lies in its undesirability. For him the Arabs took to the desert because it honed them to a state of virtue, virtue that he approved of, of course. He does warn us that the Bedouins are most greedy of gain and certainly does not relate this to the aridity of their environment. 'No, in proportion as they reside near a town,' he tells us, 'this avaricious spirit becomes more general among them.'

So now we have emerging this perception of the nomad tribesman of Arabia which was to dominate all ideas about them until very recently. I am not saying that those ideas are false; I have no idea whether they are false or not, but it is curious that this emphasis on the cleansing effects of the desert, of poverty and of hardship, does seem to increase as Europe becomes richer; just as the belief in Arab virtue grows stronger as European virtue turns into the frock-coated and black bombazined hypocrisy of the late 19th century. Consider this from an introduction written near the end of that century to the travels of Ibn Batuta, who himself criss-crossed Islam in the 14th century, knew the banks of China's imperial canal as he did those of the Euphrates, of the Niger; he came from Tangier originally. The editor of these travels in English was named William Bolting and he wrote, 'Marauder as he was, the Arab, like his half-brother the Hebrew, carried an ethical spark in his bosom which could readily be fanned into a consuming blaze. He was accustomed in the silence of the stony waste and of the stars to plunge into the depths of his own spiritual being or to await in patience some portent from the unseen.' Now Bolting wrote that, although all the early travellers had agreed that, on the whole, the nomad of Arabia was not really very religious and, until forced to it by Wahabi ascendancy, was not even very much of a Moslem in that sense.

Into the 19th century, in 1838, and we get published the findings of a man called James Welstead; he was an officer who sailed around the southern coasts of the Arabian peninsula for the East India Company; they did a survey there and he was one of the members. He talks of the Arabs that he saw, and what he praises is their plainness and simplicity, which everybody comes back to; he says, 'This freedom from pomp and ostentation, so different from other Orientals, places their character, to Europeans, in a very favourable light and is, I think, with others a reason why they esteem them higher in the scale.' This young naval lieutenant took it for granted, though in that patronising, *de haut en bas* sort of manner, which the British were then able to adopt (they could afford it), that the Europeans esteemed the Arabs more highly than any other Asiatic people; it was, of course, a curious comparison to make between the different Orientals, as if this enormous continent could be measured by a single scale. Clearly the fascination which was exerted by Arabia had shifted in a sense from the place and the places, from Mecca and its mystery, to the people who inhabited it.

However, it is true that, as the 19th century advanced, people became curiously fascinated again by the mysterious magnetism of those holy centres. It was after all a long time since Pitts had been there, Burkhardt had died young and the impact their reaching Mecca and Medina had had on Europe really had passed very quickly; it had not been very profound, people did not know about them; it was only the scholars who knew about them, as it was only the scholars who knew about the Arab travellers in the area. People really, if they thought about them at all, thought about these pilgrim centres with a sort of awed curiosity, a sort of collective intake of breath. I quote: 'There are holy shrines of the Moslem world in the far away desert where no white man, European, or Christian, could enter save as a Moslem, or even approach without certain death; they are more jealously guarded than the Holy Grail. My husband had lived as a dervish in Sind which greatly helped him; it meant living with his life in his hands amongst the strangest and wildest companions.' That was written by Lady Burton, the great Isabel, who was not entirely disinterested when she tried to create a bit of a stir. Still, she meant it; she was fascinated all her life by where her husband had been and she was writing the preface to the memorial edition of Richard Burton's own pilgrimage to Medina and Mecca. And here with Burton at last was a man who was not at all afraid to rise to the wildest demands of widespread curiosity, of sensationalism; it did not worry him at all.

We are beginning to enter the second half of the 19th century; books are no longer a matter for a self-conscious élite, everybody reads them, and here is Burton with his swift sympathy for the exotic and his readiness to take up all the attitudes of a hero; his curiously ambivalent religiosity which fitted the spirit of the time and his very rare, very unceremonious self-revelation, not to mention an implicit approval of a sort of general sexuality in all its forms which not even the concerned editing of his wife later could quite remove. Here was Burton, he was the man who could, as it were, go to Mecca once and for all; he would go there and it would be gone to. And when he is there, at last, by the draped and hidden black stone, the very core of Islam, he tells us, 'I may truly say that of all the worshippers who clung weeping to the curtain none felt for the moment a deeper emotion than did the Hadji from the far north; but to confess the humbling truth, theirs was the high feeling of religious enthusiasm, mine was the ecstasy of gratified pride.' Here is no observer coolly taking notes, though he did that, too, of course, but a person; he was a person present in the centre of his described world and he was a focus for the reader; he was an identity with which the armchair Bedouins who read him could easily identify; he could beguile them into a complete involvement. And it was this potent entity, this extra-literary presence, this character which he had created of himself which presented to the European reader his version of the Arabian nomad. He wrote that, 'the manners of the Bedouin are free and simple; vulgarity and affectation, awkwardness and embarrassment, are weeds of civilised growth, unknown to the people of the desert. The best character of the Bedawi is a truly noble compound of determination, gentleness and generosity; usually they are a mixture of worldly cunning and great simplicity.' Then he tempers his eulogy with a word about bravery: 'the valour of the Bedouin is fitful and uncertain,' pointing out that man is by nature an animal of prey – not much nonsense about the noble savage; he tells us that, 'ravenous and sanguinary propensities grow apace in the desert but for the same reason the recklessness of civilisation is unknown here.' And he describes the desert and what it meant to him as an experience: 'What can be more exciting, what more sublime; man's heart pounds in his breast at the thought of measuring his puny force with nature's might and of emerging triumphant from the trial.'

For Burton the desert was a proving ground, a sort of competitor, and in the zest with which he took up the challenge of the place he was, of course, completely Victorian. It is a notion of trial by combat as a philosophy of life which has, I think, over the decades become a most menacing doctrine, but then it summed up a most important strain in European life. If to overcome the desert was to prove oneself a hero, what was one to think of those who overcame it every day? And if the qualities one displayed in making that conquest were once, as one assumed, wholly admirable, then how deeply must they be embedded in a people who claimed such a conquest with every journey they completed?

Not everybody had the same complimentary opinion, by the way; there was a man called Palgrave, a very interesting character, an ex-army man and a Jesuit who eventually became an ex-Jesuit; he went to Arabia on a mission for Napoleon III. He travelled through the area about ten years after Burton, though he did not go to Mecca; he wrote, of another part of Arabia and of 'the miserable tribes of nomads that infest Arabia'; he much preferred the people of the towns, precisely those whom most travellers followed the Bedouins in despising. It was not a universal feeling; in Jafe for instance, Palgrave described the population's 'large developed forms and open countenance which contrast strongly with the somewhat dwarfish stature and suspicious under-glance of the Bedouins'.

Palgrave was no Burton and his attitudes did not bring him majority approval. Instead, two much more influential names appear finally to round off this pantheon of early travellers (we move into the 20th century and it gets more complicated). The first of these was Doughty who was I suppose, with Carlyle, one of the century's great unread but, unlike Carlyle, does not deserve it; he was a natural solitary, was Doughty; a sort of recluse in his later years, he wrote vast prophetic, poetic tomes, volume after volume. When he was a geology student he spent most of his time sitting on a Norwegian glacier; he had a lot of trouble in being allowed to do so, but they let him. He wandered across Europe after he had graduated and almost by chance he reached Petra, the rock city in the Middle East, now Jordan. There he learned of other carvings and inscriptions deeper in the desert and he decided that he would be the first person to see them, or at any rate the first European to see them. In 1876 he set off with the pilgrim caravan like di Vatima had done, from Damascus.

He did not go to Mecca, because he, unlike many of the others, refused to compromise with his Christianity, but he did dress in Arab fashion and he said he was a physician; he posed as a Syrian but he said he was a Christian, so he did not go to Mecca. He did find his carvings early on and sent back details of the inscriptions which nobody in England wanted, though they were published eventually in Paris. Nobody cared very much about them, for they were not very interesting and indeed they did not gain his interest; he by that time was very bored with his inscriptions, so he went on and wandered around for two years.

He was the first person really to get into the life and the skin of the Bedouin. He carried very little with him though he did have notebooks, but he finished up extremely exhausted and very ill and he nearly died. After two years he came back and settled in, among other places, Tunbridge Wells and Eastbourne, lived an awful long time and wrote enormous poems that nobody now reads.

And what news did he bring? He wrote, 'two chiefly are the perils of Arabia, famine and the dreadful-faced harpy of their religion; a third is the rash weapon of every Ishmaelite robber. Here is a dead land, whence if he die not, he, the traveller, shall bring home nothing but a perpetual weariness in his bones. The Semites are like to a man sitting in a cloaca to the eyes and whose brows touch heaven. If the outlandish person come along to strange nomad booths, let him approach boldly and they will receive him; it is much if they heard of thee any good report, and all the Arabs are at the beginning appeased with fair words. The oasis villages are more dangerous; Bedouin colonies at first, they have corrupted the ancient traditions of the desert.' And he confirms this elsewhere: 'The settled folk of the Arabian country are always envious haters of the nomads that encompass them in their oasis islands with the danger of the desert.'

And so Doughty too sets up this dichotomy and takes the nomad's side in it as most of the travellers did, between the small settlements and towns on the one hand, from this point of view vile and corrupt and dangerous, and on the other the desert, peopled by these tribes of the honourable and the uncorrupted. Of the environment he tells us, 'Commonly the Arabian desert is an extreme desolation where the herb is not apparent for the sufficiency of any creature.' The grandeur of Doughty's language seems to give these people, these gigantic Semites stretching from ordure to paradise, the status of heroes, of super-human creatures.

And the ironic thing is that Doughty was not trying to attempt a sort of lush, sub-oriental style in the manner of the later James Elroy Flecker or any of those people; he was after something completely different. He had the conviction that English over the centuries had degenerated into a corrupt mish-mash and ought to be brought back to a Spenserian, pre-Spenserian purity. Spenser was the last person who wrote a pure English and even with Milton and so forth the degradation had begun. It is this somewhat pre-Raphaelite attitude, pre-Raphaelite in the sense that he believed that there was an earlier purity in the art, which gives his book *Arabia Deserta* its curious and, in the end, compelling quality, a very strange quality, and which lends this curious mythological air to all the people and places which appear on its pages; it is well worth reading the book.

It is not an easy book to read, but once you get attuned to its style, it is really a very rewarding book, a very rich book. In fact, it is too rich because Doughty will tell you absolutely everything about absolutely everything; there is a story that when he was at the university his examiner was asked, 'Why didn't you give this extraordinary student a first class degree?'; he said, 'Well, the trouble is when you ask Doughty for a collar stud (they used to wear collar studs), he offers you all the contents of his wardrobe'.

It is true, *Arabia Deserta* is of all books the one book which is full of information that nobody is looking for. The only thing to be said about that, on the other hand, is that during the First World War when the Arab Bureau was founded in Cairo to deal with the war in the Middle East (T.E. Lawrence first worked in the Bureau before he went into the desert), they found that they had to use Doughty's book as an aid in their dealings with the Sharif of Mecca and his sons and his people; they found it, they said, constantly accurate, so that this enormous volume of information was never wrong, it simply was too much to cope with.

Finally there is another poet, Wilfred Scawen Blunt, another gigantic figure though much forgotten, called in his time the handsomest man in England; photographs have survived so we know that he really was astonishingly good looking as well as being wealthy, talented and self-willed; and that his brother died and he inherited the family fortune. He married Byron's granddaughter – no other woman, I suspect, would have done for him. He spent 10 years in the Diplomatic Service and was properly disillusioned and left it. As a poet, he is not much read nowadays, but he was well known then. But the really extraordinary thing about him is that, with a single (sizeable) exception, the opinions he held would have been totally acceptable in any Hampstead drawing room today, assuming they still have drawing rooms in Hampstead. The exception was his virulent anti-Semitism. It was probably obligatory in his class at the time, but it coloured all his thoughts about nearly everything. It was a prejudice, incidentally, which he shared with Burton. He was virtually alone, a hundred years ago, in holding the opinions that he did, but some idea of the modernity of his views can be judged by the fact that he was against imperialism, against exploitative colonialism, against the maltreatment of blacks, particularly in the American deep south. He was in favour of the independence of small nations; he was a great conservationist; he was aware of the death of many species of animal and he championed both Hindus and Moslems (particularly the latter, because of his interest in the Middle East) against the assaults of Western religion and its missionaries. He was the adversary of greed and technology.

He was a pretty accurate prophet too. He wrote to Gordon, warning him that, if he went to Khartoum, he would die; that he had been given wrong information; that he was being sent on a false mission; that it was not what he thought it was. Gordon went to Khartoum and Gordon died. Blunt foretold the end of the Empire; he castigated the British leadership then for their lack of imagination and their hypocrisy, on the one hand, and on the other for their connections, of course, with the Rothschilds. He wrote of Britain: 'the nations of the East have left their childhood, thou art grown old; their manhood is to come and they shall carry on earth's high tradition through the long ages when thy lips are dumb.' That was in the 1870s and 1880s.

He bought himself a small estate, with a very beautiful garden, not far from Cairo and he became a champion of Egyptian nationalism, which was one of the things that brought him to these opinions. There is extant a long letter from a guest who saw him in 1892, who tells how he was ushered into Blunt's presence by what he calls in his letter a 'Nubian janissary' who proclaimed 'El Sheikh'; and there was, sure enough, Wilfred in an immense white burnous like the Sultan of Morocco, says the man. His wife, Lady Anne, the Byronic granddaughter, actually was not so Byronic for she took after her grandmother more; she was a very careful scholar like her grandmother and a better linguist than Blunt. He and Lady Anne travelled through northern Arabia in the late 1870s, just after Doughty, and she wrote and he edited a book on their travels. Later they did another one on the *Bedouin Tribes of the Euphrates*, that was the title. He added his general observations to it about the nomads and perhaps a little more extensively about the horses; he was fascinated by Arab horses and bred them. The thing about him was that although he was a romantic, he was not at all carried away. 'Much has been talked,' he wrote, 'of the wonderful faculties of sight and hearing possessed by the Bedouins but I have not remarked that they excel in either; we, ourselves, were often appealed to by them when trying to distinguish objects at a distance. And if the country be uninhabited,' he says, 'the Bedouin is frightened, and of keeping a straight course for a whole day they seem incapable. Courage, though held in high esteem, is not considered essential; "God has not given me courage," they will sometimes say, "and I do not fight". He feels no delight, like men of other races, in shedding blood.' Of course, those are very splendid sentiments in many ways. 'Truth,' writes Blunt, 'in ordinary matters is not considered a virtue by the Bedouins nor is lying held shameful; "every man," they say "has a right to conceal his own thought".' And he tells us that petty thieving is rare. 'During the whole of our travels we never lost in this way so much as the value of a shilling; highway robbery, on the other hand, is not only permitted but held to be a right. A respect for law is indeed one of the leading features of the Bedouin character, but it must be understood, of their own law only. Justice, indeed, is nowhere more certain of attainment than in the desert; the poor man there never suffers wrong as a poor man. The weakest point of the Bedouin character is undoubtedly his love of money. With the single exception of a belief in God inherited from the earliest times, the Bedouins profess no religious creed whatever.' And finally he speaks of liberty and social organisation; in a chapter on this subject he says 'the individual Bedouin owes no duties even to his tribe, of which he can rid himself by a simple act of will; as long as he is with his tribe he must conform but he can withdraw at any time from its authority.'

These are the travellers, in my submission, who created for us our earliest, our most important descriptions of Arabia. Of course, there have been many influential descriptions since; we have had Gertrude Bell and Enid Starkey and T.E. Lawrence and Philby and Thesiger and Thomas and so on. But I fancy that by the beginnings of this century the terms of our fascination with Arabia had been pretty well fixed and they had been fixed by these early travellers. Only increasing familiarity with that peninsula into which we have now been forced has begun to alter them. We rely on our interpreters for our understanding of the world; we send out our scouts and we build our image of the way things are from the reports that they bring. Once we have that image it is hard to change; our fascination with Arabia has, as we have seen, deep roots; it began early on and, up to Richard Burton, it was the fascination of the forbidden, of the mysterious. It was facts, facts alone, which could and did allay our curiosity and still that aspect of our fascination (perhaps more or less completely).

But by that time a new and subtler aspect of that

fascination had begun to appear; it was with the people who seemed to embody strengths and virtues which challenged European arrogance and who lived in circumstances which undermined the increasing European faith in comfort. When one reads of African exploration, one sometimes gets the impression that the people there are being, as it were, created; they are sort of called into being by the appraisal, the regard of the white traveller. They are objects in a landscape, they have not been there as human beings, fully present, until the traveller has changed them in some way, has converted them or dressed them, has fitted them into a sort of socio-economic system of his own devising and for his own benefit.

Arabia is very different because here you have an area which is both well known on the one hand and intractable on the other; within its borders the white traveller, like any other traveller, has absolutely no alternative but to live as the nomads do. That is, he has to compete on a level with them, often without their experience and with very few of their virtues. If he travelled as the explorers did in Africa, with an enormous train and porters and the whole thing, of course, he would not have survived the brigandage of his first week. An incidental to this, which is quite interesting, is that the white man in Africa had a weapon superiority which he did not have in the desert; the desert Bedouin had firearms early, the African did not. One of the sidelights on the Vinland adventure is that the Vikings, of course, had no weapon superiority, unlike the later Spaniards when they went to America; it is a very important factor. And in the desert there was a parity of weapons just as there had to be a parity of methods of travel; it was a balance.

So here was a land already very well established – unlike Africa for instance, it was well established in European imagination – and from which there had erupted a cultural and a military force which had utterly changed history and which had a terrain so difficult that nobody, not even the Turks really, had ever been able to colonise it. Certainly no European power could or would be able to. So, for example,

the sort of unavoidable imperialist arrogance which spoiled
the relationship between the Indians and the English, which
might otherwise have been so much more fertile than it was,
could not possibly establish itself. The nomads of the desert,
once their lives had been properly reported on by people like
Doughty and Blunt, could only be regarded as people living
lives which were equal in value to, though parallel with, that
of the people in Europe and the developed West.

If one concedes that, one really must concede a little more,
because in a sense during the 100 years between Burkhardt
and Blunt, the West had been overwhelmed by the consequences of its own successes. There were the towns which
had clawed constantly at the land around them, there were
the skies which were smeared with the lowering wastes of a
million chimneys, there were the people who were crowded
into this convenient barracks of industrialism, there were the
aristocrats who had been flung aside by the porcine scramble
of the newly rich. The virtues, the songs, the health, the
stability of the old society had all been torn to shreds but all
its vices, the separation of the classes, the arrogance of
privilege, the persecution of the poor, had been maintained
and even increased. Those who had had wealth, had the
traditional skills of wealth; country skills of riding and shooting and so on. These brought involvement with the people
around them, with a tenantry, with the land and the people
who lived on the land. And although they did not perhaps
adhere very adequately to them, they did possess inherited
notions of honour, chivalry and nobility. All this had
suddenly been rendered irrelevant. And it was to people in
this situation that there was brought this series of reports.
Here was a free people with each individual his own master,
living proudly by the skills of hardship, not bound by
houses, disdainful of cities, their code half chivalric, half that
of freebooter, of brigand; it must have seemed like a vision of
perfection. There in the desert where nothing else grew,
there flowered honour, hospitality, simplicity and freedom.
It was a vision irresistible to the hemmed-in inheritors of

romanticism. The fascination of Arabia, once a matter of distance, of bizarre practices and a rival mystery, had become instead a nostalgia for the standards of Sir Lancelot and the nobility of Lyonesse.

Vestiges of that view have, I suppose, survived the oil fields and the passing of even the memory of honour in the West. Maybe what fascinates us now, as we stand like peasants with our mouths open, is wealth; and as the oil sheikhs count their shekels, if shekels they count, dollars perhaps, we mouth these figures with them. And certainly, if we have been changing, so has Arabia, of course, forced open by the logic of energy consumption; so that, perhaps, is this century's contribution to the continuing story of our fascination with the desert, with Arabia. Even in 1939 St. John Philby could write 'All I want is peace and solitude; they are more difficult to find than one would imagine even in the desert. It was not always so, but in these days of speed and spirit even the most God-forsaken spots have a potential value: if they are flat one can land on them from the air, if they are hilly they may conceal oil.' And in his day no one had even dreamt of Concorde.

8

The Conflict of Laws: Private International Law

An Introduction to the Conflict of Laws

If a case were to be brought to court in England concerning two English men, one of whom claimed a breach of contract, performed in England, in respect of English goods: no one would be at all surprised if English contract law were relied on. But if one or more of the facts of the case were to include a foreign element, another area of the law would be called upon to adjudicate: the 'Conflict of Laws' or 'Private International Law', as it is known, serves this purpose. When a foreign element exists in a case, it is suddenly necessary to determine which nation's legislative system is to be used, and if, and to what extent, a foreign legal implication may be taken into account: Private International Law is responsible for this.

Private International Law has three main areas of focus. Firstly, it defines the jurisdiction to hear the case and act upon it. If there is no jurisdiction, the matter ends there. Secondly, it classifies the action itself, and determines the applicable municipal or domestic law, in establishing the rights and obligations of the parties. The determination of which circumstances merit the recognition of foreign legal decisions and, separately, if such judgments may be enforced in the country of the jurisdiction of the court.

It is important to understand that the function of Private International Law is complete when it has chosen the appropriate system of law with which to govern the case. Its rules do not furnish a direct solution to the dispute.

Let us consider for a moment the title for this area of law. There is often a tendency to confuse it with 'Public International Law' (the Law of Nations): which governs the relations between two sovereign states. Private International Law is designed to regulate disputes of a private nature. There is a whole range of other terminology that exists to describe the same subject. Others include 'International Private Law', 'Intermunicipal Law', 'Comity', and 'Extra-territorial Recognition of Rights'. Many distinguished writers on this area of law have noted that all the titles put forward to represent it are inaccurate in one respect or another. In his work *Private International Law*,[9] Wolff explains that the chosen title is misleading as it is 'national' not 'international'. He adds that the 'Conflict of Laws' is just as much of a misnomer: for it is the task of this branch of law to prevent conflict by choosing between different legal systems. For the sake of simplicity it shall be henceforth referred to as Private International Law.

One might ask why an English court should be obliged to apply foreign law under any circumstances. Why not just apply English law and totally avoid Private International Law? The answer is that only using English Law in England, and German Law in Germany, and so on, would quickly lead to great injustice. If the court of a certain country were to apply her own laws in every case, it would mean that the outcome of the case would depend completely upon where it was actually brought.

Private International Law is not a separate branch of law as, for example, the law of contract or bankruptcy: it is all-pervading and spread through so many areas of law. This very fact makes it both fascinating and extremely complex at times.

It is not the same in all countries: and often tends to be very different from nation to nation, even in its basic composition. We are concerned here solely with the form that occurs in England. The many questions that relate to the personal status of a party often depend in England upon the law of domicil. In France, Spain, Italy and most other European countries however, matters of personal status rest upon the law of one's nationality.

There have been attempts to unify the legal doctrines of certain countries. If successful, they might simplify Private International Law immensely. However, these treaties and conventions have brought little change. Bi-lateral conventions and treaties occur between nations, and there is activity in this regard undertaken in the European Community and other community groups: the aim being to implement uniform laws in the legal systems of all their members.

The fact that Private International Law might need to consider any branch of any legislative system, makes it one of the richest and most intriguing areas of law in existence. It can address all realms of the law, from bankruptcy to polygamy. For this reason, we shall choose a few selected areas for consideration, focusing in most detail on the fundamental area of domicil.

Domicil in Private International Law

Legislative systems in different parts of the world find themselves at loggerheads in Private International Law when discussing most topics. There is disagreement not only in the defining of key terms and concepts, but also when debating the very importance and use of the most abstract ideas. It is recognised by all that one set of laws should be administered to the same person no matter where he is, or where the dispute in question arose. However, the unanimity breaks down with the considering of whether 'nationality' or 'domicil' should determine matters of personal status. English law regards domicil as of key importance, and uses it to settle disputes concerned with the family, property, and those with a corporate element. We shall look in detail at domicil and the place it holds in English Private International Law. It can be used to exemplify the differences that arise between different nations in matters of Private International Law. But its scope is more than that: for it demonstrates well the foreshortenings that exist in this area of law, and enables one to begin to determine what reforming processes might be necessary.

Actually defining domicil proves to be a difficult matter on which there is considerable disagreement. Wharton cites Sir R. Phillimore's remark:

> Domicil is a residence acquired as a final abode. To constitute it there must be: (1) residence, actual or inchoate; (2) the non-existence of any intention to make a domicil elsewhere.

In his authoritative work on domicil, Dicey mentions that:

> The domicil of any person is, in general, the place or country which is in fact his permanent home; but is in some cases the place or country which, whether it be in fact his home or not, is determined to be his home by a rule of law.

The frustration that has arisen in achieving a working definition of domicil is clearly seen in Lord Cranworth's statement (*Whicker v. Hume* 1858):

> By domicil, we mean home, the permanent home, and if you do not understand your permanent home, I'm afraid that no illustrations drawn from foreign writers will very much help you to it.

English law maintains that there are two types of domicil. That of 'domicil of origin', the natural domicil acquired at where one's parents live at the time of birth; and 'domicil of choice': the place (different to domicil of origin) where one chooses to live following childhood.

The rules that shroud domicil in English law are complicated and extensive. Cheshire & North (in *Private International Law*)[3] maintain that there are five basic rules to domicil. They say that everyone is entitled to a domicil. A legitimate child acquires the domicil of origin of his father, and an illegitimate infant that of its mother. A foundling child gains domicil of the place in which it was discovered. The initial domicil remains until such time as an individual takes another domicil. Even in circumstances where he has left his domicil of origin (or other acquired place of domicil), with the distinct intention of never going back: a new domicil is not truly acquired until he actually moves to some other place permanently.

No provision exists in English law by which an individual may be domiciled in two places at the same time. Generally in a situation (such as in the United States of America), where both Federal and State-based legislative systems exist, one is usually said to be domiciled in the State.

Various nations have specific legal systems that legislate over particular sections of the society. Although there is, as in India, one law for Hindus and another for the followers of Islam: all nationals of the country are governed under the umbrella of Indian Territorial Law.

An individual who ascertains that he has adopted a new domicil of choice may have to prove that if necessary. It is not until sufficient proof is given that the domicil will be respected. The person must show that his new domicil is permanent and that he intends to stay there for ever.

The fact that one might specifically remain in a certain place at length, perhaps on a yearly basis, for the purpose of claiming residence there (and thus enabling one to benefit from the tax laws of that place): does not necessarily hold good. New complications constantly arise with the complex tax situations and other circumstances in which people find themselves.

The most detailed and specific considerations of each case must be taken into account. And in situations where a person applies for domicil in a new country, if any suggestions or provisions exist whereby he might in some event return to his domicil of origin (or previous domicil of choice): in general the application should be turned down.

With reference to matters of intention to remain in a place

permanently, Lord Westbury stated in *Udny v. Udny* (1869), that:

> Domicil is a conclusion or inference which the law derives from the fact of a man fixing voluntarily his sole or chief residence in a particular place with the intention of continuing to reside there for an unlimited time ... It must be a residence not for a limited period or particular purpose, but general and indefinite in its future contemplation.

In 1930 and the extraordinary case of *Bowie v. Liverpool Royal Infirmary*, the strength that domicil of origin is seen to hold in matters of English Private International Law was made apparent. The situation was such that the will of a certain George Bowie was only to be seen as valid if at his time of death Mr. Bowie was domiciled in Scotland.

Bowie, a Glaswegian by birth, with domicil of origin there, lived in Scotland until about his forty-seventh year. After that he moved to Liverpool to live off the fortunes of his brother. Twenty-one years later, on the death of his brother, Bowie lived with his sister, also in Liverpool. She died in 1920, leaving Bowie to live in Liverpool until his death some seven years later.

Having departed Scotland initially, Bowie never returned there; and only left England for two short trips. He was said to have taken great pride in being from Glasgow, and even went so far as to have a Scottish newspaper delivered each week. While alive, he had steadfastly upheld the decision never to return to Glasgow. He even prepared his own funeral arrangements to take place in Liverpool.

It would seem that Bowie had been resigned to living in England, and one might conclude the fact that he had obviously earned a domicil of choice in England. But when the case was brought before the House of Lords, it was decided with an overwhelming majority that George Bowie had never gained a domicil of choice anywhere. They maintained that, at the time of his death, he had died with his Scottish domicil of origin.

Domicil of the Deceased

When attempting to decide the domicil of someone now dead, great care must be taken to include all information that hints at whether the chosen place of abode was deemed by that person to be permanent. Scholars note that when deducing whether the deceased intended to stay at his selected domicil for a perpetual period: that no point is too trivial. But in real life it often proves impractical and impossible to attend to all the minute details called for.

Matters such as what type of person he was and whether he was taken by whimsical occupations come into play. Factors which indicate as to whether one intended to remain domiciled in a certain place for ever are numerous. For example: had he made any specific announcement or declarations, particularly in writing, during his lifetime? Has he kept citizenship to his previous place of domicil? Had be bought a house or kept substantial property in the disputed place of domicil? Had he bought a place in which to be interred? Did he participate in local political activities or did he vote during his life-time in the place in question?

Substantiating a Change in Domicil

In English courts it is deemed that one needs a much greater quantity of material to substantiate a case whereby one is attempting to resign one's domicil of origin: than if one is merely transferring from one domicil of choice to another. However, it is seen as a far easier matter to acquire and prove a transference of domicil between two places that exist under the authority of one Sovereign State: as if one changed domicil of origin in Wales, to a domicil of choice in the Isle of Man.

Under the authority of English law, one cannot gain a domicil of choice and right to abode in England if one has broken the English law on entry into the country: as, for instance, situations in which an illegal immigrant has entered unlawfully. This proves to be a good example of one of the variances between English Private International Law, and that of other nations. In Canada, for example, an illegal immigrant is entitled to a domicil of choice in the country, even though he has made an unauthorized entrance.

Although one with an English domicil of origin might acquire a domicil of choice in a foreign country, and thus abide by the laws of that nation: he may continue to remain subject to the English Sovereign in a certain capacity.

Diplomats & Domicil

In his book, *A Treatise on Private International Law*,[8] John Westlake Q.C., touches upon the situations of diplomats living abroad whilst serving their government.

> So far as the question of domicil lies between two British places, these rules follow from the circumstance that the service of the crown involves no lasting tie to one part of the British dominions rather than to another. And when one of the places in question is politically foreign, the person residing there in the diplomatic or consular service of the British crown, the rule that a previous British domicil is not necessarily lost by such residence still applies. If the service be diplomatic, it might perhaps be deemed incompatible with its duties to acquire the foreign domicil; but there would seem to be nothing to prevent a person in the consular service from acquiring a domicil, if he so minded, in the country where he is employed, it being of frequent occurrence that foreigners are chosen for such employment in their respective countries.

Domicil of Origin v. Domicil of Choice

The domicil of origin is awarded a most venerable status in English law. As in the case *Bowie v. Liverpool Royal*

Infirmary, it can at times be almost impossible to persuade a court that a new domicil was taken: even in situations where the most outright evidence seems to point to the conclusion that a change in domicil actually occurred.

At times when one has relinquished one's domicil of choice, the domicil of origin is always available for resurrection. It can be a sensitive issue as one might find oneself redomiciled to one's domicil of origin: with which one might have broken all ties for life that one had had. This feature of the revival of domicil is not adhered to by, among others, the United States of America, New Zealand or Australia.

Domicil of Dependants

Children with domicil in England are prohibited from obtaining a domicil of choice different from that of their parents. At the age of sixteen, youths are allowed to make a change in their domicil, and to gain their first domicil of choice.

The exception, when a minor may obtain independent domicil from that of his or her parents, may be achieved when he has entered a legal marriage before the age of sixteen. Although such a case cannot exist concerning an English child, it can in situations where children below sixteen were married legally outside the United Kingdom: such as in an Islamic country. If the marriage is recognised by English authorities then the couple may gain domicil in England.

A parent is permitted to apply for a domicil of choice for its offspring. When a father makes a change in his domicil, the change is transferred to the status of his legitimate children. This can happen even in cases where the children do not actually reside in the same country as his illegitimate children. The laws that sustain a decision regarding the domicil of an infant, in extenuating circumstances, are exceedingly complicated.

It is important to note that in the event that parents gain a new domicil of choice following their child's birth, the infant also gains the new domicil, as a domicil of choice. If the father dies, his offspring (if under sixteen years of age) generally obtain the domicil of their mother.

English law usually stipulates that an individual suffering from a mental abnormality cannot make changes to his place of domicil. Those in whose custody he has been placed are also prohibited to making a change in the patient's domicil. But a father's change in domicil will still be transferred to child, even though he has a mental disorder. And if the individual (who is over sixteen years of age) has had a mental abnormality from childhood, the father's change in domicil will continue to be transferred to him. But in situations in which the patient has acquired a mental disorder after the age of sixteen, his domicil does not change in alignment with that of his father: it is unchangeable. However, a court acting in the interests of the mentally disordered person may, it is thought, alter the person's domicil if it means affording to him a more congenial environment.

The Drawbacks of Domicil and Areas for Reform

Domicil rests upon the concept that substantial evidence will and must be produced to show that a person in question intends to keep the newly chosen domicil for life. Cases arise in which a man finds himself with a domicil that in no way is representative of his true domicil: following the revival of his domicil of origin. There are times where applications for domicil are refused even when a person has lived in a country for much of their life: if there exists the faintest glimmer of a chance that that person will abandon the domicil of choice.

The problems that arise with the very defining of domicil can make the concept awkward and complex to use. Many of these problems concerned with it prompt people to embrace the idea of residence before that of domicil. 'Ordinary residence' is seen as a connecting element in numerous situations from immigration to social security. It is residence in a place for educational, professional or commercial reasons. One is not expected to stay in that place for ever; but must physically spend time there more than regularly. 'Habitual residence' need not be so permanent as ordinary residence: but although a frequent presence must be maintained, no long decision is necessary. These two types of residence are seen by many to be almost one and the same.

The laws pertaining to domicil evolved with England's relations first between its union partners (Ireland, Scotland and Wales), but later developed further with those nations within its Empire. The concept of being domiciled outside the Empire was not recognised until 1823. Many of the laws that regard domicil in English law are outdated, ambiguous, and no longer applicable to modern ways of living. Attempts to alter the fundamental make-up of domicil's legislation have faltered. However, less radical adjustments are expected to be agreed upon.

Such reforming measures highlight the need for two areas in which to legislate, one directed at the domicil of children, and one concerned with that of adults. Other reformatory alterations that have been proposed are for example: superseding one domicil of choice only when another has been established. Some call for the necessity for a concrete intention to be existent for a new domicil of choice, to be dropped. It is hard and often impossible to say that one intends to reside at the chosen location for time immemorial. There have also been ideas put forward to replace the domicil of origin with a simpler 'domicil of birth'. The idea that the father passes his domicil to his legitimate children, and not to illegitimate offspring, has also been criticized as outmoded.

Although it certainly is necessary to adjust the criterion surrounding the way in which one might change one's domicil, it is important that a situation does not arise in which alterations may be achieved with too much ease.

Torts in Private International Law

In situations where a case is brought to court in England concerning a tort that has been perpetrated outside England, Private International Law is responsible for determining which country's legislative system will be used in the case.

Usually a choice is made between *Lex loci delicti* (the law that stands at the place where the wrong was committed); or *Lex fori* (the law of the place before whose courts the case has been brought to trial); or a mixture of the two may be adopted.

The case of *Philips v. Eyre*, which was brought to court in 1870, is seen as a test case, and is key in treating cases of this nature. The Governor of Jamaica was having damages brought against him, in an English court, following his alleged imprisoning of the plaintiff at a time of insurrection in Jamaica. It was found that the Governor's actions had been vindicated following the passing of a colonial act of indemnity. Willes J. on passing judgment, remarked:

> As a general rule, in order to found a suit in England, for a wrong alleged to have been committed abroad, two conditions must be fulfilled. First, the wrong must be of such a character that it would have been actionable if committed in England ... Secondly, the act must not have been justifiable by the law of the place where it was done.

Both Lex loci delicti and Lex fori have disadvantages: particularly the latter. For with it, there is a tendency for 'forum shopping' to take place: where the plaintiff can go to bring an action wherever the law is most in his favour. Some feel that a more flexible approach to the subject should be developed: perhaps the doctrine of the proper law of tort. Concerning such a doctrine, Morris wrote:

> If we adopt the proper law of tort, we can at least choose the law, which, on policy grounds, seems to have the most significant connexion with the chain of and circumstances in the particular situation before us.

The scope for complex situations is unlimited. For example, if an arrow is fired at the border of Germany and France, and kills a man, we must decide within which of the two countries the crime was committed. For although the arrow was released from the bow in Germany (and the death occurred in France), it is not a crime on its own to release an arrow from a bow. Lex locus delicti has been disputed to be that place at which the injury was administered: but also as the place from which an action initially began, going on to cause injury.

Maritime Torts in Private International Law

Private International Law is brought into use frequently with the collision of two vessels at sea. It is of prime importance, firstly to ascertain whether the collision took place within the territorial waters of a particular nation, or in the open sea.

In cases where the encounter occurred in territorial waters, the doctrine is applied by *Phillip v. Eyre*. That State in whose waters the collision took place is seen to be that in which the tort was perpetrated. When a tort is committed on one vessel, and one vessel only, then generally the national law of the country from which the ship originated is applied. If a tort that took place on a foreign vessel is brought to court in England, the plaintiff must not only prove that the offence was actionable under the vessel's national law, but also under English law.

The most common method used to adjudicate in situations of collision for cases brought to court in England, is using 'General Maritime Law'. The name is however, misleading, as it is not a neat and cohesive legislative system. In consequence difficulties arise when attempting to decide the limitations of General Maritime Law, and under what circumstances it is not applicable.

Sovereign and Diplomatic Immunity in Private International Law

A system exists whereby those with status as a Head of State or those who hold various diplomatic posts enjoy immunity from most civil and criminal jurisdiction which would otherwise apply. As individuals, when operating in foreign countries, they gain immunity through Private International Law from everything from parking fines to murder.

Heads of State and those of certain diplomatic rank cannot be sued in an English court, although they may very well be in the country at the time. Sovereign States are seen as egalitarian in status, and it is commonly understood that one such state cannot and will not bring action upon another Sovereign State, its officers or property. The case of the *Parlement Belge* is recognised as a test case and exemplary in this area. It concerned a steamer that belonged to the Belgian Government, which had crossed the Channel with post, goods and fare-paying passengers. Whilst venturing through the harbour at Dover it struck an English tug which was moored in the harbour. When the case came to court, the judgment was that, as the Belgian steamer was the property of the Belgian Government, it was immune from prosecution.

A Head of State who actually came to England and engaged in felonious behaviour, whether in his own name or under the guise of another: would be exempt from being charged with any crime. A Sovereign is also exempt from prosecution in cases in which he actually owns the property in question, has custody over it: or in situations whereby the State has ownership of the thing in question.

Whilst residing in England in 1894, the Sultan of Johore, who was living under the name 'Baker', promised to marry an English woman, then rescinded his vow of marriage. The woman, who was unaware that the Sultan, alias Baker, was a Sovereign, attempted to sue him for breach of promise

(*Mighell v. Sultan of Johore*). (Since 1968 one can no longer be sued in this regard.)

Sometimes it is disputed as to whether the Sovereign in question is actually who he maintains he is. In such cases, if the court does not know the defendant, it is expected to find out who he is without a long antagonistic struggle. When there is a person of high-ranking title in question, the matter is referred to the Secretary of State for Foreign Affairs, or to the Commonwealth Relations Office (if the defendant comes from a nation of the Commonwealth).

In the United Kingdom there are three categories of persons entitled to the privileges of diplomatic immunity. The first are diplomatic agents, who are totally exempt from the civil and criminal jurisdiction of English courts, both in official and private acts. They are exempt also from dues and taxes, and their immediate families fall under their blanket of full diplomatic privilege as well. Members of the technical and administrative staff, such as typists and clerks are immune from civil jurisdiction, but only in respect to acts done in the scope of their duties. Members of the service staff, that is to say butlers, cooks, maids, chauffeurs and the like, are also immune to all civil jurisdiction of English courts, in the course of their work.

Those Who May Not Sue

As we have seen, there are those whom no one may bring a case against. Situations also arise in which there are those who are prohibited from bringing action against others. At times of war, when the United Kingdom has a national enemy, this alien foe cannot sue under the jurisdiction of an English court. His actual nationality does not come into it, for the matter rests on the question where he lives, or from where he conducts his affairs.

A British Citizen, or one from an uninvolved nation, living by choice in the State that is seen as hostile to the United Kingdom, or such a person who is living in a State controlled by the hostile nation: is dealt with as an enemy party. (The same obviously goes to a member of the enemy who is residing in the United Kingdom.) Such an enemy cannot begin proceedings against another individual, nor can he carry on a case that was begun before the state of war ensued.

Such alien foe are liable to be sued, but when the case is brought to court, they are free to challenge the allegation or grounds upon which the case has been brought.

Private International Law and Family Law

The subjects of the legitimacy of marriage and matrimonial disputes (divorce, child custody and so on), when a foreign aspect is present, often need the scrutiny of Private International Law. The amount of legal information that accompanies such actions is substantial. The municipal laws which govern, what in England is classified as 'Family Law', differ greatly throughout the world: perhaps more so than most other areas of the law. Marriage and divorce are closely connected and associated with morality and religion. The ultimate goal of Private International Law may be said to be the 'Harmony of Laws': if this is the case, it will certainly be fraught with difficulty as regards marriage and divorce. In consequence of legal disharmony, in one country a couple may be legitimately married but, in another, this union may be seen to be void. The same may be true of disparity of capacity and procedure in a divorce action. Perhaps one of the most complex, controversial and fascinating areas of Private International Law, although at times confused with moral and religious prejudice, is that of polygamous marriage. It is here that Private International Law may be seen in its element, and complex doctrines have been developed to justify the use of one legal system to the exclusion of all others.

Under English law marriage is only recognised as such when it is of a monogamous nature. The law stipulates that a marriage at its time of inauguration must be dedicated to proceeding in a monogamous way. In the case of *Hyde v. Hyde*, Wilde J.O. noted:

> I conceive that marriage as understood in Christendom, may for this purpose be defined as the voluntary union for life of one man and one woman to the exclusion of all others.

The case of *Mehta v. Mehta*, which came to court in 1945, proves interesting. The ceremony through which marriage was achieved was seen to be monogamous: for it was performed by a certain sect of Hinduism which allowed only monogamous marriage. The husband, however, could have entered a polygamous relationship if he had reverted to the main orthodox stream of Hinduism (which at the time permitted polygamy).

The court adjudicating on the case, heard that a woman domiciled in England underwent a ceremony in Bombay with the defendant. The woman maintained that she had been led to believe that the ceremony, which was performed in a language she did not understand, was one of conversion into Hinduism. Later she realised that the event had also been that of her wedding.

Circumstances in which a case is brought to court in England, with an element relating to Islam, often prove exceedingly delicate.

Lex loci celebrationis (the law that prevails in the place in which the marriage took place), ultimately decides whether the marriage is to be polygamous or monogamous in nature. In places where either type of marriage is a possibility, the religion of the ceremony is usually the deciding factor. For instance, if a Christian marriage took place in Kuwait, it will be bound by the Christian laws of matrimony.

Marriage is seen as a binding contract which is entered into by two parties following mutual agreement. Legislation governing that of a matrimonial agreement is usually that of the *Lex domicili*, immediately before the marriage took place. The legality of any marriage is governed by the principle that it is only legitimate if seen to be so by the law of the place in which it has been entered into. Thus the aphorism *Locus regit actum* pertains.

Annulment of a Marriage

There are numerous situations in which a marriage may be annulled. One set of reasons force the union to be void, and through another set it may be made void if various conditions exist. For instance, a marriage is automatically invalid if one of the parties is already married, or if either one is under the age of consent. The wedlock may be terminated if one party refuses to consummate it, or if the female was pregnant when the ceremony took place, and was made so by another man. It is of the utmost importance that it is ascertained as to whether to union is automatically void, or to be taken to be void on the wishes of either party. The circumstances that provide a basis for annulment under English law, do not necessary apply in the legal systems of other nations.

Many have suggested that the laws in which marriage and divorce are shrouded are old-fashioned and still too intertwined with those of religion. There have been calls for the breaking away of some of the legislation, which is at times unnecessarily complicated and archaic. Under the judgment of canon law, a contract into marriage cannot be disunited. In its eyes, the union was either extant or was never so.

Usually, as we have seen, a wife is entitled to acquire the domicil of her husband. But in cases where the marriage has been annulled, the wife is free to choose if she wishes to acquire the domicil of her former partner.

Termination of a Marriage by Divorce

Not until 1857 was an English court empowered to put an end to a legitimate marriage. The Privy Council's arbitration in the case of *Le Mesurier v. Le Mesurier*, of 1895, gave precedent to the jurisdiction adopted by English courts in granting divorce. In the course of the case it was propounded that the only test for jurisdiction may be the place of domicil of the husband at the time at which the case is initiated. The Privy Council decided that the court of Ceylon in question was incapacitated in granting a divorce to a pair of individuals, who, although living in Ceylon, were at the time domiciled in England. The Council stated:

> ... the domicile for the time being of the married pair affords the only true test of jurisdiction to dissolve their marriage.

Concluding Remarks

The relevance of Private International Law cannot be disputed in a world of instant communication and global markets. The ability to travel anywhere, not only cheaply, but quickly, means that many businesses and private relationships with a foreign element are established every day. It is inevitable that some of these relationships will end in disputes, resolvable only by recourse to law. More and more conflicts as to competing systems of law are bound to arise, particularly where there are substantial doctrinal differences in the legislative systems which might apply. As the domestic legal systems of the nations are adjusted to address local and contemporary issues, it is unrealistic ever to expect a unity of legal doctrines as between nations. In consequence, the imperfectly interacting legal systems will always require some acceptable procedure to resolve competing claims. It is not fanciful and far-fetched to envisage a unification of the doctrines relevant to the choice of laws, given only that time, attention, and economic relevance strongly suggest to the governments of nations that this area of law should be perfected in the interests of all concerned. Unlike other areas of law, there is considerable resistance to evolutionary change.

Private International Law might in many ways be said to be in its infancy. There is a great deal of scope for diligent work in this area, which is both highly complex and extremely important. Perhaps the greatest danger to the rapid advancement of this area of jurisprudence is that of bureaucratic inertia: which must be watched for with vigilance and uprooted wherever possible.

SELECT BIBLIOGRAPHY

1 *Polarized Law*, T. Baty, Stevens & Hayes, London, 1914.
2 *The Conflict of Laws*, J.H. Beale, Harvard Law Review Publishing Associates, Cambridge (Mass), 1935.
3 *Private International Law*, Cheshire & North, Butterworths, 1987 (10th Edition).
4 *International Private Law or The Conflict of Laws*, W.M. Hibbert, Oxford University Press, 1918.
5 *The Principles of Private International Law*, A. Nussbaum, Oxford University Press, 1943.
6 *Private International Law*, J.A.C. Thomas, Huchinson, London, 1955.
7 *A Treatise on the Conflict of Laws, or Private International Law*, F. Wharton, Kay & Brother, Philadelphia, 1881.
8 *A Treatise on Private International Law*, John Westlake Q.C., Sweet & Maxwell, London, 1890 (3rd Edition).
9 *Private International Law*, Martin Wolff, Oxford University Press, 1945.
10 *Introduction to the Study of International Law*, T.D. Woolsey, Sampson Low, London, 1875.

9

The Ainu: First People of Japan

On Hokkaido, the northernmost island of Japan, there live the remnants of a people known to themselves as *Ainu*. Only a handful of their race is still pure, and the few that remain live in bitter poverty. Their elaborate traditions, epic tales and etiquette are all but forgotten. These last Ainu are all that are left of a society that once dominated Japan and its neighbouring islands.

The Ainu are a very ancient people. They have been likened to the aborigines of Australia and the native Americans. Similarities have been found to exist between them and these people, as well as various tribal groups in Siberia.

By some they have been known as *Aino*, but this is a complete misnomer. It means a mongrel in Japanese (who started the misnomer to degrade the Ainu). The word Ainu in their own language simply means 'man'. (*Inu* is similarly used incorrectly on occasions: it is the Japanese word for 'dog'.)

The reasons why the Ainu and their civilization have all but vanished are endless. The world has changed and they have been unable to adapt. Their systems of education, philosophies and their ideals were at odds with those around them, and those of the modern world. Yet their isolated communities could not remain detached: in the end the people under whose jurisdiction the Ainu fell, sought to change them. They were restricted in their hunting and prevented from practising their ancient rites and ceremonies. Gradually their land was taken away and the last

172

Ainu found themselves a homeless people. They had no understanding of city life, but had nowhere else to go. They had no grasp of politics or of modern Japanese ways. Like other ancient peoples in a modern world, they had no voice with which to make themselves heard. And with no written script, most of their thoughts, ideas, traditions, songs, and legends disappeared with them.

Although there are a few hardy Ainu still in existence, scarcely any are thought still to live in the traditional Ainu manner. Sadly, even these diehards are soon expected to become a people of the past. It is for this reason that this monograph will refer to the Ainu people in the past tense.

Ainu History

A study of place names throughout Japan (as well as in Saghalien, the Kuriles and parts of Siberia), shows that at one time or another the Ainu were widely dispersed. (Indeed, Mount Fuji itself has been said to derive its name from the Ainu word 'Fire Goddess'.)

The last remnants of the Ainu exist today in the southern-most parts of Saghalien and in some areas of Hokkaido. Their existence was recorded when the first Japanese Emperor, Jimmu Tenno made his crossing from Kyushu to Yamato in 660 B.C. In his fascinating work *Ainu Life and Lore*[5], the Venerable John Batchelor noted that their language has been deemed in many respects to be derived from Aryan tongues. (Batchelor spent most of his life with the Ainu, learning their ways and documenting them in full. He first ventured to Hokkaido as a young lay preacher and lived there until his death in 1940s. Although a missionary, Batchelor seems to have had no qualms in writing of the Ainu's traditional religious beliefs.) He suggests that the Japanese first knew these aboriginal people by the name *Tsuchi-gumo*, which means (in Kanji – i.e. Chinese characters), 'Earth-spiders'; as well as *Ebisu*, barbarians. Batchelor propounded the theory that 'Earth-spider' is essentially the same as 'pit-dweller', which the Ainu certainly were. They are known to have lived through the hostile Japanese winters in man-built pit houses.

The Ainu were a people with no method of writing and hence no literature. But perhaps even more detrimental to their society, this meant that they had no reliable way of recording their own history. The Japanese, who had adopted Chinese characters, set down in writing, records of their battles and campaigns. The Japanese accounts were obviously biassed in favour of their own warriors. They portrayed the Ainu as repulsive barbarians. The Ainus' epic tales on the other hand, give only a very diluted impression of what their ancestors had been through. The Ainu had suffered devastating defeats at the hands of the well-equipped Japanese and countless numbers of them had been slaughtered in battle. Nevertheless, the Ainu stood determined to overcome the Japanese invaders, displaying enormous bravery, but their weapons were greatly inferior to those of the Japanese. Their armour was no more than leather and bamboo at best. They did not have the technology or know-how to craft such weaponry as was being produced by the Japanese smiths.

In the year 720 A.D., one Ainu attack was of such force that the Japanese were compelled to send warriors from nine provinces to contain the attack. In the event the Ainu were forced to retreat to an area just north of Sendai. The year 776 A.D. saw a massive and consolidated Ainu attack on a great Japanese garrison near Sendai. The Ainu won, slaying the commander of the fortress and many of his men. Stories of the Ainus' ferocity spread terror through the islands.

Battles and skirmishes between the Japanese and Ainu continued until 855 A.D. It was then that a civil war began between different Ainu factions, severely weakening them. In these confrontations, every able-bodied individual would turn out. The men would fight the men, whilst the women-folk were expected to fight the opposing women. Surprise attacks by one community on another were made at night.

They were called *topat-tumi*. It was known for almost the entire male population of a village to be killed in this way. The women were seen as capable warriors and were taken along on such raids.

In their subsequent rebellion of 878 A.D., they were no match for the Japanese. From that time on, the Ainu were gradually driven further and further north and so forced to inhabit the less habitable parts of Hokkaido. They became a vanquished people. Restrictions were laid down one after another, dividing and diluting Ainu society and destroying their heritage. They lost their lands, traditions and at last they lost the most precious thing of all: their identity.

Ainu Physical Characteristics

A great many of the earlier visitors to Japan and her neighbouring islands, such as Saghalien and the Kurile chain, were obsessed with the way the Ainu looked. They were very different from the Japanese and the most startling difference, which has been remarked on constantly, is the growth of their hair.

They have been called the 'Hairy Ainu' by many who travelled amongst them. They grew long thick beards, and it was thought to be distinguished to do so. Their hair was indeed thicker than that of the Japanese, and more apt to curl naturally. It is now known that the Ainu were not much more hairy than most Europeans, but when compared to their neighbours, the Japanese, the difference was striking. Some of the early photographers who took pictures of Ainu villagers 'retouched' their photographs, adding more body hair. Then they claimed a likeness between the Ainu and some of the primates.

In complexion, the Ainu were generally lighter than the Japanese. Their skins were tanned or copper-coloured, depending on which area they inhabited. They were much stockier than the Japanese and more muscular on the whole. The men were about five feet five inches high and the women

nearer to five feet. They were nothing like the giant Neander-
thal types described by early explorers of the region. The
descendants of the Ainu, now mostly interbred with the
Japanese, are taller: due to improved diet.

An Ainu referred to another Ainu as 'a person of the same
eye-socket', thus distinguishing him from a Japanese. Their
eyes were not as almond-shaped as the Japanese, but their
faces were rounder. It was deemed comely to have curly hair,
which was known as 'hair of a deity'.

It was very important to an Ainu that his hair should not be
cut or reduced in length. They believed the hair to have
certain concealed powers. Thus it was a terrible ordeal for an
Ainu to have his head shaved. When the Japanese resorted to
this, the Ainu were convinced that their lives would be
shortened, just as their hair had been. But the Ainu themselves would carefully clip the hair before it reached the
shoulders. They cut it in the shape of a crescent at the back of
the neck. It was of paramount importance to make certain
that no hostile power ever happened upon any of the clipped
hair. As in the beliefs of Voodoo in Haiti, it was thought that
by using such a personal thing as a person's hair, a spell could
be cast to harm the person himself.

When drinking their libations or sipping soup, Ainu men
raised their long moustaches with the aid of a 'moustache
lifter'. These were made from pieces of wood some nine
inches long and no more than an inch wide. Some would be
plain and others ornamented and used on ceremonial occasions. One end would be tapered to a point and immersed
into the drink. A few droplets of the beverage would be
caught in this way and offered to the gods out of respect and
so that their thirst too might be quenched.

In certain situations it was deemed proper by the Ainu,
and indeed necessary, to cut off all one's hair. If a woman's
husband died she was expected to shave her head and look
sorrowful. She would then cover her head with a hood.
Before head-shaving developed, a widow was supposed to
pull out the hair from her head and never let it grow back.

Ainu widows and widowers were not traditionally permitted to remarry following the death of their spouse, as it was thought that the deceased partner would be waiting in the next world.

Ainu Etiquette

It was of extreme importance in Ainu society to ensure that the younger generations were versed in the complex formalities of Ainu etiquette. The correct protocol was at times very detailed, and few outside the Ainu community ever knew the appropriate salutations and mannerisms required in a particular situation. To those around them, the Ainu were looked upon as a savage, barbaric people with no manners let alone a system of etiquette. But the Ainu's courtesy and civility to each other was very great. For example:

When arriving at a friend's house, a low coughing sound is made by the visitor. If there is a door drawn across the entrance of the dwelling it must not be moved by the guest. It is evident that the family are at home if a piece of matting is suspended in the entrance. It was considered quite discourteous to peer into another's house through the eastern window, as that was a sacred opening.

When the owner opens the door, the guest follows him into the house, having removed his foot-coverings. They go to the middle of the hut and sit cross-legged, facing each other. When in another's house, a visitor should move with slow deliberation, never rushing. The visitor begins the throat-clearing once again and presses his palms and fingers together. The hands are held in this position, raised to chest level, with one of them pushed out further than the other. Sitting so, the hands are rubbed across each other slowly, with gentle movement. The host returns the salutation in the same way: and they continue to do this as they inquire into each other's fortune and health. When the hands have been rubbed together in this way for quite a while, both men run their fingers through their beards and continue to make rasping sounds with the throat.

The process of this salutation is repeated as the guest begins to tell his host the reason for his visit. The host reciprocates the gestures. Finally, when the official business has been discussed, the men rub their beards one last time and speak informally.

Women salute men in a different way. A guest removes her head-cloth when entering the house of another. This piece of cloth is placed over her left arm, whilst her mouth is covered with her right hand. She runs her right index finger up the left hand, arm, and up to her face. Then she waits for permission to speak. Male Ainu did not salute Ainu women in a formal way. A woman was expected always to walk backwards to the door when in the company of men. It was thought rude for her to show her back to an Ainu man.

When a woman was reunited with her sisters, relatives or close friends after a long absence, they would greet by weeping on each other's necks. And whilst doing so they would explain in a kind a chanting fashion what they had been doing in the time that had elapsed.

Much of Ainu etiquette was aimed at women, who were obligated to behave with a certain reverence when in the company of men. All, except widows, were supposed always to remove their head-covering in front of a man (especially indoors), as well as to get out of the path of an approaching male. Their general form of greeting to one of the opposite sex was to stare at the ground and cover their lips with one hand.

The Ainu were a very sensitive people, and a breach in etiquette was seen as a very serious offence. If a guest came to visit for a few days, but overstayed his welcome, he was prompted to leave in the following manner. The host would prepare a meal known as *tolkootha*. Comprising meats and vegetables, it means 'the feast of being sent back, the mouth having been cooked for'. The visitor would usually get the hint and leave, there being no ill-feelings between the two parties. If he still did not get the message, the hosts would go to stay with a neighbour until he finally went away.

Ainu Women

As already apparent, the womenfolk of the Ainu were expected to act reverentially towards men. These women, as in many developing societies, were burdened with the most arduous responsibilities. It was their chore to till the ground, to raise the young, to prepare the food, and even to weave the cloth from the fibres of elm bark.

The Ainu men were responsible mainly for fishing and hunting, although subsequent restrictions by the Japanese prevented them from carrying out these activities. They would often be heard complaining that the women stood about chattering far too much. They told a story to make the point:

> When the Creator of the world was doing his work he dispatched two gods to Hokkaido. One was male and the other female. The male was allotted the eastern side, and the female, the western side. They both set to work making the place habitable. Time passed and the female happened to meet the sister of Aioina, (the first Ainu), with whom she began to converse. The females chattered and chattered about all sorts of things for a very long time. Meanwhile the male deity had completed his half of the island, which was smooth and quite habitable. The female deity suddenly realised that much time had passed and she rushed to complete her chore. Her slovenly and hurried work meant that the western side of Hokkaido remained rugged. The male god castigated her, and it is said that she began to cry. Hers were the first tears that the world had known.

Perhaps the strangest of all Ainu practices was the tattooing of a wide moustache upon the face of each woman. Various other parts of the body, such as the forehead, forearms, backs of hands, and the fingers below the knuckles were also tattooed.

One woman performed the procedure on another. Men were never tattooed. It was seen as something done to make women beautiful and it was carried out thus:

Bark from an ash tree was soaked in water. Meanwhile a fire was kindled with birch bark, and over it was suspended an iron pot. The birch bark created a thick soot which clung to the base of the pot. One woman cut grooves into the area of skin to be tattooed on the other. A little of the soot was rubbed into the wound, after which a rag dipped in the ash bark liquid was dabbed on the lacerated area. This process was so painful that only a little could be done at a time. The first area to be tattooed was the middle of the top lip and around it. Then the lower lip was begun, and the two areas worked on alternately until they joined up. (This was usually done upon the engagement of the girl.)

There was a certain amount of pressure from the older Ainu women for the younger generation to be tattooed, as they had been. Some girls are also said to have requested it, as all their friends had had the operation and they did not want to be left out. The blue-black colouring is impossible to remove as it is not formed using a needle, but by actually slicing the top layers of the skin.

The Ainu said that they learned the technique from the dwarf-like pit people who once inhabited Hokkaido. There are many legends connected with tattooing. Some Ainu maintained that women had a lot of evil blood in their veins and that tattooing was an effective way of draining away this fluid. They would say in support of tattooing, that covering the mouth with it prevented sinister forces from entering the body. Old women were known to re-tattoo their faces and recolour the designs on the other parts of their bodies. This procedure was known as *pashka-oingara*.

So many myths existed about the tattoo, making its presence a social imperative, that the Japanese authorities and Christian missionaries had a very hard time stopping its use.

The Japanese thought it an extremely ugly mutilation of the skin, and were disdainful. On the other hand, Ainu children were told that horrific events would befall them if they were not tattooed. With the growing interaction between Ainu and Japanese, Ainu women realised that other women were not tattooed and that they could go about unmutilated like them. The strange custom ceased around the turn of the century.

Ainu Society

For centuries the Ainu lived in quiet isolation, having been forced to retreat to the wilds of Hokkaido. They survived there, living according to their ways and their philosophies, in a society which they had developed around their requirements, one generation passing down the necessary knowledge to the next. The young would be instructed on how to make fetishes and worship the gods.

No monarchy ever presided over the Ainu. Each village was a self-governing unit watched over by the elders of the community. A chief and two sub-chiefs were appointed by the villagers. The leader had certain responsibilities, such as presiding over the activities of the Bear Festival, and his dwelling was generally used for the community's religious meetings. The Ainu did not usually construct special religious buildings. The chief would lead hunting expeditions as well as trade sorties and he was expected to give final judgment on matters in dispute. But most importantly, his job was to ensure that there was harmony in the community.

Ainu Dwellings

Ainu communities were generally located around the banks of a river. Each hut was constructed on a little land of its own. Being made from reeds and wooden poles, fire was always a great risk for, once alight, there was no way to stop the blaze, and so, for safety's sake, a safe distance was maintained between one building and the next. The roof and sides of each hut were thatched with reeds woven onto a rugged framework of poles. One hole would be made in the south-facing wall, and another in the wall facing east. The latter was sacred. Nothing was ever thrown through it and it was an horrendous breach of etiquette to peer through it.

In her famous book entitled *Unbeaten Tracks in Japan*[2], Isabella Bird wrote of a large, well-built Ainu hut:

> The usual appearance is that of a small house built on at the end of a larger one. The small house is the vestibule or ante-room, and is entered by a low doorway screened by a heavy mat of reeds. It contains the large wooden mortar and pestle with two ends, used for pounding millet, a wooden receptacle for millet, nets or hunting gear, and some bundles of reeds for repairing the roof or walls. This room never contains a window. From it the large room is entered by a doorway, over which a heavy reed-mat, bound with hide, invariably hangs. This room in Benri's house is 35 feet long by 25 feet broad, another is 45 feet square, the smallest measures 20 feet by 15. On entering, one is much impressed by the great height and steepness of the roof, altogether out of proportion to the height of the walls.

A hearth in the centre of the main room heated it and provided the cooking facilities. The fire was ventilated by a hole cut in the thatch. A pot-holding hook was rigged up for cooking. There was no need for a chimney. As in a Japanese house, there was almost no furniture. Mats were spread on the floor for sitting, and some houses had raised sleeping platforms. One area would be set aside for the family treasures. They would not have consisted of gems or precious metals, but of more constructive implements. Lacquerware bowls and ancient swords were highly prized, the swords being passed from one generation to the next. The Japanese, it is said, confiscated the blades of these weapons to keep the Ainu at bay.

The Law

Laws were decided by members of the village as a whole. They judged according to the traditions, and, by such principles, ruled what action should be taken against any lawbreakers. As the Ainu had no means of writing, their whole legal system was verbal.

Punishments for wrongdoers were wide ranging and favoured physical punishment. It seems that the Ainu had no gaols in which to incarcerate offenders. The death penalty was not used, as death was not seen in Ainu society as a punishment. The level of pain inflicted on the criminal was in relation to his misdeeds. Beatings were the most common; but being put in disgrace was also seen as a severe punishment. If a crime was repeated, the culprit was likely to have the tips of his ears and nose cut off and then be hounded from the village.

Murder was dealt with by cleaving the tendons of the feet with a knife. Thus the victim was preventing from walking, and as a result was unable to work and forced to crawl about for the rest of his life. It is said that a punishment just as severe was the banishing of the offender to what the Ainu called 'the place without birds or trees': thought to be Siberia.

Methods for trying the miscreant were many, the object being to get an individual to confess. They were known to involve torture in many instances and it was not uncommon for a law-breaker to take his own life rather than go through the ordeals or trial.

Some villages favoured making the offender climb into a large pot of water, heated by a fire. He would only be released upon admitting his crime, or with the agreement of the audience that he had suffered enough.

Trials for women and girls frequently differed from those of the men. One method was to make them smoke several pipes of tobacco in succession. The ashes were then put into a receptacle with water and the criminal was forced to drink it.

If she was unable to carry out the task, she was proved guilty thereby.

Ainu Clothing

The Ainu had no sheep from which to take wool and no cotton plants from which to produce thread. However, they had developed from being a people clothed only in furs and hides. The climate of the Ainus' environment ranged from blistering heat in the summers, to the almost arctic conditions of winter. The solution was elm bark which provided them with a cloth loose enough to 'breathe', and warm enough in winter to keep them from freezing. From the fibres of the young bark they made a thread, and from this thread they wove their *attush*. Attush means 'fibre of the elm', and is the name they gave to the long robes they wore.

In the early spring, bark was removed from the elms and put in warm water to be soaked for about ten days. It gradually became soft: allowing the strands of fibre to be easily separated, and then laid out to dry. A coarse thread was prepared from the fibres and it, in turn, was woven on the Ainu's most prized possession: the *kamakap* or loom. It was a simple device which could produce a crude material, yet quite adequate for the Ainus' needs.

It was the womenfolk's responsibility to do the weaving. They also dyed the attush and embroidered the farbic with symmetrical patterns of curved and straight interlocking lines. The dyeing was done by steeping the garment in a solution produced from oak bark stewed in water, followed by a process of leaving it in an iron-rich marsh for seven days or so. By this time it would have become a rusty-black, known as *kunnep*, the black thing.

Every Ainu attush was ornamented with neat designs. But what appeared to be mere decoration had a more important purpose. Like the tartans of the Scottish clans, the Ainu designs were each unique to one village community. Thus an outsider in their midst would be known immediately.

Women and men wore attush with different patterns, the women's being more highly decorated. It is said that the men were very particular about the way their women stitched their garments. If the needlework was not deemed to be of a high enough standard, they told the women to unpick it and begin again.

The Ainu of Saghalien wore belts fashioned from leather, from which they suspended brass rings. The Hokkaido belts were made simply from elm bark fabric.

In the winter, leggings and headdresses were worn. The attush were modified, with skins of bear, deer, dog and so on attached to the back. Gradually, as the Japanese authorities prevented the Ainu from hunting, skins ceased to be available. The Ainu began to dress with the pieces of Western clothing that became available in more recent times. The women, who usually wore a soft undergarment below the attush called a *mouru* or 'soft cloth', favoured one of the velvety textiles of the Japanese. For these the Ainu had to pay in money. As soon as material was imported into their community, they lost the know-how to weave attush from elm bark. In any case, the new generations of Ainu were reluctant to wear such coarse attire.

Food

The eating habits of the Ainu people changed drastically as the Japanese restrained them from hunting, and drove them from their lands. Until the latter half of the 19th century there was generally enough food for all. The Ainu never over-fished the rivers, or hunted for more meat than they could eat. What they caught was smoked under the eaves of their huts and then put in a store house. These separate buildings stood on stilts, so as to keep the food dry and vermin free. Vegetables and supplies of millet were also stored in this way.

Turtles were seen as especially important. Many groups of Ainu did not eat them, but looked upon them with great reverence. If they came upon one, they would take it ashore and give it a large amount of sake to drink, before taking it back to sea.

Sardines and herrings were favoured by the Ainu, as were walruses and porpoises if they could be caught. Each year tens of thousands of fur seals migrate past Hokkaido, en route to Siberia, where they breed. The Ainu would pick off a few, eat the meat and use the skins to barter for rice and other commodities. Acute over-hunting of these and other creatures in and around Hokkaido, has reduced their numbers drastically.

There do not seem to be a large number of medicinal plants that were known to the Ainu. Many of their treatments centred around invocations of the gods. But a few plants had a wide range of applications. Mugwort (artemisia) in particular, the leaves of which were plucked in early spring, was used to make medicinal concoctions and was thought to be a great life preserver, and taken for all kinds of conditions.

Bear Festival

Certain events in the Ainu calendar required great feasts to be arranged. For these, invitations were sent out to other communities, and very special delicacies were prepared, such as chestnuts served with fish eggs. The Bear Festival was the greatest occasion in the Ainu year.

This ritual is perhaps one of the strangest practices of any ancient people. Certainly it has been a source of shock and surprise for the visitors to Ainu society who have witnessed it. Extensive preparations were made for the festival. It is said that the women would shave their spouses' foreheads and the backs of their necks. Tattoos were recoloured and the best clothes were brought out. The women made millet dumplings, while the Ainu men set about making fetishes for the celebration.

The bear is the most ferocious wild animal that the Ainu

knew. It was respected above all other creatures, as an embodiment of strength and power. A year or so before the ritual took place, a bear cub would be caught by the members of the community. They would take it home with them to the village where it would be brought up for a year. When the cub was of a certain size (the larger the better), it was taken out of its cage. A cord was fastened around its neck, and by means of this it was paraded about for all to see. The Ainu men would begin to worship the cub when all had gathered. The crowd danced and clapped their hands, as the elders addressed the little bear cub. They explained what the festival would entail: telling it that it was to be sent back to its ancestral abode. It was a great honour indeed for the bear cub to go through this ceremony. The village elders told the bear that they hoped it would not bear a grudge against the Ainu, for they were glorifying it in this way because of their love for it.

The Ainu asserted unequivocally that the cub was not being killed, but sent to meet those who had preceded it.

Isabella Bird who travelled alone throughout Japan in the 1870s, witnessed the Bear Festival. Her fascinating eye-witness account is quoted here:

After the capture the bear cub is introduced into a dwelling-house, generally that of the chief, or sub-chief, where it is suckled by a woman, and played with by the children, till it grows too big and rough for domestic ways, and is placed in a strong cage, in which it is fed and cared for, as I understand, till the autumn of the following year, when, being strong and well-grown, the Festival of the Bear is celebrated. The customs of this festival vary considerably, and the manner of the bear's death differs among the mountain and coast Ainos, but everywhere there is a general gathering of the people, and it is the occasion of a great feast, accompanied with much *sake* and a curious dance, in which men alone take part.

Yells and shouts are used to excite the bear, and when he

becomes much agitated a chief shoots him with an arrow, inflicting a slight wound which maddens him, on which the bars of the cage are raised, and he springs forth, very furious. At this stage the Ainos run upon him with various weapons, each one striving to inflict a wound, as it brings good luck to draw his blood. As soon as he falls down exhausted, his head is cut off, and the weapons with which he has been wounded are offered to it, and he is asked to avenge himself upon them.

Miss Bird's account differs in several ways from other descriptions as witnessed by foreigners to Hokkaido. A common practice was to shoot the cub with blunt arrows, just to annoy it. Strangulation was also important in various Ainu communities: they would throttle the bear using a cord and two pieces of wood. However, this was done in such a way as to avoid actually killing the animal. The custom of strangling was outlawed by the Japanese in the early years of this century. Other spectators to the festival noted that a knife was plunged into the bear's neck in order to kill it. The blood that spurted out of the mortal wound was collected in a jar, then passed around to be drunk warm. Spilling even a drop of the sacred fluid was seen as a horrific sin. Some of the animal's flesh also was consumed raw by those present.

When the bear cub was quite dead, the east window of the chief's hut was broken in, to form an aperture through which the creature's carcass was carried. The bear would be skinned (and the head removed if this had not already been done). Its nose was removed and put near the hearth. The cub's flesh was cut from the bones and boiled up into a stew. A little of this dish was set around the remains of the carcass, together with dumplings garnished with herbs.

At this point the Ainu elders (women not being permitted to take part in such serious religious matters), would don their ceremonial head coverings, and dance about.

The bear's body would be offered, garnished and cooked to the animal's head. Fetishes were also presented in homage to the dead cub. Then the Ainu would wait in polite silence before announcing that they would eat with 'him'. A few morsels of the meal would be dropped into the fire as a token of respect to the fire god, and then the feast would begin.

The bear's skull was attached to the top of a long pole, and looked upon in reverence as the most important fetish of the community. It was known as *keu-mande-ni*.

The Ainu completed this festival every year in their small villages for centuries. They believed most earnestly that they were honouring the cub and treating it with the utmost respect. They saw the ceremony as a way of letting the creature know their love and devotion to it. For the Ainu, the ritual was not horrific in any way, having been raised in the belief that it was doing a service to the bear cub. Perhaps their sincere belief that such a practice was benefiting the creature enabled them to act as they did.

Kamui and Ramat

There was not an organised priesthood in Ainu society. The head of each family was responsible for attending to the household's duties towards the deities. Frequent ceremonies were held for occasions that ranged from hunting trips to marriages.

To the Ainu it was fundamental to keep content those spirits which controlled their world. They called their gods *Kamui*. It is a strange word, and its applications were very wide. Something that was inordinately beautiful was also Kamui. A huge mountain was *Kamui nupuri*; an immense wind, *Kamui rera*. But when inverted, *Nupuri Kamui* would mean: 'the spirits of the mountain'. (Thus Kamui could be used as a noun or an adjective.)

The first Ainu man was *Aioina Kamui*, (Kamui there being added as a term of respect). It has been suggested that the Ainu, who were a polytheistic people, were not always so. (It seems likely that the Japanese word for a god, *Kami*, may have been borrowed from the Ainu.) The Creator of the world and the owner of heaven was *Pase-Kamui*, while those deities beneath him were collectively called, *Yaiyan Kamui*. Thunder was this Great God's voice, lightning was his glory and the Milky Way was the River of God.

Malicious forces were plentiful, and known as *Nitne Kamui*. Even though they were pernicious in their activities (such as spreading disease), they were worshipped all the same, for fear that they might take reprisals. The Ainu maintained that Nitne Kamui were not actually worshipped as they only pretended to invoke them, to keep them at bay.

It was believed that almost every object, whether tangible or intangible, had an immortal life; and that spirits were present in everything from a wave on the ocean to a bowl in a hut. These spirits would make sure that the object would behave as it was expected to. *Ramat* was the soul and heart that was in each object. If someone died, or a house was destroyed by flames, the Ramat was thought to escape and thus be able to travel on somewhere else. When a man died he was buried with items that might be of use to him in his future life – bows, arrows, bowls and so forth. Each was placed beside him, but was broken first, so as to allow the Ramat to be released, just as the dead person's soul had been. The Ramat was warned that soon it would be time for it to move on. So just before killing an animal, the Ainu would explain in a small ceremony that it should make ready to be liberated. It was very important to address Ramat with great respect, as offending it might cause it to respond with *turenbe*, divine magic.

Vines were thought to be filled with Ramat. Old Ainu men with stiff joints and aching bones would put circles fashioned from vines through their ear lobes. (These were quite different from the simple pieces of red material that Ainu men generally wore through their ear lobes.) They maintained that the divine vines, being malleable and flexible, would restore these qualities to the rest of the body.

Ainu Fetishes

If an Ainu wanted to attract the attention of a divine one, to worship it or obtain its assistance, he would make a fetish and offer it to the deity. These fetishes were known as *Inao*, 'that which conveys a message'.

An important fetish, always present in an Ainu dwelling, was the *Chisei koro inao*. It was dedicated to the ancestral guardians of the home and was usually placed in the position of greatest honour: the north-east corner of the main room.

The womenfolk, in most cases, were not permitted to participate in the ceremonial fetish-making and invocation. An exception might be the making of offerings to a departed spouse.

On the birth of a baby, a fetish was constructed to call upon the deities to watch over the infant. The Ainu believed that the first man had a spine of willow wood, and that their spines were also of willow wood. The fetish was made of a piece of willow stick, to which were attached a large number of willow wood shavings.

To one not versed in fetish construction, these different charms might all look much the same. Each would generally be formed by affixing shavings onto a stick. Then the fetish would be placed outside the dwelling and invoked. Millet beer was presented to the deities in attendance.

Skulls of all types of birds and animals could be petitioned, as mediators to the deities. The skulls of bats, foxes, owls and albatrosses were all used by the Ainu in this way. Other methods of appeasing the gods were practised as well as fetish making. Through some of them one was thought to be able to increase one's natural powers. Thus swallowing a bear's eyes was believed to give the participant extraordinary sight.

Fire Worship

The goddess equated with the fire made in the hearth of a home was known as *Fuji*, the ancestress. She was seen as a purging element, and was always treated with the utmost respect. Etiquette corresponding to her worship and devotion was complex as it would have been disastrous to cause such a sacred lady to become enraged.

Nothing was ever thrown casually into the hearth fire, such as household debris or tobacco ash. The burning material was never poked with a poker or removed whilst burning.

Ainu Superstition and Magic

The Ainu were extraordinarily superstitious and obeyed in the minutest detail the traditions passed down by their ancestors. They also seemed to update their superstitious convictions when necessary. For example, with the introduction of photography, the Ainu affirmed that, if photographed, their eyes would be forced to remain open through all eternity. It was also thought that through some sinister action, the process would bring about the end of their life in some way.

Dr. B. Douglas Howard, author of *Life with Trans-Siberian Savages*[12], travelled amongst the Ainu of Saghalien. He told of the occasion that he showed the Ainu photographs that he had taken of themselves. They were driven into a state of fury and came to his hut brandishing weapons. There was no other choice than to put all the photographs and equipment into a large pile and set light to it. Of the spectacle Howard wrote:

> Inao (fetishes) were stuck in the ground all around the fire, and following their intimations, while they stood back in great alarm, I threw my poor Kodak, my pictures, all my apparatus, on the fire, and stood calmly looking on till nothing was left of them but ashes.

Making Rain

The northernmost areas of Japan are subject to lengthy dry spells that have caused horrendous famines. For months at a time rain does not fall and in consequence the Ainu developed rain-making processes. One Westerner reported witnessing a pet dog being paraded around the village, decorated with bright rags of cloth and flowers. The animal towed a container of water. The name of this procedure was *shiriwen hokki*. The observer noted that on that night there was a heavy storm.

Another method of inducing rain was to put out sieves on poles and challenge the deities to fill them. Yet another was to dunk mugwort leaves in water and shake the excess water onto the soil.

Restoring Life

If it was known that an Ainu was soon to die, those around him would expel clean water from their mouths gently over the invalid's head and chest. It was hoped that this might restore life.

In the same way, during an eclipse, Ainu have been seen to shake water into the air to rejuvenate the ailing sun or moon.

Witchcraft

Ishirushina was an Ainu word meaning 'the binding up of a spirit through a spell'. By this magic, the assistance of sinister forces was gained, to both good and evil ends. Ailments were said to arise when such spirits had entered one's body. A remedy for stomach pain was made by mixing the scrapings from a dried albatross' beak, in water. This concoction was then drunk and the pains were supposed to withdraw. (The albatross was seen as one of the most important marine deities.) It was a general belief in Ainu society that the more foul-tasting a potion, the more successful its results. They would state that, if the medicine was not pungent, it would not drive the malicious spirits away.

In another procedure, miniature images of a particular Ainu would be constructed and nailed to a tree through the figure's heart or face. Invocations by the maker of such a doll would be presented, requesting the demons to bring an end to the person in whose likeness the doll was made. It was understood that the invisible fiends would hear such a plea and come to take the victim's life. He who tampered with such an effigy when nailed up, would be struck with a curse.

Snakes also played an important role in Ainu magic. They were thought to be demons, and a large number of superstitions surrounded them. For example, if a person slept with his mouth wide open, it was believed that a snake would be capable of slithering in through the orifice to take possession of the victim's body.

An Ainu man seeking revenge would seek out a snake and make a pact with it. In return for fetishes and worship dedicated to it, the reptile would undertake to kill a chosen person. It was thought that snakes were particularly fond of goading women to the point of insanity.

Such was the power snakes were thought to possess that snake skins were kept by some to use in amulets and to foretell the future. Killing a snake would mean that the demons within it would enter its killer, with grave consequences.

Shamans in Ainu society were known as *tusu-guru*. They were versed in matters of magical concern and people were frightened of them because of the powers they were said to be able to manipulate. Amongst their activities was the exorcism of evil spirits, hypnotism, and allowing demons to speak through them. They could also supposedly send their soul to the land of the dead to bring back the soul of another. Being such a superstitious people, the Ainu could not challenge these shamans. Realising their power to cause terror, some of these shamans took great advantage of the unsuspecting Ainu.

The Departed Ainu

For over a thousand years the Ainu lived in their isolated communities on Hokkaido. Having been beaten back to this northerly land, they had comparatively little interaction with Japanese society, Hokkaido being until recently very much cut off from mainstream Japan. It is geographically and climatically inhospitable, so that Japanese settlements were slow to move into the area.

With the growth of Sapporo, the capital of Hokkaido, and other large cities, the Ainu could no longer remain unaffected by Japanese civilization. Sudden profound changes to Japanese society itself in the closing years of the 19th century, brought catastrophic change to the Ainu.

But the decline of the Ainu and their world really began during the times of friction with the Japanese more than a millenium before. The Japanese forces had pursued a policy aimed at the extermination of the Ainu. The case is similar in many respects to that of the American Indian tribes, similarly persecuted by the incoming Colonists.

Like the native Americans, the Ainu had no immunity to the new diseases, such as smallpox, brought by the invading Japanese. As they had only the most rudimentary knowledge of medical science, the Ainu population was decimated. Again like the American Indians, the Ainu had a low tolerance to alcohol, and the Japanese abused this weakness. They would pay the Ainu labourers in alcohol. Their resulting inebriation wasted their time, the little money they could earn, and ate away at their natural vigour. Their social structure was destroyed in part by the craving for alcohol: etiquette and propriety, so important to the Ainu, were eroded most severely.

Altercations amongst the Ainu developed over trivial matters, sparked by alcohol and money. The Ainu had never had a currency system, but it became of increasing importance to purchase both Japanese luxuries and alcohol. As these new-found extravagances were obtained, the Ainu quickly lost the knowledge and will to create their traditional attush, clothing. Similarily, they no longer required bows and arrows as guns were available.

Ainu women were often more than willing to marry Japanese men, as it promised them a life of less arduous toil, and modern comforts until then unknown. It has been noticed that these mixed marriages produced children who were physically weaker than their parents. These offspring, with only one Ainu parent, were not schooled in the details of Ainu etiquette and traditional beliefs. As there were no books in the Ainu language, traditions and lore had always been passed down orally. But with the breakdown of Ainu society, few still had the time to relate these drawn-out tales.

Those who strove to keep their lineage pure Ainu, could only wed their offspring to closer and closer relatives. In consequence, mental and physical illness resulted, greatly weakening those pure Ainu strains.

Land was another problem. The Ainu's traditional lands were slowly removed by order of the Japanese. The Ainu were not recognised and thus their estates were subject to appropriation. As land became more and more scarce the Ainu were compelled to move to the rugged western flank of Hokkaido. Forced to exist on their crops alone, after the passing of legislation to forbid hunting, the Ainu found their harvests failing due to the poor, over-tilled earth.

Living in ways to which they were not accustomed, the Ainu grew weaker and weaker. They were unable to tolerate city life, for they were a people bonded with nature. They hated being cooped up, which became their fate. Japanese who lived in Sapporo and other cities in Hokkaido would talk of Ainu employees suddenly getting up, leaving, and never coming back. One Ainu explained this restlessness by saying that the cry of the mountains beckoned.

SELECT BIBLIOGRAPHY

1 *Alone with the Hairy Ainu or, 3,800 Miles on a Pack Saddle in Yezo and a Cruise to the Kuril Islands*, A.H.S. Landor, John Murray, London, 1893.

2 *Unbeaten Tracks in Japan*, (Volumes I & II), I.L. Bird, John Murray, London, 1880.

3 *The Ainu of Japan*, Rev. John Batchelor, Religious Tract Society, London, 1892.

4 *The Ainu and their Folk-lore*, Rev. John Batchelor, Religious Tract Society, London, 1901.

5 *Ainu Life & Lore: Echoes of a Departing Race*, Rev. John Batchelor, Kyobunkwan, Tokyo, 1930.

6 *Ainu Cult and Creed*, N.G. Munroe. Routledge & Kegan Paul, London, 1962.

7 *Illness and Healing Among the Sakhalin Ainu*, Emiko Ohnuki-Tierney, Cambridge University Press, New York, 1981.

8 *Songs of Gods and Humans: the Epic Tradition of the Ainu*, D.L. Philippi, University of Tokyo Press, Tokyo, 1979.

9 *Les Ainous: Peuple Chasseur, Pecheur et Cueilleur du Nord du Japon*, Crédit Communal, Bruxelles, 1989.

10 *Japan's Minorities: Burakumin, Koreans & Ainu*, G.A. de Vos & O. Wetherhall, Minority Rights Group, London, 1974.

11 *The Ainu Ecosystem: Environment & Group Structure*, Hitoshi Watanabe, University of Washington Press, Seattle, 1973.

12 *Life with Trans-Siberian Savages*, Dr. D.B. Howard, Longmans, Green & Co., London, 1893.

13 *Ainu Folklore*, Carl Etter, Wilcox & Follett & Co., Chicago, 1949.

14 *Concerning the Ainu in Kamchatka*, A.F. Majewicz, V.A.M., Pozan, 1981.

15 *The Bear Worshippers of Yezo and the Island of Karafuto*, Edward Greey, Boston, 1884.

16 *Primitive Culture in Japan*, N.G. Munroe, Transactions of the Asiatic Society of Japan, (Volume XXXIV), Yokohama, 1906.

17 *The Ainu of Yezo*, Japan Magazine (pp.439–443), Tokyo, November 1912.

18 *Together with the Ainu: A Vanishing People*, M.I. Hilger, University of Oklahoma Press, Oklahoma, 1971.

19 *On the Arrow Poison in use Among the Ainos of Yezo*, S. Eldridge, Transactions of the Asiatic Society of Japan, (Volume IV, pp.78–88), Yokohama, October 1875.

20 *The Ainu of North Japan: A Study in Conquest and Acculturation*, Shinichiro Takakura, Transactions of the American Philosophical Society, (New Series Volume L), Philadelphia, 1961.

10

Cults in 19th Century Britain

ROBERT CECIL

There has never been a time of which we have record when Christendom has not been vexed by controversy about dogma or church organisation or both. This applied as forcibly to 19th century Britain as to earlier centuries, even though religion was under threat and Christians might have been expected to close ranks against the assaults of infidelity and secular ideology. Variations of belief flourished, partly because religious tolerance was gaining strength, especially after the emancipation of Roman Catholics in 1829, and partly because scientific discoveries, coupled with historical and textual criticism, had cast doubt on the literal truth of the Bible. The human mind, throwing off its shackles, or in some cases reluctantly prised loose from traditional authority, was resuming that enquiry into man's origin and destiny which seems to be innate in us all. Perennial interest in the mystery of life and death justifies our concentrating on this aspect of heterodox thought, where the invasive influence of cults was at its strongest.

Whilst new heresies, as we shall shortly see, were making their appearance, there was also the revival of an ancient heterodoxy that was as old as orthodoxy itself. Indeed adventism, or belief in Christ's Second Coming, had formed part of the belief of some of the earliest Church Fathers. It had originated as a Jewish Messianic myth, but had acquired some special connotations in the morbid and ingenious minds of certain early mediaeval Christians. Whilst the mythic picture varied at different times and places, certain eschatological features, loosely based upon the Book of Revelation, were common to most of them. The signs and portents of the Second Coming included a 'time of troubles', marked by war, drought, famine and pestilence, during which the Antichrist would dominate; after these trials Christ would come in his glory, greeted by saints and martyrs, both living and dead, and would preside over the Last Judgment. Those who survived this final ordeal would inherit the New Jerusalem, where 'there shall be no more death, neither sorrow, nor crying, neither shall there be any more pain: for the former things are passed away'.[1]

One of those who accepted this prophecy, whilst interpreting it in his own way, was the Swedish visionary, Emanuel Swedenborg (1688–1772), who made a special study of Revelation. He believed that the Last Judgment had occurred in 1757 and that at the date of his death in London men were already living in 'the last days'. A startling series of events in Europe had created a climate favourable to such beliefs. The execution of Louis XVI, the reign of terror and the short-lived triumph of atheism in France convinced many who, in more sober times, would not have been regarded as visionaries, that the course of human history had changed abruptly. Had events merely become unpredictable, or were men witnessing 'signs of the last things', which had indeed been predicted? We, who live at a period when waves of hysteria about thermo-nuclear destruction intermittently sweep the country, can have some appreciation of men's state of mind in those days. Clergy preached sermons identifying Napoleon with Antichrist and devising anagrams linking him with Apollyon. Extreme Protestants commented with mixed glee and foreboding on the expulsion from the Vatican of Pope Pius VI; they had long associated the Roman Church with 'Babylon the Great, the Mother of Harlots'; it looked as if her day of reckoning had come. Shortly before the French Revolution there had been a resurgence of Martinists, Rosicrucians, Masonic Lodges of the Egyptian Rite and the like, and this underworld had been haunted by the shadowy figures of Cagliostro and the Count of Saint-Germain.

Britain had nothing equally piquant to offer, but here, too, it was a period when a disturbed and credulous public would lend an ear to any charismatic figure with an inner urge to assume the prophetic mantle. One aspirant to such a role was Richard Brothers, a half-pay Captain, who in 1794 published *Revealed Knowledge of the Prophecies and Times*. He stressed the incidence of revolution, earthquake, pestilence and the downfall of the Pope, after which all men would become one family. This was too much for the authorities, who placed him in an asylum. One of his assumed titles was 'Prince of the Hebrews'. Extermination of the Jews had formed part of certain mediaeval eschatologies; this had been transformed in a more humane era into conversion of the Jews, which thus became a sign of 'the last days'. In 1815 a society aiming at the conversion of the Jews was founded and in some minds became linked with the pretensions of the British Israelites, who held that the British were indeed the Lost Tribes.

Brothers' career overlapped that of Joanna Southcott (1750–1814), the daughter of a Devonshire farmer and author of four books of prophecy between 1801 and 1804. She claimed the powers of the angel, described in Revelation (ch. VII), who 'sealed the servants of the Lord in their foreheads'. Those so sealed would, at the Second Coming, be gathered up alive into heaven. As if this were not enough, she was also:

> ... 'the woman clothed with the sun', of whom it is written, 'and she brought forth a man child, who was to rule all nations with a rod of iron: and her child was caught up unto God, and to his throne.'[2]

After a number of false pregnancies, she died without having produced the Messiah, who was designated the Shiloh, or Prince of Peace. Five years after her death a group of her followers proclaimed the Shiloh in London; they were led, according to the Newgate Calendar, by Samuel Sibley and his wife. Their message was not one of peace and joy; they cried 'Wo! Wo! to the inhabitants of the earth, because of the coming of the Shiloh!' The inhabitants in the immediate vicinity became incensed and the Adventists had to be rescued from the mob. A decade later a crippled shoemaker, named Zion Ward, who edited a weekly, *The Judgment Seat of Christ*, emerged as the new leader. In 1832 he was imprisoned for blasphemy and died five years later.

One historian of this period, following the Marxist practice of interpreting religious phenomena from an economic base, has attempted to relate the rise and fall of these minor millenarian waves to cyclic movements of the economy:

> . . . it was certainly a cult of the poor . . . There is a sense in which any religion which places great emphasis on the after-life is the Chiliasm of the defeated and the hopeless.[3]

Like many other Marxist interpretations, this one is strong in theory, but weak on facts. If despair of well-being in this world were the motivation, one would expect the millenarians and their followers to be drawn predominantly from the lowest economic and social category. This is demonstrably not the case. Sibley was a watchman and his followers are described as 'journeyman mechanics and labourers'; Ward was self-employed. Thackeray, who was a shrewd social observer, mentions two Adventists among the employees of the devout Mrs. Sophia Newcome, whose 'mansion at Clapham was long the resort of the most favoured of the religious world'.[4] One of these is the housekeeper; the other is the head-gardener; it is not the illiterate, lower servants, but the half-educated, upper servants, who are touched by this obsession. The millenarian myth that was to begin, much later, to appeal to the proletariat was Marxism itself, which has all the essential characteristics: violence, directed against the rich, who have indulged in usury (profit-making); the triumph of the virtuous poor (proletariat), and the final establishment on earth of egalitarian peace and harmony (withering away of the state, classless society etc.). 'For it is the simple truth that, stripped of their original supernatural sanction, revolutionary millenarianism and mystical anarchism are with us still.'[5]

The fact is that in the first half of the 19th century all classes of society were in some degree touched by millenarian ideas. We can see this most clearly by briefly examining the best organised group, namely the Catholic Apostolic Church (CAC). The two leading figures in the first phase were the Scots Minister and friend of Carlyle, Edward Irving (1792–1834); and the wealthy banker and one-time M.P., Henry Drummond (1786–1860). Drummond owned a large house at Albury in Surrey and there convened in 1826 a meeting of those interested in the unfulfilled prophecies of Scripture, which seemed on the verge of realisation. One of those attending the meeting was Irving, who in the previous year had begun preaching 'the Second Advent' from his pulpit in the Regent Square Church in North London. He and his followers believed that one of the signs that the Second Coming was imminent would be the Pentecostal gift of tongues (*glossolalia*) and powers of healing. In 1830 allegedly miraculous cures of consumption occurred in a family living near Rosneath, Dumbarton, and in the following year people, mainly women, began to 'speak with tongues' and prophesy in Irving's Church. This led to his eviction in 1832; his excommunication from the Church of Scotland and his death followed in 1834. After his burial a number of women, clothed in white, stood round his grave in the belief that he would rise again.[6]

Drummond and his friends, drawn mainly from the Anglican and Presbyterian Churches, did not regard themselves as discredited by the excesses of the 'Irvingite' glossolalia. They acquired their own church in Gordon Square and co-opted twelve Apostles, who constituted the ruling body of the CAC. Each Apostle was empowered to 'seal' 144,000 of the righteous, this being the number prescribed in Revelation (Ch. VII). By 1851 there were 37 churches in Great Britain with an estimated 8,000 members. Each Apostle also had

assigned to him an overseas area, or 'tribe', which he was
supposed to visit. There was, for example, a small colony in
Malta, grouped round the Rt. Hon. J. H. Frere, who had at
one time been H.M. Minister in Spain (1800–1809). His
brother, Hatley, is mentioned in a letter of 1844 written from
Malta by John Holt, a Lancashire J.P., who was on a sailing
trip round the Mediterranean:

> At Athens we were joined by Mr. Frere, a brother of Rt.
> Hon. J.H. Frere, the intimate friend of Canning, who in
> 1813 published an interpretation of prophecy and has a
> very confident expectation that 1847 is to be the end of the
> Christian dispensation – the date of the advent of our Lord
> and the battle of Armageddon, and the period of pouring
> out the Seventh Vial . . . and a Mr. Fletcher who has been
> sent out by the Archbishop of Canterbury and who has
> been two years at Antioch, Damascus, etc. on a visitation
> to the Nestorian and other Eastern Christian Churches,
> mentions persuasions and appearances which convince the
> Turks that in this year – 1260 of the Hegira – Constanti-
> nople is to fall . . . In the East a feeling is abroad that we are
> in the Times of the End.[7]

The CAC had no monopoly of millenarians; some, like the
Earl of Shaftesbury (Lord Ashley), remained within the fold
of the established Church, which found it necessary to
combat their views. Archbishop Whately of Dublin opposed
their heterodoxy in one of his books; Samuel Waldegrave,
Bishop of Carlisle, devoted the Bampton Lectures in 1854 to
refuting the tendency. In 1848 John Holt, back in London,
attended a series of meetings at Exeter Hall, which had
become a major centre of Low Church propaganda. In a
letter to his sister-in-law, who seems to have been less enthusiastic about the end of the world, he listed some of the
speakers who had touched on this great theme:

> I conceive you may not reciprocate these sentiments on
> that portion of unfulfilled prophecy which I believe is

having its accomplishment in these contemporary events – and especially in my conviction that we live on the eve of the millennial morrow. I wish you had heard the many distinguished men that I have lately listened to on this subject, earnest, sober, learned, honest, prayerful, deep students of prophecy – McNeile, Stowell, Bickersteth, Cumming, Villiers, Lord Ashley, Freemantle, Daniel Wilson, Goodhart and other . . .[8]

To some Adventists, the deferment of the Second Coming was a serious test of faith. Edmund Gosse, whose parents were Plymouth Brethren, has vividly described the confusion in his father's mind:

Our thoughts were at this time abundantly exercised with the expectation of the immediate coming of the Lord, who . . . would suddenly appear, without the least warning, and would catch up to be with him in everlasting glory all whom acceptance of the Atonement had sealed for immortality . . . The world, after a few days' amazement at the total disappearance of these persons, would revert to its customary habits of life . . . My father lived for nearly a quarter of a century more, never losing the hope of 'not tasting death', and as the last moments of mortality approached, he was bitterly disappointed at what he held to be a scanty reward for his long faith and patience.[9]

The self-constituted elect faced domestic problems, which pressed less severely upon more orthodox Christians. These are illustrated by the following letter, addressed in 1879 to my grandfather by a kinsman, Samuel Cecil; it displays an inimitable admixture of worldliness and other-worldliness:

You know our hope – that girding ourselves to be prepared for the Lord's coming in his own way, we shall at his coming be accounted worthy to escape those things that are coming on the earth. How far our faith may avail to include our children in the blessing, now that they have arrived at age to choose for themselves, we cannot tell. But if the parents should be taken and the children left, would you kindly undertake the oversight of their interests until they come of age? Our property being nearly all vested in Trustees, there must be someone to whom they must be authorised to pay the dividends, until they can themselves give receipts ... Earnestly hoping that this may all be unnecessary – that we may be all, as one family, taken away from the evil to come; and earnestly longing that you may yourself be a partaker of the same glorious hope, as I am, as ever.[10]

The expectation seems to be that, however terrible the evil to come, it would not prevent the Trustees from paying out dividends – an impressive tribute to Victorian confidence in the stability of contemporary financial institutions. Eschatological speculation was undoubtedly promoted (though in what degree it is impossible to assess) by study of the works of Swedenborg, which gradually became more widespread. For Swedenborg, however, the Last Judgment had coincided with his own visionary experiences and had not been marked by the clangour of the Last Trump with the dead rising from their graves, as in a painting by Stanley Spencer. Judgment, for Swedenborg, would be an almost imperceptible process of separation between sheep and goats. This would take place in the world of spirits, an intermediate point between heaven and hell; unlike purgatory, it was not a world where reparation and repentance were possible, but one in which characteristics that had become dominant in life would reassert themselves after death with inescapable results. Those who gravitated to hell did so because it was for that their lives had fitted them. All who went to heaven became angels; there was no independent order of angelic beings.

One effect of this teaching was to bridge the immense chasm that had opened, in Evangelical Christianity, between life and death; death-bed remorse and absolution lost their significance. Mental and moral states, which men had developed in their lives, accompanied them through the gateway of death into the world of spirits, so much so that some, who had recently died, were scarcely aware of the transition from this world to the next. Swedenborg claimed to know this from his frequent and detailed conversations with angels. To all who had been subject to his influence, death not only lost its sting; it also lost its finality as a mark of punctuation. An early disciple, William Cookworthy (1704–1780), likened death to 'putting off an old coat to put on a new one'. On his death-bed he said to his daughter, 'Is this the death, which I so long dreaded? This great, this mighty change! What is it? Why, ceasing to breathe, that is all!'[11] The sculptor, John Flaxman (1755–1826), was also a Swedenborgian; when he died, his friend, William Blake, said of his death, 'I cannot think of death as more than the going out of one room into another'.[12] This attitude intensified interest in the dubious borderland between life and death that was in any case developing during the first half of the century, under the influence of the Gothic novel and the relaxation of Christian orthodoxy.

Blake was not an uncritical Swedenborgian, but until his death in 1827 he held fast to certain basic ideas, which he had found in Swedenborg's works, as these became available in English translation from 1783 onwards. Blake perceived that the institutionalised churches had perverted the message of Jesus by laying so much emphasis on death, judgment and the intercession of clergy. The moral problem confronting man was not connected with what he believed or what religious rites he observed; the root question was what attitude he took up towards the sufferings of his fellow men. This would determine his moral state and whether he carried heaven or hell around with him; no amount of sly hypocrisy, or lip-service to Christian platitudes, could conceal his true state, which, as in Swedenborg's world of spirits, would in due time stand fully revealed. Blake's *Songs of Innocence and Songs of Experience* bore the subtitle: 'showing the Two Contrary States of the Human Soul'. In his *Songs of Innocence* he mainly extolled children, because their responses had not been corrupted by deceit and dissembling, which were the fruits of adult experience. Such experience would prove fatal in the world of spirits, where the false antithesis between appearance and reality would vanish, 'because no one there is permitted to have a divided mind, that is to speak one thing and will another'.[13]

Blake's vision of heaven was also Swedenborgian. He wrote in *The Book of Los*: 'The eternal world is one of mutual cooperation in which all forms of life are nourished and supported by all other forms, as in the economy of the individual human body.' Swedenborg in his *Heaven and Hell* had been even more specific, describing heaven as 'a whole angelic society' which, 'when the Lord manifests himself as present, appears as one object in human form'.[14] All participating in this angelic society would fulfil particular functions, corresponding to the functions of the different organs of the body. Indeed, he continues: 'The whole natural world corresponds to the spiritual world, not only in general, but also in particular.'[15] The doctrine according to which God was a Grand Man (Adam Kadmon), composed of the totality of perfected humanity, was of Cabalistic origin and had been delineated by the 17th century mystic J.G. Gichtel in his *Theosophica Practica* (1696). It is probable that Swedenborg's concept derived from Gichtel's, or that both shared a common origin. Such thinking reinforced the trend towards narrowing the gulf fixed by orthodox theology between God and man, thus paving the way for the various cults of humanity that were to emerge later.

It was not to be expected that such radical rethinking of Christianity would make rapid strides. Swedenborg himself modestly observed on his death-bed that 'from and after the year 1780 it will spread very much'.[16] His antagonism to established churches suggests that, for spreading his beliefs, the last thing he would have done would have been to found a church. His followers thought otherwise. They had at first met together as the Theosophical Society, but in 1787 they reconstituted themselves as the New Church, which later became the New Jerusalem Church. In the U.S.A, the New Church Society opened its doors in Baltimore in 1792. One of those in England who opposed the new development was the Rev. John Clowes, who for over 50 years was Rector of St. John's, Manchester. De Quincey writes affectionately of him as 'holy, visionary, apostolic . . . translator of Swedenborg and . . . organising a patronage of other people's translations . . .'.[17] Clowes, it may be assumed, held that Swedenborg's ideas would make more rapid progress among his fellow pastors if not emanating from a rival church. This view would have gained strength in the decade following Clowes' death in 1831, as spiritualism came into prominence, encountering clerical hostility, but finding supporters among students of Swedenborg. In Le Fanu's overtly Swedenborgian novel, *Uncle Silas*, the heroine's father, although a great landowner, is depicted as attracting the disapproval of the local clergy because of his Swedenborgian leanings. It is recorded that, when Ruskin's friend, Thomas Dixon, loaned one of the prophet's books to William Rossetti, the latter's pious mother promptly burnt it.[18] In 1879 there were 70 New Jerusalem Churches in Britain. By that date, the Swedenborg Rite was also firmly established in Masonry, having been imported from North America, and by the end of the century there were estimated to be 13 such lodges in this country.

There was another powerful ingredient spicing the cultist brew that was beginning to intoxicate impressionable minds. It had originated with Franz Mesmer who, well before the French Revolution, had created a sensation in Vienna by postulating the existence of 'magnetic fluid' and a force denominated 'animal magnetism', which could be employed in healing. This theory, too, had links with Cabalistic tradition. Medical research was already interested in electricity, though unclear what curative function it could fulfil, and it was at first supposed that electricity might have some affinity with the magnetic fluid. The hostility of orthodox doctors was soon aroused, however, when it became apparent that in some people the mesmeric trance was accompanied by inexplicable manifestations of paranormal powers. The medical profession in the early decades of the 19th century was engaged in a struggle to divest itself of its dubious association with apothecaries, bonesetters and others, whose practice seemed to rest upon no scientific foundation. At the same time, the more scientific practitioners themselves enjoyed minimal success in their efforts to check disease and alleviate suffering; they were in no mood to tolerate the interference of mesmerists, hypnotists and somnambulists (as they were then sometimes designated), whose claims seemed to be even more extravagant than those of the existing subculture of 'quacks'. Given the prevailing enthusiasm for all things supernatural, orthodox doctors feared that the new craze might carry all before it.

One of those who took up the cudgels on behalf of 'science' (as he understood it) was Dr. Samuel Hibbert, who was a member both of the Royal Medical Society of Edinburgh and of the Philosophical Society of Manchester. In his book, published in 1824, he attempted to formulate a 'philosophy of apparitions', which would be rational and materialist. His main thesis was that all psychic experience had its origin in disorders of the blood, brain or nervous system; any manifestation, however well attested, that could not be so explained was dream or delusion. He then analysed a few carefully selected cases, in which ghostly visitations, or 'second sight' could plausibly be ascribed to epilepsy, delirium tremens, incipient lunacy or the action upon the blood of some stimulant or depressant. One of the agents so examined was the 'febrile miasma', which, according to Hibbert, 'has been found possessing its greatest degree of virulence' at Cadiz and Malaga. Whether this location had been chosen in order to account for Spanish mysticism does not become clear, although a derogatory mention of St. Teresa of Avila occurs later. He is particularly scathing about death-bed visions – 'the mere phantasies of ... diseased imagination'.[19] On the other hand, he defends himself against charges of impiety by excluding Scripture from his purview:

> Concerning the manner in which the Deity, for signal purposes, has formerly chosen to hold an immediate communion with the human race, it would be irrelevant to offer any observations.[20]

It was prudent on the part of the medical profession – never renowned for its piety – to keep on the right side of the clergy, who had their own reasons for denigrating those claiming ready access to the mysteries of the supernatural. By the 1850s, spiritualism had been imported to these shores from the U.S.A., linking the hypnotic trance to belief in survival. Swedenborgians had for some time been using mediums in the hope of holding conversations with angels, as the founder of their faith had done, and the most famous of all the mediums, Daniel Home, arrived in London in 1855 with an introduction to a leading Swedenborgian, Dr. J. Garth Wilkinson.[21] Home, who took no money for his displays and was never detected in any kind of fraud, always insisted that his chief aim was to refute materialism by demonstrating the truth of immortality. As he wrote, 'I have a mission entrusted to me. It is a great and holy one.'[22] Ruskin, who in the 1870s attended seances organised by Lord Mount-Temple at Broadlands, admitted, 'I could never have recovered my faith in Christianity except for spiritualism'.[23]

In 1856 Home's psychic gifts deserted him. Befriended by a wealthy Polish family, he travelled with them to Rome; after studying Catholic doctrine, he was received into the Church and admitted to a private audience with the Pope. His spiritual adviser, Father de Ravignan, rashly assured him that, since Home was now a Catholic, there would be no recurrence of his psychic experiences. Before long, however, he resumed his life as a medium and from that time was consistently reviled by the priesthood. He fared no better at Protestant hands. When he had first reached England and was living near London, 'the good clergyman of Ealing found it his duty to publicly preach against me, and to attribute the manifestations to the devil'.[24] The Rev. Charles Kingsley was equally hostile, denouncing in one phrase, 'Spirit-rapping, Holloway's Pills, Table-turning, Morison's Pills, Homoeopathy, Parr's Life Pills, Mesmerism, Pure Bosh . . .'[25] This tirade adds to the irony of the fact that in 1932 a medium, named Charles D. Boltwood, claimed to be in touch with Kingsley and to be receiving biblical revelations from him.[26] One suspects that, in addition to table-turning, a certain amount of grave-turning must have taken place.

It is not difficult to understand the opposition of priests and pastors. If spiritualism made inroads among the faithful, mediums would begin to constitute a rival source of guidance. For this role most of them were manifestly unfitted; more and more of them were being revealed as frauds, for whom a comfortable living in this world was more important than disclosure of truth about the next. It was held against them that their deception was practised at the expense of the bereaved, who were specially vulnerable. Both medium and the message came in for criticism. Lord Tennyson was deeply committed to the doctrine of immortality and his brother, Frederick, was a convinced spiritualist; but the Poet Laureate remained doubtful:

I grant you that spiritualism must not be judged by its quacks; but I am convinced that God and the ghosts of men would choose something other than mere table-legs through which to speak to the heart of man . . .[27]

Moreover the banality of most spirit messages marked them as unlikely to emanate from any level more exalted than that of the minds of the medium and those taking part in the seance. No one seems to have examined the possibility that it was precisely this form of interaction at a subconscious level that was occurring. There is a psychic phenomenon, well known in the East and recorded in Sufi lore, by which a mind finely attuned can 'pick up' from other minds information stored in them, but normally inaccessible. That this might be the process in operation was largely excluded by the obsession that the messages must be coming from the dead and that the void to be traversed was that of death itself, rather than one attributable to ignorance and lack of perception.

All the contemporary criticisms are summed up in Browning's *Mr. Sludge 'The Medium'*, in which the leading figure is presented as 'a vulgar and contemptible mountebank'. It is commonly believed that the poet intended to portray Home, whom he and his wife had known in Florence. Browning never claimed to have caught Home in deception, nor is it certain that to have done so would have much shocked him; the poet had a penchant for shady characters, whose colourful careers he could display. What seems to have alienated him was the impact of Home's powers upon the impressionable mind of Elizabeth Browning. This would be enough to explain Robert Browning's attitude, without necessarily accepting at face value Home's account of the seance at which there occurred the levitation of a wreath, which came to rest upon the head of Elizabeth, ignoring that of her more famous husband. In any case, *Mr. Sludge*, whilst it mercilessly attacks fraud, falls short of asserting that there can be nothing else to spiritualism. Sludge admits that he cheated, but insists that unaccountable things do happen:

> This trade of mine – I don't know, can't be sure,
> But there was something in it, tricks and all!

G. K. Chesterton was probably right to conclude that 'Browning's aversion to the spiritualists had little or nothing to do with spiritualism'.[28]

As a means of checking infidelity, spiritualism had serious drawbacks, which churches were quick to detect. Orthodoxy still held that the dead were sleeping till the Day of Judgement, when their fate would be finally determined. The souls with whom spiritualists, like Swedenborgians, made contact seemed already to be in heaven, where life bore a marked resemblance to life on earth. It was only too apparent to the clergy that belief in hell was on the decline; the assumption that everyone automatically went to heaven was not necessarily beneficial; there was much to be said for maintaining the traditional tension between being saved and being damned. Moreover there was a great deal more to religion than belief in immortality. One of those who thought in this way was the writer George MacDonald (1824–1905). As a young man, he had been a Congregationalist Minister, though never touched by Calvinism or belief in predestination. In one of his early novels he expresses what was undoubtedly his own view about spiritualists;

> Offered the spirit of God for the asking ... they betake themselves to necromancy instead, and raise the dead to ask their advice, and follow it, and will find some day that Satan has not forgotten how to dress like an angel of light ... What religion is there in being convinced of a future state? Is that to worship God? It is no more religion than the belief that the sun will rise tomorrow is religion.[29]

Among men of religion there was a suspicion that spiritualism was not a life-line thrown to true faith in an age of infidelity, but rather an incursion of materialism. Christianity had always rested, in the last resort, upon revelation; spiritualists, on the other hand, were claiming to supply proof. In doing so they were in step with the spirit of the age; everywhere, it seemed, men were laying bare the secrets of the natural world and harnessing them to their uses. Why, they asked, should not the unseen world, too, be forced to disclose its mysteries? By tapping this new source of illumination, it might be possible to construct a spirit world that would satisfy man's reasonable hopes and enable him to discard the confused and outdated imagery of the Bible.

At this point in the controversy a remarkable and exotic personality involved herself in it. Madame Helena Petrovna Blavatsky was a widely travelled Russian woman, who in 1873 at the age of 42, travelled to the U.S.A. and there teamed up with Col. Henry S. Olcott; together they founded the Theosophical Society and began to investigate the claims of spiritualism. Mme. Blavatsky had formidable qualifications as an investigator, since she could produce many of the unexplained manifestations that had given mediums their notoriety. She agreed with them that such phenomena showed the inadequacy of materialist assumptions about the nature of the universe, but she rejected their claims to be in touch with the dead. On the contrary, Mme. Blavatsky held that her manifestations demonstrated the power of living Masters, or Mahatmas, who were using her to counter self-destructive tendencies in Western civilisation; her task was to restore the balance by reintroducing the wisdom of the East. The two Mahatmas to whom she primarily owed allegiance lived in Tibet under the patronage of Panchen Lama. Theosophy, however, cannot be dismissed as no more than an attempt to propagate the doctrines of Mahayana Buddhism. Stress was certainly laid on reincarnation; but no religious faith was excluded and the brotherhood of mankind was emphasised. It was expressed in the brotherhood of the Masters themselves, whose onerous task it was to sustain the world in being, despite the intemperance and unreason that had stained recorded history.

Sadly, it was intemperance and unreason that marked the early years of the Society in its relationship with the world outside, and this downward trend accelerated after its removal to British India in 1879. The Mahatmas were not willing to reveal themselves openly; like the *Abdals* of Sufism, theirs was an occult brotherhood. It was perhaps inevitable that in Western minds this would arouse suspicion and excite more interest in hidden identities than in the teaching itself; at Adyar, Madras, local Christian missionaries accused European Theosophists of betraying the white man's faith. The wrath of the spiritualists had already been evoked by Mme. Blavatsky's dismissal of what she termed their 'necromantic evocations'.[30]

In 1882 another body interested in spiritualism and

psychic phenomena, the Society for Psychical Research, had come into existence. Its founders were three Cambridge academics, Prof. Henry Sidgwick, Frederic Myers and Edmund Gurney, who joined forces with Prof. William Barrett of the Royal College of Science in Dublin. Their hope was that it might be possible to use scientific methods to analyse all psychic phenomena, including telepathy and clairvoyance. In this hope they were to prove mistaken; the phenomena concerned usually occur in cases of heightened emotion and thus are not susceptible to repetition under controlled conditions, such as scientists demand. Upon many scientists, the paranormal has an impact comparable to that of a loadstone upon a magnetic field; in the face of the unfamiliar and unexplained, their minds seem unable to retain that degree of objectivity to which science lays claim.

Representatives of the S.P.R. met Mme. Blavatsky and Col. Olcott, who visited England in 1884, and it seemed that a working relationship had been created. The S.P.R. decided to pursue further investigations in India and selected for this purpose a young Australian lawyer, Dr. Richard Hodgson. It was an unfortunate choice: Hodgson had no experience or understanding of Eastern peoples or religions. He arrived in Adyar before the return of Mme. Blavatsky and fell into the hands of disaffected elements, supported by local missionaries. The result was a biassed report, which was published by the SPR without further examination in the following year[31]. It was a serious blow to the prestige of the Theosophical Society, for which the recruitment of its future President, Annie Besant, failed to compensate. Mme. Blavatsky removed to London in 1887 and there published two volumes of her major work, *The Secret Doctrine*. She died in 1891 broken in body and to some degree in spirit. Whether or not one ascribes long-term importance to the Theosophical Society, its emergence marked the beginning of an era in which Eastern ideas and traditions increasingly came to fill the gap left by the exhaustion of the Judaeo-Christian legacy. It is a process that in our day has been carried much further by the work of Idries Shah and the release of a flood of literature about Sufism.

Meanwhile the medical profession was still trying to come to terms with the disquieting connexion between Mesmerism and the paranormal. In Paris the experiments of Jean-Martin Charcot had convinced him that hypnotic phenomena were 'simply hystero-epilepsy, artificially induced'.[32] This conclusion demystified hypnosis to his satisfaction, so making it more acceptable to medical science; but it also disqualified it from general use. The fact that it could be beneficially employed, for example, with patients allergic to the anaesthetics in common use, did not interest doctors as much as the preservation of what they regarded as their scientific integrity. All that could be conceded was that mind and personality were revealing themselves as more complex than had earlier been realised. This was dramatised in 1886 by R.L. Stevenson in a story, the merits of which brought it before a wide public. *The Strange Case of Dr. Jekyll and Mr. Hyde* might almost have been written as a case-book illustration of Blake's 'two contrary states of mind'. Jekyll's last testament records:

> I thus drew steadily nearer to that truth, by whose partial discovery I have been doomed to such a dreadful shipwreck; that man is not truly one, but truly two. I say two, because the state of my own knowledge does not pass beyond that point. Others will follow . . . and I hazard the guess that man will be ultimately known for a mere polity of multifarious, incongruous and independent denizens.

The 19th century had not recorded progress in its search for God and the Infinite; but it was certainly making advances in the discovery of Man.

Whilst insight was being gained into diseases of mind and personality, perception was growing on the other side of the Atlantic that mind also had power to cure. 'Mind-cure' was the term originally employed for what in the hands of Mary Baker Eddy became known as Christian Science. Like

Buddhism, Christian Science was preoccupied with pain and death; but the response was not to escape into Nirvana, but rather to deny the reality of these facts, fundamental as they are to life as we know it. Mrs. Eddy (1821–1910) began her spiritual journey by rejecting the Calvinism of her upbringing. She married young and in 1843 her prayers failed to save the life of her first husband, who died of yellow fever; but the doctor who attended him assured her that her prayers had prolonged her husband's life. Her own health was poor and for three years she was a patient of the faith-healer, Phineas P. Quimby. In 1866 she suffered a fall on an icy street that was thought likely to prove fatal. She lay in bed with the Bible open at the passage:

> And behold, they brought to Him a man sick of the palsy, lying on a bed: and Jesus seeing their faith said unto the sick of the palsy: Son, be of good cheer, thy sins be forgiven thee.[33]

Mrs. Eddy got up and made a recovery that her friends regarded as miraculous. From 1867–1879 she practised as a healer and was reputed to have restored to life a child who had been given up for dead. At the end of that period she decided, for reasons that remain unclear, to found a church, which by the end of the century was firmly established in the U.S.A. Progress in Britain was slower; but the first Church of Christ, Scientist, opened its doors in London in 1897.

Use of the word 'Scientist' was presumably dictated by the fact that science was the new gnosis; for similar reasons Marx attached the adjective to his brand of socialism. It is more puzzling, however, to understand why Mrs. Eddy named her science after the Christ who suffered for men and died on the Cross. In her terms, this sacrifice would seem to have been meaningless, since Christ died to redeem the human race from sin, whilst in Mrs. Eddy's eyes sin, like death itself, was unreal. In an authoritative work on Christian Science death is described as:

... part of the belief in material life, and therefore unreal in the strict meaning of the word ... Those who have passed through the experience called death in no wise lose their individuality ... those whose affections and interests have been centred on the material, will find that they have but entered on a fresh dream of material living and dying.[34]

From the same source one learns that Mrs. Eddy 'passed away without pain or struggle' in December 1910. It cannot be said that her religion, whilst it may well have aided the living, has contributed to our understanding of the mystery of death and survival. It was, however, an antidote to more dismal creeds and, as such, was welcomed by William James:

> Mind-cure might be briefly called a reaction against all that religion of chronic anxiety which marked the earlier part of our century in the evangelic circles of England and America.[35]

One may regret that the early Christian Scientists, like the followers of Swedenborg, decided to found a church, thus ignoring the long history of discord, rivalry and doctrinal distortion that has plagued institutionalised religions. If Mrs. Eddy had stayed with her original concept and the designation Mind-cure, her less ecstatic followers might have anticipated some of the promising research undertaken in recent years by such American neurobiologists as Professor Robert Ornstein and his colleague, Dr. David Sobel. Their research has shown how much the maintenance of good health and the prolongation of life depend upon mental attitudes, and how great a role can be played by the brain in keeping us well and resistant to the onset of disease.[36]

NOTES AND BIBLIGRAPHY

1 Revelation, XX, 4–5
2 Ibid., XII, 5

3 *The Making of the Working Class*: E.P. Thompson (Gollancz 1963), p. 381

4 *The Newcomes*: W. M. Thackeray (Nelson, 1902), ch. II

5 *The Pursuit of the Millennium*. N. Cohn (Paladin, 1970), p. 286

6 *Irving and his Circle*: A.L. Drummond (Clarke, 1935), p. 231

7 Author's family papers.

8 Ibid.

9 *Father and Son*: E. Gosse (Penguin, 1970), pp. 205–6

10 Author's family papers.

11 *New Church Worthies*: D. Bayley (London, 1884), p. 48

12 Ibid., p. 140

13 *Heaven and Hell*: E. Swedenborg (Dent, 1940), sec. 508

14 Ibid., sec. 69

15 Ibid., sec. 89

16 *The Rise and Progress of the New Church*: R. Hindmarsh (London, 1861), p.39

17 *Autobiographical Sketches*: T. de Quincey (London, 1853), p. 133

18 *Four Rossettis*: S. Weintraub (Allen, 1978), p. 204

19 *Sketches of the Philosophy of Apparitions*: S. Hibbert (Edinburgh, 1824), p.111

20 Ibid., p. 87

21 *Natural and Supernatural*: B. Inglis (Abacus, 1979), p. 256

22 *Incidents in My Life*: D.D. Home (New Jersey, n.d.), p. 127

23 *MacDonald and His Wife*: G. MacDonald (Allen, 1924), p. 335

24 *Incidents in My Life*, op. cit., p. 64

25 *The Water-Babies*: C. Kingsley (London, 1863), ch. IV

26 *The Beast and the Monk*: S. Chitty (Hodder, 1974), app.2

27 *Tennyson: Poet and Prophet*: P. Henderson (Routledge, 1978), p. 189

28 *Browning*: G. K. Chesterton (Macmillan, 1951), p. 93

29 *Annals of a Quiet Neighbourhood*: G. MacDonald (London, 1867), ch. XV

30 *The Real H. P. Blavatsky*: W. Kingsland (J.M. Watkins, London, 1928), p.123

31 Kingsland, op. cit., reproduces the report in an appendix.

32 *Natural and Supernatural*: op. cit., p. 392

33 Matthew, IX, 2

34 *Christian Science and its Discoverer*: E.M. Ramsay (Boston, 1935), pp. 88–9

35 *Varieties of Religious Experience*: W. James (Longman, 1903), p. 95

36 See, for example, *The Healing Brain*: R. Ornstein & D. Sobel (Macmillan, 1988)

11

From Kafiristan to the Land of Light

Nestled amongst the vast ranges and the valleys of the Hindu Kush there is a land which until recent times was unexplored and unknown. It was populated by a people thought to be more barbaric than any other, who, it was said, were in league with the Devil. No one was sure from whom these Aryan people were descended and some have speculated that their ancestors might have been the troops of Alexander the Great or those of Tamerlane. This region became known by the surrounding Islamic peoples as *Kafiristan*, Land of the Infidels.

The Kafirs lived in their isolated society for many hundreds of years, unaffected by the progress and changes sweeping through Central Asia. They continued to develop their own forms of art, invoking their gods as their ancestors had done for centuries. Strange systems existed that allowed social mobility: the foremost of these judged a man's importance by the number of Muslims he had slain.

As Afghanistan slowly turned into an integrated union of tribal groups, one ruler after another looked towards Kafiristan. Each realised the importance of conquering what was seen as an uncivilised people. It would be a triumph for Islam, but more than that: it would lessen the risks of an attack by the Kafirs. And it was the Achilles heel of Afghanistan, should the British continue their attempts to conquer the Afghans.

It was in 1895 that the great Afghan statesman, King Abdur Rahman Khan began his systematic conquest of

221

Kafiristan and its people. He was tired of the Kafirs' raids on Muslim settlements, and he understood the advantages that taming Kafiristan would bring. For almost five years he carried out his campaign of conquest and subsequent conversion of its people to Islam.

Roads were built linking Kafiristan to the rest of Afghanistan. Schools were set up to educate the people and to teach them to read and write – matters of which they were ignorant. Afghans were encouraged to resettle in this rugged province. But most significantly the ancient ways and beliefs of the Kafirs were denounced and condemned. Archaic idols of the Kafir gods were torn down and destroyed, their festivals were prohibited and wine was made illegal. All this was replaced by newly erected mosques from which the virtues of Islam were extolled.

When all this had been done, Abdur Rahman renamed this former land of infidels. These new people of Afghanistan had embraced Islam and seen the Light. Thus their land was awarded the title *Nuristan*, The Land of Enlightenment.

Geographical Position of Kafiristan

Kafiristan encompassed an area of over 10,500 square kilometres, and lay between the latitudes 34° 30′ and 36° north and between longitudes 69° 20′ and 71° 20′ east. To the north lay Badakhshan and to the north-east the Lutkho valley of Chitral. Chitral proper and Lower Chitral were to the east, and the Kunar valley made the border to the south-east. Today the boundaries of Nuristan are similar, but the area has decreased significantly, as has its population since the time of the conversion to Islam.

Much of Kafiristan lay above 1500 metres and therefore not only did it experience cooler weather than most of the rest of Afghanistan; it also enjoyed a reasonably moist climate, influenced by India's great summer monsoon. Immense banks of cloud hover above Nuristan even in the driest weather and this moisture makes possible the growth of forests, while other parts of Afghanistan are infertile.

Five great rivers flow through Nuristan: the Alingar, Presun, Manangul, Tsargul, Waigul and Pittigul. Each rushes to join with the Kabul River, either directly to the south (as in the case of the Alingar) or after mixing with the waters of the Kunar River.

Nuristan is made up of a succession of uneven principal valleys, which are hazardously steep. It is this system of rugged valleys that has given Nuristan, and Kafiristan before it, great security from attack.

In winter, howling winds tear through some valleys, while others are strangely unaffected by such gales. The heavy snowfalls of October do not thaw until the end of March is near. During these freezing months of the year the passes become impossible to negotiate. Each valley is isolated from the next until the spring. The snows sever Nuristan's connection with the outside world, and prevent wars until the thaw in spring.

The Kafirs developed eye protectors of their own design, similar to those of various Eskimo tribes. They are fashioned from small scraps of wood with slits cut to protect the eye from direct sunlight. The Mongoloid eye-shape is a natural protector against glare.

There is little actual rainfall in Nuristan; most of the precipitation occurs as snow which falls extremely heavily during the winter months. Towards the end of January, avalanches are commonplace, blocking routes between villages and even obstructing the flow of the rivers.

During Amir Timur's excursion through Kafiristan in 1393 (documented by the Zafar Nama of Sharaf-ud-Din and translated by Raverty), we are told that Timur waited until the night to travel when the snow's surface was frozen:

Notwithstanding the sun was in Gemini, and the air warm, the snow was so deep that the horses' legs sank into it so that they could not get on. Timur therefore continued his advance up the mountain range in the night, at which time the snow froze, and, in the day time, when the snow began to thaw, halted, placing the few horses with the force on woollen clothes and felts to keep them from sinking into it, and again commenced to push on towards the close of day.

Spring arrives in April. The trees turn a shade of light green and the rivers' water-line rises substantially as the snows begin to melt. Agricultural activities can begin again as the ground thaws out.

Kafiristan was home to thick forests and many kinds of fruit; olives, apricots, mulberries and grapes grew on the steep valley slopes. The rivers were abundantly filled with fish (which the Kafirs refused to eat, saying that they existed by eating filth, and were thus inedible). Markhor, the wild goat of the Himalayas, once roamed the sheer hillsides; there were ibex too, and leopards, bears and urial, the wild sheep of Asia. But these creatures, together with the once exuberant vegetation, have thinned out and disappeared. Some animals such as the snow-leopard were hunted vigorously by the Kafirs, for it increased the status of a Kafir to have killed many. Other creatures such as the wild boar were once butchered, but following conversion to Islam, their meat was forbidden.

Origins of the Kafirs

The history of Kafiristan remains sketchy at best until the 19th century. Few dared to cross into it for fear that they might not reach the other side. Instead, they wended their way around the surrounding highlands in an attempt to avoid Kafiristan's inhospitable climate, people and terrain.

There have been many hypotheses in the last century, and even before, concerning the origins of the Kafir people, because their traditions, customs, etiquette, and, until recently, their religion, were very different from those of any other Central Asian people. Some scholars have suggested that the Kafirs were descended from the *Arom* people, or that they had originated in the Arab land of Salarzai. Last century it was a popular notion that they were a people with Grecian roots, the descendants of Alexander's men.

It is no easy task to trace the beginnings of a race who seem never to have had a system of writing, and who have always been at war with those around them. One can analyse the Kafir languages or study their peculiar traditions to glean a hint of their enigmatic past. However, no single credible lineage is revealed.

The Kafirs' society was divided into various groups, all isolated from one another within Kafiristan and most of them at war with each other. One Kafir language was either dissimilar or completely foreign to the next. There were five principal languages: Kati, Ashkun, Waigai, Paruni and Wa-mai: and the words for even such basic concepts as 'man', 'father' or 'mother' were quite different in two settlements a few miles apart.

The ideologies of the Kafirs were made up of an extraordinary collection of beliefs. They included ancestor worship, a form of fire worship, and the invoking of a large number of deities, of whom idols were made. It seems probable that they were influenced by various sources at different times in their history.

Elphinstone, in the early years of the last century, sent a man to find out more about the Kafirs. Several months later he returned with a detailed account of the Kafir people and society. Elphinstone's book was published in 1815.[1]

It was not until September 1885 that Colonel William Lockhart of the British Army crossed the Hindu Kush through the Zidig Pass and journeyed through the land of the Katir Kafirs; seemingly the first expedition by a European into Kafiristan. Lockhart's purpose was to gather secret intelligence. However, six years before, a young Englishman named William Watts McNair, supposedly dressed as a tribesman of the Hindu Kush and posing as a doctor, had entered some of the outer valleys of Kafiristan.[15] Alexander

Burnes was another early adventurer in Central Asia. In his work *Travels into Bokhara*[14] published in 1834, he wrote:

The Kaffirs appear to be a most barbarous people, eaters of bears and monkies and fighting with arrows, and scalping their enemies.

The most famous and reliable study of the people of Kafiristan before Abdur Rahman's conquest of the land, was made by Sir George Scott Robertson. His work *The Kafirs of the Hindu Kush*[3] was published in 1896, just as Kafiristan was being opened up. The fact that Robertson's investigation was completed before the Islamic conquest makes his work valuable and fascinating. Although he was a military man, Robertson's study is anthropological in nature. Robertson suggested that the Kafirs were descended from an archaic Indian people from the eastern part of Afghanistan who had spurned tenth century attempts at conversion to Islam, and retreated to the impenetrable valleys of the Hindu Kush.

On the question of the Kafirs' Grecian origin, Robertson wrote:

If there be points of resemblance between the present Kafir and the ancient Greek sacrificial observances, and if certain of their domestic utensils – such, for instance, as the Wai wooden dish-stand – may seem to be fashioned in Grecian mould, it may fairly be conjectured that some of the Kafir tribes, at any rate, are still influenced, as the ancient Indian populations of Eastern Afghanistan were also influenced, by the Greek colonists of Alexander.

Biddulph's book *The Tribes of the Hindoo Koosh*[13], printed in Calcutta in 1880, mentions the Kafirs and their putative origins:

Beween Chitral, Afghanistan, and the Hindoo Koosh, the maps show a large tract of unknown country under the name Kafiristan, concerning whose inhabitants the wildest conjectures have been formed. The fact that, while surrounded on all sides by fanatical Mahommedans, with whom they are in a chronic state of war, they have been able in spite of all attacks to preserve both their independence and their faith intact, and that their customs and their traditions, which differ from those of their neighbours, furnish some grounds for the assumption that they at one time enjoyed a higher state of civilisation than they do at present, has been sufficient to stimulate the curiosity of travellers and ethnologists. Conjectures have been hazarded that the Siah Posh people are of Greek descent, while a recent Russian author (Terentieff) has confidently asserted that they are incontestably of Slav origin; and the natural subjects of the Czar.

Whilst positioning troops at the fort of Kullum in central Kafiristan, Abdur Rahman claimed to have discovered a stone with the following words etched on it:

The Great Mogul Emperor Timour was the first Muslim conqueror vanquished the country of this unruly people up to this point, but could not take Kullum, owing to its difficult position.[i]

It might seem as if the Afghan ruler had concocted the story of this find to boost his own notoriety. However, Charles Masson, writing in the Bombay Geographical Journal of 1840 (i.e. before Abdur Rahman's purported discovery) made mention that *Taimur* (Tamerlane) had indeed left a marble slab engraved concerning his attempted conquest of the Kafirs.[i]

People of Kafiristan

The word *Kafir* is used very loosely. It represents various tribes who were almost completely independent of each other and many of whom had little in common. They had however, one determining factor: their absolute refusal to comply with Islam.

None of these different tribes seem ever to have had a single term with which to describe all the peoples of

Kafiristan. They would instead use the specific name for the tribe being discussed.

The Kafirs have been called 'Red Kafirs' by some. The use of 'red', Shakur[12] explains, signifies 'cruel' in Pashtu.

Two names have been designated to differentiate between the two main peoples of Kafiristan: *Siah-Posh* and *Sufed-Posh*. Schomberg suggests that these were contrived by the British: Siah-Posh referring to all Kafir people, and Sufed-Posh to those Kafirs who had accepted to live under the cloak of Islam. The Siah-Posh are known as the 'Kafirs garbed in black'. The main Siah-Posh tribes are the Madugul, Kashtan and the Kam. Sufed-Posh are the 'Kafirs garbed in white', i.e. the Presuns, Wai and the Ashkund.

Masson mentions one early report of the Kafirs, that might have been made by Tamerlane himself:

The infidels are described as 'strong men' as large as the giants of Aad: they go all naked, their kings are named Oda and Odashooh: they have a peculiar language which is neither Persian, nor Turkish, nor Indian, and know no other than this.

In complexion, most people in Nuristan are generally light; blond or red hair is not uncommon, as are blue or green eyes. The eyes tend to be fairly close together and the nose prominent. The people of Nuristan, and Kafiristan before them, are extremely hardy. The exceptionally rugged countryside of their region, coupled with the freezing winter weather and their own lifestyle, have produced a people unsurpassed in stamina. They can scale the steep slopes of a valley in deep snow with the ease of an athlete and trek for many hours at high altitudes.

The British in late Victorian times were intrigued and obsessed, it seems, with the notion that what they saw as a primitive Central Asian people could be so similar to them both in looks and in conduct. From the 1880s onwards, it became a popular activity to go and investigate the civilisation of these strange mountain people. Lord Aberdare is quoted as saying in 1889:

> The Kafirs are described as strong, athletic men with a language of their own, the features and complexions of Europeans, and fond of dancing, hunting, and drinking. They also play at leap-frog, shake hands as Englishmen, and cannot sit cross-legged on the ground.[ii]

Kafirs practiced a form of head shaving: the whole head was shaved, except for a round area some four inches in diameter at the back. This was known as the *Karunch*. Children would have their heads shaved about a month after birth. The Karunch was abandoned shortly after the adoption of Islam.

The bright mountain light and the rigorous conditions and climate has always led to the premature ageing of the people of the Hindu Kush. Smallpox during the Kafir times scarred many faces, sometimes hideously when the victim had succumbed to rubbing the spots. Robertson mentions other afflictions that were not uncommon:

> ... a terrible ulceration which frequently attacks the bridge of the nose, the cheeks or the lower eyelids; also in the Bashgul Valley, goitre which seems almost exclusively confined to women.[3]

All accounts of the Kafirs seem to agree that they were a people of extraordinary mental ability and intelligence. It was baffling to invading commanders that a people with weaponry so primitive could be capable of such extraordinary tactical comprehension. Numerous accounts mention the Kafirs' astounding powers of memory. This factor proved invaluable during the years of war with the Soviet forces, when the people of Nuristan had to master the latest arms and weapon systems.

Various records exist that describe the Kafirs' passion for lying. Robertson (op. cit.) wrote the following:

> The Kafirs are very untruthful. A successful lie excites

their admiration, and a plausible liar is to them a sensible, sagacious man. Their want of veracity, is most striking on first acquaintance, for they, like so many other wild or savage people evidently hold the belief that telling the truth, merely because it is the truth, must necessarily be harmful to them.

Throughout Afghanistan, hospitality and politeness are of the utmost consequence: the Kafirs and their descendants, the Nuristanis, are certainly no exception. Social etiquette has always been very convoluted. A guest or visitor is waited upon with great deference and respect, and the elders of the community are held in reverence.

Slaves

The Kafirs' practice of keeping slaves was something that angered the Afghan government, which was trying to bring an end to slavery. It is possible that many of the slaves were people from other tribes captured in battle, or the descendants of such people. It is likely that many had been taken in previous raids on Muslim communities, and thus were followers of Islam. Late 19th century scholars suggested that perhaps the enslaved populace in Kafiristan were a people crushed by the Kafirs centuries before: perhaps a more ancient people of the Hindu Kush than the Kafirs themselves.

The slaves were apparently forbidden to attend the shrines to particular deities, or to tread in hallowed places. They were sold from time to time and it seems as if slaves were used in bargaining procedures with other tribes. A slave's offspring became the property of his master. Robertson (op.cit.) gives details of the rules for the artisan class, *Bari*, who were slaves. They were the carpenters, the blacksmiths, leatherworkers and so on, whilst their womenfolk wove the cloth, making clothing and rugs. If they were working for their master they were not paid, but if labouring for another they were paid by him, and were allowed to keep their earnings.

At the time of the Islamic conquest, the enslaved populace of Kafiristan were freed but forced to become Muslims.

The Islamic Conquest of Kafiristan

In order fully to understand the reasons that led the Amir Abdur Rahman Khan to open up Kafiristan, it is useful to examine the position of Central Asia during the latter years of the 19th century.

Russia was pursuing a policy of expansion in Central Asia: a matter that began to worry the British, who saw their own position and influence in Central Asia diminishing. Britain knew that in order to secure for itself a strong position in Central Asia it would have to ally with Afghanistan, which has always been the key to controlling Central Asia.

With this in mind the Viceroy of India, Lord Lytton, set out in 1876 to make an ally of the Afghan ruler Amir Sher Ali. One year later, in 1877, Britain looked set for war with Russia over the Dardanelles and exactly at this time, Russia also began trying to develop an agreeable relationship with Afghanistan. To put pressure on Sher Ali, Russia sent troops to the Afghan border.

Britain grew concerned and sent an ultimatum to Sher Ali, who refused it. In November 1878, the British began to march on Afghanistan. Sher Ali turned to the Russians for assistance against the British: but the Russians withdrew. Sher Ali himself retreated to Russia, leaving his son Mohammed Yaqub Khan as sovereign.

The British, who had begun to seize key Afghan cities, negotiated a treaty with Yaqub Khan, but six weeks after the British mission had arrived in Kabul (in July 1879), they were stormed whilst at the Bala Hissar fort. Nearly all were killed. Consequently three British armies moved to retake Kabul and other chief cities. Yaqub Khan was imprisoned as the British looked for a solution.

The British then aided Abdur Rahman Khan to succeed to the throne of Afghanistan. They pledged financial support in return for a guarantee that, as the ruler, Abdur Rahman would promote the modernisation of the country.

Sher Ali had attempted to conquer Kafiristan, the last stronghold of agnostics left in the country. It was seen as both necessary and a popular course of action. But Sher Ali had failed, thereby boosting the Kafir sense of superiority.

However, the idea of converting the Kafirs to Islam and the popularity that he would thereby acquire, were not the only reasons Abdur Rahman had for invading the region. In his autobiography he gives three other objectives. The first was that the Russians were approaching Kafiristan and looked very much as if they themselves would take the area, and pretend to form it into an independent nation. Secondly he feared that, were this to happen, the Russians might persuade the Kafirs to retake other areas of Afghanistan such as Jalalabad, that were once under Kafir control. Thirdly, as a matter of national security, it made Abdur Rahman uneasy to have a hostile people along the entire north-eastern flank of the country.

Abdur Rahman wanted to open up Kafiristan, to promote trade, to end the Kafirs' practice of slavery, and to put a stop to their inter-tribal warfare with other regions.

In his autobiography, Abdur Rahman states:

My idea was to make the people [of Kafiristan] my peaceful subjects by kindness and clemency. To accomplish this, I had several times invited many of their chiefs to come to Kabul, and sent them back overloaded with rupees and other rewards, so that they should go and talk about it with their countrymen. They were such savages, however, that they used to exchange their wives for cows with the neighbouring Afghans, and thus ensued many disputes whether the cow or the woman were of greater value. They did not appreciate my kindness, and with the money I had given them, bought rifles to use in fighting against me.

Abdur Rahman decided that to attack Kafiristan in the winter months was his best option, when there was thick snow. He had several reasons. Firstly, he knew that the Kafir strategy would be to scale the mountain peaks in order to shoot downwards. In winter, climbing the pinnacles would be arduous, if not impossible, whilst carrying heavy weaponry. Secondly, if he invaded when the mountain passes were not snowbound, he thought that word would be sent to the Russians requesting assistance: thereby giving them a perfect excuse to take the whole region. Abdur Rahman depended on the skilled army that he had under him and trusted in their ability to take Kafiristan.

Thirdly, he knew that as the Kafirs were a people of great courage and mettle, a battle fought in the summer was likely to result in far higher casualties. Lastly, it was of the utmost importance to Abdur Rahman that the battle for Kafiristan be fought and won by his men before news of the attack could filter out to people such as Christian Missionaries or even the Russians, who would interfere.

Thus it was that in the autumn of 1895, Abdur Rahman put together a great deal of military hardware and supplies in secret. He divided his forces and equipment into four divisions. The largest was put under the charge of Captain Mahomed Ali Khan. It was to proceed through the Panshir to the fort of Kullum: the strongest fort in Kafiristan. General Ghulam Haider Khan led the second contingent from the east. General Katal Khan moved southwards from Badakhshan; and a small unit under the direction of Faiz Mahomed marched northwards from Laghman.

According to Abdur Rahman, there was nothing unusual in having these units in place before the surprise attack: as each was close to the border of Afghanistan, its presence was not unexpected. On the appointed day, the order was given for each of the divisions to proceed to take Kafiristan from the appropriate direction. It took some forty days to achieve the conquest.

During the invasion, various Kafir leaders crossed to Chitral to ask the Mehtar of Chitral (to whom they still paid an annuity), for assistance against Abdur Rahman's army. The Mehtar had no intention of becoming mixed up in the war, or allowing people from Chitral to be involved. All sorts of inter-tribal clashes and feuds could have begun. The British, who were overseeing matters in Chitral, did not want to see friction begin on the border either.

It is recorded that, during the invasion, a number of Kafir leaders approached the Afghan Commander-in-Chief. They said that their people would follow Islam and learn about it, as well as paying to Abdur Rahman the annuity that they had been paying to the Mehtar of Chitral: if his forces would withdraw. The Commander however rejected their offer, insisting that, for him to retreat, the Kafirs would have also to give up the equivalent of a tenth of all their produce in revenue; they would have to allow the region to become fully accessible; and finally they must supply a number of men to the Afghan army. The Kafirs preferred to fight on. Accounts of the invasion agree that Abdur Rahman was only willing to end his campaign when he had secured the total submission of the Kafirs. He prohibited the killing of any children under the age of seven, but no Kafir older than that age was safe unless he or she adopted the ways of Islam.

Another Kafir delegation went to the Mehtar of Chitral. This time they asked that if they were overcome by Abdur Rahman's forces, their people could be allowed to settle in Chitral: the Mehtar had no objection. However, the then Viceroy of India realised that an influx of Kafirs would cause problems for India and he intervened, saying that an inflow across the border would be wholly undesirable. All the same a great many Kafir women and children crossed into the Chitral region. The descendants of many of them remain there today, and in some cases continue to practise their ancient beliefs.

Artisans were sent from Kabul to Kafiristan to construct a mosque in each village. Abdur Rahman took members of each village hostage, usually the patriarchs, as security against reprisals. They were held near Kabul at the Aliabad camp, where they were taught the ways of Islam and instructed in the Persian language. A policy was instituted whereby every so often the hostages could return to their villages whereupon a new contingent would take their place.

The Afghan government announced that in the fighting, it had lost some six hundred soldiers, and the Kafirs some ten thousand. Ghulam Haidar ensured that 1500 Kafir captives were dispatched to Kabul as well as about one hundred camel loads of pillaged booty. Many of the prized Kafir heirlooms, such as their silver drinking bowls, disappeared from Kafiristan in this way.

Various communities in Kafiristan fought on, and were still not under the government's control by the spring of 1896. In the Ramgul region, the Kafirs managed to regain villages which had initially been lost. A substantial number of Afghan troops had been killed in avalanches or had frozen to death: being unaccustomed to such bitter cold. Some contingents of Mullas who had come to convert the Kafirs were killed in ambushes. Abdur Rahman sent about 2500 families of nomadic peoples such as the Safis and the Kochis to settle in Kafiristan.

During the months subsequent to the conquest there were numerous uprisings and revolts by the Kafirs as they came to terms with the penalties imposed upon them by Abdur Rahman Khan. They overthrew army posts, destroyed roads and the new infrastructure whenever they could. In late December 1897, Abdur Rahman sent a message to the Kafirs who had fled to Chitral. It guaranteed that they would be given complete freedom if they returned at once to Kafiristan. Few complied.

Of his methods, Abdur Rahman wrote:

When I conquered the country of Kafiristan in 1896, I

ordered that no prisoner of war should be sold as a slave,
and also that no one should be allowed to marry a Kafir
woman against her will. I compensated by presents of
money those people who had captured prisoners as their
booty and thus were entitled to keep their gains of victory,
and I then released the prisoners and set them free.

By 1898 many Kafirs were professing a superficial dedication to Islam, but in secret they still worshipped their
idols. Further problems arose with refugees crossing the
Afghan border into India. The British grew increasingly
nervous that the border was not being maintained.

Following his conquest of Kafiristan, Abdur Rahman was
bestowed with the title *Ziya ul Millat wa Din*, the Light of the
Nation and of Islam.

Kafir Society

Various important elements of Kafir culture and civilisation
are noted below. Reference is made to practices that were
unique to the people of Kafiristan. In religion, language,
architecture, music, and in social matters such as food and
community structure, the Kafirs were very different from
the other peoples of Afghanistan. As in many societies, this
variation from those around them has brought them persecution and subjugation.

Kafir Religion

The creed of the Kafir peoples incorporated elements of idol
worship, fire worship, and supplication to an extensive pantheon of gods. All of these are abhorred by Muslims, being
completely at odds with all that Islam preaches.

The names given to deities in various parts of Kafiristan
varied from place to place. Gleaning an understanding of
their complex religious system was made more difficult because Kafirs were usually reluctant to confide the intricacies
of their belief to outsiders, although Robertson mentions

that some communities were reassured by hearing that he was a 'Kafir', an infidel, just like them.

The oral legends and explanations of the religion were never, it seems, committed to writing until recently. They must have evolved through time and been affected by the limited number of aliens who had come in contact with the Kafirs.

Writing about the people of the Bashgul valley just before the forcible conversion of Kafiristan, Robertson says:

> The older people are devout in their respect for all the gods, but Bashgal Kafirs seem ready to abandon their religion at any time without much regret. They leave it, as they return to it, chiefly for motives of material advantage, and rarely appear to trouble themselves about religious convictions.

Kafirs certainly did believe that there was a heaven and a hell. They maintained that the universe was split into *Urdesh*, the home of the immortal ones; *Michdesh*, the earth on which we live, and *Yurdesh*, the underworld, which was where all human beings ended up. This nether world might be reached through a gorge in the earth which was guarded by *Maramalik*, the sentinel. *Imra* was the creator, and held the position of greatest importance. He was the architect of all things and the God of gods and men.

The spirit of a dead person was thought to go to the underworld. If the person had been evil and malicious during his life the spirit would pass to *Zozuk*, hell. If he had been a good person, the soul would go to *Bisht*, that section of Yurdesh that we would know as paradise. Death was not seen as a frightening event and thus the Kafirs faced danger with equanimity.

Imra had made everything in heaven, earth and hell. He created the devils (including *Yush*, the most powerful devil), as well as vast numbers of other spirits. Imra had many characteristics of the Kafir people. There were endless stories told of the deities and their exploits, especially of

Imra. It was said that Imra grew tired of the evil spirits, so he assigned *Moni* to destroy them. One escaped and was at last hunted down by Moni, who slew him. But from the corpse rose seven more fiends, which Moni slaughtered with the steel of his blade.

Smooth stones were worshipped by certain groups of Kafirs, some having imprints which were said to be the mark of Imra's hand. They were put outside temples and were even placed on the Kafir style of altar. Rocks were placed as memorials to honour the dead: some were thought to have been created by the gods themselves.

The Kafir religion was sometimes undermined by outsiders who came and dared to do things which the Kafirs had always maintained would bring certain death – such as peering down into a sacred pit. When the offender did not die, the others began to question the bases of their faith. Indeed, the Kafir conviction that certain actions would bring death just encouraged Muslims and other outsiders to break the rules and, by challenging the superstitions, to prove them invalid.

Certain deities, such as Imra, would have their own shrine, since it was deemed appropriate that such an important deity should have a shrine of his own. As the god of combat and warfare, *Gish* was another favourite who was often furnished with his own shrine, especially by the people of the Bashgul valley. Created by Imra, he had existed in the guise of a man on earth, where he had been renowned as the fiercest warrior of all time.

Sacrifice

The gods were kept happy by the frequent sacrifice of all sorts of creatures. The particular ceremony itself determined which animal was appropriate for sacrifice. Usually sheep or goats were used, but it was not uncommon for a cow or bull to be killed. Before a sheep or a goat could be offered up, it had to shake its whole body, the result of having water poured in one ear and down the spinal column. This indicated that the appropriate deity had accepted the animal as satisfactory. The ancient Greeks too, are alleged to have poured water over a sheep: if it shook itself, the oracle might be approached. The Thugs of India had a similar practice.

Numerous scholars have suggested similarities between Hinduism and the Kafirs' religion. A great disparity however, is the fact that Kafirs considered it quite acceptable to slaughter cows as sacrifices: animals which are held by the Hindus to embody the greatest divinity.

Sacrifices were made to demons as well as to deities, as it was thought that evil fiends could be dissuaded from bringing disaster to the community by sacrificial offerings.

On occasions such as large feasts, substantial numbers of animals were ritually slaughtered. The religious leader of the community is said to have tied a scrap of material around his forehead, cleaned his hands and removed any coverings from his feet, before proceeding. A goat was brought and once it had shaken itself in the way described, it was held firmly by the horns. A dagger slit the creature's throat before cutting the spine, the oesophagus and the trachea. A receptacle was used to catch a little of the blood, which was poured onto the fire and, during the ceremony, verses were chanted by the priest. The head of the animal was severed from its body, and in some communities it was thrust into the flames for a few moments until lightly charred.

The carcass was dismembered and cut up, before being cooked on a fire made with cedar wood. It was then eaten by those present.

Marriage

Kafir marriages were relatively simple. When a man wanted to get wed, he engaged the assistance of a close companion to approach the girl's parents to secure their agreement, and to negotiate the necessary fees. When this had been accomplished, the girl's admirer went to her house, where there was a sacrifice in celebration and the union was sealed.

Couples were betrothed as children, but adolescents would generally marry following puberty. Kafir society was polygamous, with four or five wives as the usual upper limit for a man. If these spouses became friends they would live in the same house, but if there was infighting the husband would have to provide each with a separate house. Widows might be taken into the custody of the dead man's brother if he so wished.

A bridegroom was expected to pay a certain sum in livestock or other valuables to the father of the bride, this bridewealth payment being known as *Malpreg*. The total payment could be made up of parts, and there was a strict scale for the value of each object used in payment: a silver cup was worth a certain number of goats; a dagger was worth so many – and so on. The Malpreg had to be paid in full before the actual union of the couple could take place.

In return, the bride's family was expected to supply a dowry, known as *Bakawa*. It was not necessarily composed of such tangible things as constituted the Malpreg, or as valuable. It might take the form of grain, butter or other foodstuffs; clothes for the girl during the first few years of marriage might be supplied, and some jewellery perhaps.

Even before Abdur Rahman's conquest, merchants had begun to cross into Kafiristan selling little trinkets, mirrors and glistening but worthless jewellery. The Kafirs had not seen such baubles and swapped heirlooms and their own valuables for them. In this way many ancient Kafir relics disappeared; and at the same time, many modern baubles became possessions sought after for a dowry.

Childbirth

In Kafir society, there was a special place on the outskirts of the community to which a pregnant woman, and women at the time of menstruation, would go to stay in seclusion. They were known as *Sawart-ama* in Kafiristan (and are called *Bashgali* by the Kalash of Chitral).

Whilst they were at the Sawart-ama, women were seen almost as if they were infected in some way. No members of the community would dare go near the site for fear of contamination. If circumstances arose in which this code was broken, the intruder would have to go through a process of vigorous cleansing, and a goat would be sacrificed to ensure that purification was complete.

When it was necessary for a woman to visit those in the Sawart-ama, she would be expected to enter naked. On leaving, she would have to wash her body thoroughly. Food would be left outside the dwelling for the women inside to collect and any pot or pan that came in contact with the women confined there was regarded as contaminated.

Just before childbirth an old woman would come from the village to deliver the child. She would strip off her clothes before entering the confines of the house and depart as soon as the infant was born. In some parts of Kafiristan a midwife would live in the Sawart-ama. After the birth, another month was spent in the Sawart-ama before mother and baby returned home.

When a woman died whilst at the Sawart-ama, she would be interred close by. Male members of the village were not permitted to be present at the funeral and, in any case few from the village would attend.

Abdur Rahman saw to it that these houses of seclusion were destroyed at the time of the conversion to Islam. Their removal overnight demonstrates one of the problems that Kafir society faced at the time of the conversion. Ancient traditions were being swept away, and those who had lived by them became confused and bewildered.

Death

Kafir practices concerned with death were quite different from those in the Islamic world or elsewhere among the peoples of Central Asia. The corpse of the deceased was neither cremated, nor buried in the ground: it was placed to rest in a wooden casket and left in a certain area designated as a graveyard. Several members of the same family or lineage (known as *Matr*) were placed in the same coffin. The corpse of a child who had not yet passed puberty was simply placed, without ceremony, in the appropriate container at the graveyard. The dead person was laid to rest fully clothed, and additional items of clothing might also be included.

The importance and the rank of the dead individual would decide the degree of formality and ceremony to be observed. When an important member of the community died, everyone would come to the house where the corpse lay, and the procedure of mourning would begin.

Robertson (op.cit.) describes the scene when the head woman of a village had died:

> In the centre of the concourse, on a bed supported at each corner by a slave, lay the body of the deceased, covered over with bright-coloured turbans. The head was adorned with a kind of crown of sprigs of juniper-cedar, and monstrous imitations of feathers made by fastening bits of red cotton round sticks. The eyebrows, closed lids, and grey cheeks were exposed to view. The blinker silver ornaments were placed one on each side of the head, as with the body in a lying posture they could not be fixed as they would be worn during life. On the feet were dancing-shoes fringed at the top with markhor hair. At the foot of the bed were a second pair of dancing-boots of similar make. Festoons of wheat hanging from the bed proclaimed to all that the deceased during her life had given freely of her substance.

The distinctions and merits of the dead were then extolled in orations by those in attendance. Others present circled the bed in a curious type of dance, whilst there was lamentation from all.

Where a man had died in battle and it had not been

possible to retrieve his whole corpse, his head would be severed from the body and returned to the family. This was of great importance. The head, in such cases, would be adorned and a turban wrapped around it. A body fashioned from straw and finely dressed would be placed with it. Sacrifices of goats and sheep would be made in honour of the dead man, and would be accompanied by feasting and dancing, as well as lamentation.

At length, the head would be placed in the appropriate casket and the straw effigy, made to represent the deceased, would be ceremoniously set alight at the place of interment.

The importance and distinction of the lineage of the departed Kafir would be recited and philanthropic deeds performed in life would be mentioned. In some cases the litter on which the body lay would be raised shoulder-high and paraded about to the sound of drums and dancing.

Thieves who removed ornaments and clothing from the caskets, and were discovered, were dealt with by the families of the dead. Slaves did from time to time steal in this way. It was understood that anyone who robbed the graves of the dead would fall ill and die in some spectacular fashion.

The coffin boxes at the cemetery were generally not repaired. As they were crafted from wood they did in time disintegrate, revealing their contents. There are records that the Kafirs hung flags, made from shreds of cloth, near the coffin; a practice that occurs in other parts of Afghanistan as well as in other societies throughout the world.

Effigies

Some twelve months after the death of a Kafir of a certain standing, it was the practice for an effigy to be fashioned in his memory; the erecting of the image generally being chosen to coincide with a period of feasting in the community. The commemoration banquet was funded by the family of the deceased – an extremely expensive occasion, for in some cases, many hundreds of people would attend, expecting to be fed. If an elaborate effigy was planned, the feast would be expected to be both long and opulent.

The effigies were carved from one piece of wood and could be anything from a few inches in length to life-size. The deceased person was depicted standing, sitting, riding a horse, even straddling two steeds, or riding a two-headed mount. The facial features of the carvings were precise, and lightly coloured stones were sometimes used for the eyes. All manner of accoutrements such as weapons and supplies, were attached to them. These effigies were not universal throughout Kafiristan: some communities did not have them or know what they were.

The Kalash people of Chitral continued to make these effigies until recently, but the practice has almost died out and recent effigies are not crafted with the same attention to detail as in past centuries.

Another kind of memorial was in the form of a column of wood that sprouted from a stone base. At the top of the column, there was a carving similar to the ones already mentioned. Up the column itself, nicks were gouged into the wood, each one representing an enemy whom the departed warrior had slain during his time on earth.

Of these columns the Fazl Huq and Nurulla journey of 1859 established that:[iii]

> In order to show how many people they have killed, each man erects a high pole on the outskirts of his village, with a rude figure of a man on the top of it. For every man he kills he bores a hole in it and knocks in a peg. If he kills a woman, he bores only a hole, without any peg. A Bahadar or Surunwali always occupies the highest place at feasts, and receives a double portion.[19]

Clothing

Kafir costume in general was quite different from the dress worn by the Islamic peoples of Afghanistan and Central Asia, their clothing being designed to stand up to the fierce winter months of the Hindu Kush. Other clothing was worn for festivals and ceremonies of religious importance. Kafir dress was made by local tailors, as was the material itself.

There are records of a certain man who wished to go about wearing trousers of a brilliant red colour. The man had first to give several cows to his community in order to gain permission to dress in the strange manner he liked.

Certain parts of Kafiristan had no cotton and people made all their clothing with wool, or bought cotton imported from outside Kafiristan. Warriors had of course no uniform, but those who had slain a number of foes would wear as a wrap some cloth from the turban of a slaughtered Muslim.

Before the Islamic conversion, few men wore hats or head coverings, although on the wooden grave effigies the male figures were almost always shown wearing a turban. In recent years the *Pawkul*, or *Chitrali cap*, has become popular. It is made of wool and is rolled up, but can be unrolled to cover the ears. Goat skins strapped at the waist were at one time commonly worn by herdsmen, or by those in mourning. These goat skins were of great value in keeping out the bitter winter winds. Men traditionally did all the stitching and sewing of the garments, a custom that remains unchanged today.

In some villages the women would wear a cotton cap on the back of their heads, some with cowrie shells embroidered onto them. But the strangest head covering was worn by Katir women. It had two 'horns' radiating from the top and is certainly an ancient tradition. Around 520 A.D., the Chinese traveller Sung-Yun wrote of the people of Ye-tha (thought to be the people of Sirikol in Hunza):

> The ladies cover their heads, using horns, from which hang down veils all round.[iv]

Of the horned head-wear Biddulph tells us:

> The Bushgali women wear a curious head-dress, consisting of a sort of black cap with lappets, and two horns about

a foot long, made of wood wrapped round with black cloth and fixed to the cap. This curious fashion does not seem to have been always confined to these tribes, or it may be that they were more widely spread than at present.[13]

A heavy coat known as a *Budzun* was worn both by men and women, but particularly by women. Wealthier women would have an undergarment, perhaps of cotton. A well-known item of Kafir costume are the leggings which give the legs some protection whilst tramping through snow. Fisher notes in his book *Afghanistan and the Central Asian Question*[11], that the name *Siyahposh* (the same as Siah-Posh), means black-legged and derives from their goat-skin leggings. Black clothing was very common and favoured amongst the Kafirs.

Some groups of Kafirs dressed very differently from the norm. For example, the Presun villagers wore a heavy padded costume with horizontal striations that stretched to the knee.

During festivities, some Kafir men would wear turbans that rose to form peaks. Feathers were sometimes stuck into the wrappings of the turban. The most prized costumes were the silk robes fashioned in Badakhshan.

In recent times, the clothes of the people of Nuristan have been influenced by those worn in the West, as well as by the costumes of the Islamic World. The Pakistani *shalois cemise* are also worn by some people. Traditional knowledge and skill in the making of clothes has almost disappeared: and the peculiarities of Kafiristan such as the horned bonnets have vanished as well.

Weaponry and Warfare

The Kafirs were a bellicose people, at war with almost all regions surrounding their own. As the last enclave refusing to embrace Islam, they were resolute in their resistance. To kill a Muslim in battle was deemed to be a glorious achievement and it was one of the main ways to increase one's social status. As described, monuments were constructed to list the battle record of the most oustanding warriors.

Ambushes and quick raids were the Kafirs' favoured method of attack. In this way they were capable of hauling away a great deal of plunder. Muslim merchant caravans and convoys were looted when passing near to Kafiristan, and the very idea of crossing the Land of Infidels was seen as absurd. On such forays, the Kafirs were quite prepared, it seems, to kill both the women and children of the enemy. Wounding the opposing forces was also commendable.

For Abdur Rahman, a conquest of Kafiristan was the perfect opportunity by which to gain popularity. He would be appealing to his subjects by converting to Islam what he saw as a barbaric and heathen people, and also by making the north-eastern sector of Afghanistan safer for them to travel through. As the Muslims were so set against the Kafirs, Abdur Rahman could only gain by quashing the infidels.

The Kafirs' bravery is evident when one examines their traditional fighting implements. Until very recent times they had only daggers, bow, arrow, and spears to use in battle and their weapons were not of the high quality available in other parts of Central Asia. Iron is thought to have been almost wholly imported. Blacksmiths were seen as having a very low social status and would not therefore have been encouraged to excel at their profession. There are a significant number of early accounts speculating about the large quantities of gold in Kafiristan. Of this suspected gold Masson wrote:

> It is also universally believed that gold is found in large quantities in this country (Kafiristan), and it is fancied that it grows with the grain. The metal is pale coloured, and called *Tilla Kahi*, or straw coloured gold ... The rivers flowing through Kafiristan, undoubtedly bring down gold with them.

The *Katara* was the favourite weapon of the Kafirs. It was a dagger some twelve inches long, and in some cases, double-sided and slightly curved. The hilt was separated from the blade by a guard, and there was a second protection at the base of the hand grip. Scabbards were fashioned from iron or brass. The main way to cause death with a Katara was to swing the left arm of the Muslim upwards and thrust the blade into the left flank of the body. Instant death could also be brought about by sinking the blade deep into the base of the neck.

Spears and shields were used in war, but it seems that axes were only used in ceremonial occasions, and in battle as a last resort. The bows were long and flimsy, but each arrow had a triple-sided point some two inches in length. The fact that the blade had three sides made it extremely painful and difficult to withdraw. Writing in 1815, Elphinstone says of the Kafir weapons:[1]

> The arms of the Caufirs are a bow about four feet and a half long, with a leather string, and light arrows of reeds with barbed heads, which they sometimes poison. They wear also a dagger of a peculiar shape on the right side, and a sharp knife on the left, with which they generally carry a flint and some bark of a particular kind, which makes excellent tinder. They have also begun to learn the use of fire arms and swords from their Afghaun neighbours.

The war against Communist forces in Afghanistan has taken the people of Nuristan at a single step from the most rudimentary pieces of weaponry to the complexities of the most modern battle systems. As the war proceeded, the Nuristanis taught themselves how to use and maintain captured Soviet arms, as well as those donated from abroad.

Feasts and Festivals

Kafir society revolved around feasts and festivals. The former were of great consequence for many reasons. Feasting marked important events in Kafir life: such as marriages, births, comings of age, deaths, victories in battle, as well as religious observances. But their significance was greater than that, since elevation of status in the community was directly related to the giving of feasts. A feast-giver would win the acceptance of his fellow villagers, who would recognise him as a man of elevated status. Permission to do certain things (as we saw with the man who wanted to wear red trousers) was also gained by giving feasts.

The main distinction that can be made concerning the celebrations is that to some feasts only member of the family were invited; at others the whole community arrived expecting to be fed. The food served would vary for each type of feast. When adolescents came of age, the family, or *matr* (line) of the youth would attend. When a boy reached maturity he would be presented with a dagger and a leather belt; a girl would be given clothes and perhaps jewellery.

At a funeral, the convocation was much more formal. If the deceased had been a great feast-giver himself, tales of his generosity were recounted. Funeral feasts were imperative if a family's social reputation was to remain untarnished. They could be lavish, and consequently enormously expensive; indeed so costly that a family could be plunged deeply into debt. If a great warrior had died, his family would provide perhaps dozens of cows and goats for the community to feast upon. Members of the matr would donate what they could. In many cases the death of a close relative meant the family being condemned to economic hardship for years to come. Again, the erecting of an effigy to commemorate the death of an individual was marked by the throwing of a prodigious banquet. This was so expensive that the cost significantly contributed to the passing of the custom of effigy erecting altogether.

Merely hosting banquets did not of itself bestow heightened status, but it did make the host a candidate for higher rank.

Wine

The making and drinking of wine set the Kafirs firmly apart from their Muslim neighbours, who were disgusted that grape juice should be fermented to form liquor. The Kafirs' reputation as a wild, untameable people was further fuelled by tales of their over-indulgence. Grapes were trodden by foot in a rough type of vat, or a natural basin in the rock, the juice being allowed to ferment for a short period before being drunk. The pulp was dried and eaten.

Early accounts of the Kafirs suggest that they did little else but swill down their alcoholic concoctions. Elphinstone remarked:

They all, both sexes, drink wine to great excess: they have three kinds, red, white, and dark coloured, besides a sort of consistence of a jelly, and very strong. They drink wine, both pure and diluted, out of large silver cups, which are the most precious of their possessions. They drink during their meals, and are elevated, but not made quarrelsome, by this indulgence.

Three hundred years before Elphinstone wrote this, Baber is said to have noted in 1514:[16–17]

So prevalent is the use of wine among them, that every Kafir has a *khig*, or leathern bottle of wine about his neck. They drink wine instead of water.

Abdur Rahman's men destroyed all apparatus for producing wine, together with all the Kafirs' supplies and today the knowledge of producing wine is all but lost: this being an excellent example of how information can be lost in a short span of time.

Some reports have claimed that wine was still being made in Nuristan until recently, but it is now virtually certain that this has ceased for good, the war with the Soviet Union having increased devotion to Islam and Islamic beliefs.

But the large silver goblets, called *Urei*, of which Elphinstone spoke have been found to exist still. Many of these prized heirlooms are thought to have been carried away as loot by the invading Muslim forces of Abdur Rahman, while others were probably sold to traders in subsequent years. Edelberg and Jones's book *Nuristan*[24] contains a photograph of two Kafirs with silver cups, taken in September 1953.

*   *   *   *

Abdur Rahman's invasion of Kafiristan altered not only the course of that isolated Kafir society: but it heavily influenced other Central Asian communities. Large numbers of Kafirs fled as refugees to what was then India and is now Pakistan. Their descendents are still to be found around Chitral in the Hindu Kush. They live in isolated communities and have, to a considerable extent, managed to resist the pressures of conversion to Islam. The Islamic World took heed of Abdur Rahman's conquest, pledging to continue what the Amir had set out to accomplish. Other isolated communities in Central Asia, branded as pagan, also heard of the conquest: and feared that they would be next.

The Afghan Amir brought to an abrupt end rituals, ceremonies and traditions which had taken centuries to develop. He destroyed the wine vats, removed all customs not in accord with Islam, and had the Koran taught to both young and old. Many Kafir practices and beliefs went underground in order to survive, but through propaganda and indoctrination, Islam took over at all levels of society. Those who did not conform were brutally disciplined. Any tradition, person, or institution seen as adverse to Islam was purged.

The Nuristanis still speak of the time when Abdur Rahman's soldiers stormed their lands and they remember those events as if they occurred yesterday. Some keep hidden the ancient silver urns handed down through generations. Others have tried to keep alive archaic Kafir traditions, in secret. It would be virtually impossible for a people so long at odds with another, to embrace the religion, customs and outlook of their conquerors.

In the days before Kafiristan was renamed 'Nuristan', there was a favourite poem. It told the story of a father who had sold his son to the Muslims. When the boy grew up he slew fourteen Muslims and went back to the village of his birth. On his return, his mother sang:

> *Parolé bélé bató warmélawé*
> *Badal lowe bele amá bato lousousawe*
> *Urá pras sagor aman bato warmeláwe*
> *Awár paras dandako partus tatakotáwe*
> *Pa sheristan gangare suta.*

Well done, my lad! Well hast thou fought!
My old blood was drying up for grief for thee,
When thy father sold my high-spirited boy.
And thou hast killed fourteen men and come home again,
With the bells tinkling on thy feet.[v]

NOTES

i Abdur Rahman had the following words etched into the same stone: 'In the reign of Amir Abdur Rahman Ghazi the whole of Kafiristan, *including Kullum*, was conquered by him, and the inhabitants embraced the true and holy religion of Islam', and engraved a verse from the Koran, which means 'Righteousness and virtue have come, and untruth have disappeared.'

ii From: *Memoir of William Watts McNair*. See Bibliography[15].

iii It is worth mentioning Fazl Huq and Nurulla briefly. They were two Afghans converts to Christianity who set out in 1859 from Peshawar to preach the Bible to the people of Kafiristan. They encountered many problems during the crossing through Muslim territory to Kafiristan, and were in danger of their lives. Some of those in whom they confided their Christian faith blackmailed them, with threats of exposure. For some of the journey they donned women's garb and travelled disguised in *bukhas*. Eventually they reached Kafiristan and attempted to convert the Kafirs to Christianity but, after two months away from Peshawar, they decided to return as the snows were soon to arrive.

During their expedition through Kafiristan they made notes on the people and country. Their journal was written, we are told, in lime juice, so that the sheets looked blank. However, having reached Peshawar, the pages were warmed over a fire, and the words became dark and readable.

In one community, the two were surprised to find twenty-eight Muslims who had been invited to be the guests of the Kafirs. The Muslims had killed some Kafirs from the same village many years before, but this had apparently been forgotten. Fazl Huq and Nurullah were suddenly led away from the feast by their friend. Then:

> The Kafirs brought a drum and pipes, and began to sing and dance, throwing their hands and feet about, the women looking on. Then suddenly, without one moment's warning, each Kafir knife was unsheathed, and seen poised high above his head, and, with a loud whistle, four or five Kafirs rushed on each Mohamedan, stabbing him in every part, and all had sunk down dead, covered with many wounds. They then beheaded them and threw them all down into the rivulet below . . . the blood feud was still unremoved, and the Kafirs had never forgotten their own, murdered long before.

From: *The Church Missionary Intelligencer*, December 1878, (reprinted from July 1865). See Bibliography[19]

iv From: Beal's Travels of Buddhist Pilgrims.

v From: *The Church Missionary Intelligencer*, December 1878 (reprint from July 1865) See Bibliography[19].

SELECT BIBLIOGRAPHY

1 *An Account of the Kingdom of Caubul and its Dependencies*, Hon Mountstuart Elphinstone, (Longman, Hurst, Orme, Brown, and John Murray), London, 1815.

2 *Kafirs and Glaciers*, R.C.F. Schomberg, Martin Hopkinson Ltd., London, 1938.

3 *The Kafirs of the Hindu Kush*, Sir George Scott Robertson, Lawrence & Bullen Ltd., London 1896.

4 *The Life of Abdur Rahman*, (Volumes I & II), Edited by Sultan Mohamed Khan, John Murray, London, 1900.

5 *Men of Influence in Nuristan*, Schuyler Jones, Seminar Press, London & New York, 1974.

6 *Afghanistan of the Afghans*, Sirdar Ikbal Ali Shah, Diamond Press, London, 1928.

7 *Afghanistan*, Louis Dupree, Princeton University Press, New Jersey, 1973.

8 *A Journey Through Nuristan*, Wilfred Thesiger, The Geographical Journal (Vol. 123 pp. 457–464), London, 1957.

9 *A Hidden Race Roaming in Unknown Kafiristan*, Sirdar Ikbal Ali Shah, Conquest Magazine, (Volume III, No. 26), London, December 1921.

10 *The Emergence of Modern Afghanistan*, Vartan Gregorian, Stanford University Press, Stanford, 1969.

11 *Afghanistan and the Central Asian Question*, F.H. Fisher, James Clarke & Co., London, 1878.

12 *The Red Kafirs*, M.A. Shakur, Peshawar, 1946.

13 *Tribes of the Hindoo Koosh*, Major J. Biddulph, Office of the Superintendent of Government Printing, Calcutta, 1880.

14 *Travels into Bokhara*, Alexander Burnes, John Murray, London, 1834.

15 *Memoir of W.W. McNair*, J.E. Howard, Keymer & Co. Ltd., London, 1889.

16 *A Narrative of Journeys in Balochistan, Afghanistan and the Punjab; including a residence in those countries, from 1826 to 1838*, C.E. Masson, London, 1842.

17 *Papers on Afghanistan, containing the narrative of journeys performed in that and the adjacent countries, between 1827 and 1830*, C.E. Masson, Transactions of the Bombay Geographical Society, Volume 5, Bombay, 1840.

18 *The Religions of the Hindukush*, (Volume I), Karl Jettmar, (translated by Adam Nayyar), Aris & Phillips Ltd., Wiltshire, 1986.

19 *Afghan Missionaries in Kafiristan*, Fazl Huq and Nurulla, Church Missionary Intelligencer (Volume III pp.724–733), London, December, 1878. (Reprinted from July 1865).

20 *On the Siah-posh Kafirs*, E. Downes, Church Missionary Intelligencer (Volume X pp.277–287 & pp.307–314) London, September & October 1874.

21 *Kafiristan*, Sir George Scott Robertson, The Geographical Journal (Volume IV pp.193-218), London, 1894.

22 *Notes on Kafiristan*, H.G. Raverty, Journal of the Asiatic Society of Bengal (Volume XXVIII pp. 317–368), Calcutta, 1859.

23 *Kafiristan*, Sir George Scott Robertson, Encyclopaedia of Religion and Ethics, Edited by James Hastings, (Volume VII pp.634–636), T & T Clark, Edinburgh, 1914.

24 *Nuristan*, L. Edelberg and S. Jones, Akademische Druck – u. Verlagsanstalt, Graz, 1979.

12

The Gateway of the East End

Introduction

The East End of London, one of the most deprived parts of the capital, home of the docks and gateway to successive waves of immigrants from the Huguenots to Somalis, has always been an area of poverty, exploitation, change and transition. Right on the doorstep of the prosperous City, the East End has a uniqueness of character evolved from a rich and turbulent past. Its humour and optimism transcends hardship, generations and redevelopment.

Until the end of the 1960s, the economic and social fabric of London's East End was dominated by port and river activities. For this reason the docks, now known as the *Docklands*, are a fascinating reflection and illustration of economic growth, decline and renewal, of social and political class systems, and of attitudes to inner city development.

Roman to Medieval

The first enclosed wet dock, mentioned by Pepys in 1661, was at Blackwall, but maritime activity dates back far earlier.

London was a port before it was a city. To the Romans it was a twist in the river, where the waters were shallow enough to anchor the galleys which brought troops necessary to support a controlling garrison. The first port was of moorings cut into the clay of the river bank and strengthened by stakes. River activity took place on high ground west of what is now Docklands – in the district which is now the City of

London. The river was much wider then and the islands of Bermondsey would have been partly under water at high tide. Place names dating from Saxon times indicate that Wapping, Shadwell, Bermondsey, Radcliff and Rotherhithe were occupied at this time.

Historians believe 'Wapping' to be an old-English place name, dating from the fifth century. The area was then marshland on the river bank, to the east of the ancient village which the Romans had developed into the prosperous walled town of Londinium. A British monk, Gildas, writing in Latin around the year 550, tells of King Vortigern's request for the Saxons to deliver the kingdom from the Picts and Scots following the Roman withdrawal. The Saxons, considered a race 'hateful to both God and men', sent an initial force of three warships known as *Cyuls*. These were long narrow vessels with a single square sail. It is not clear where the Anglo-Saxons put ashore in their cyuls and constructed their wattle-and-daub huts once they had repelled the interlopers; but original chronicles of Wapping or 'Waeppingas' clearly refer to a Saxon hamlet somewhere on the river's edge.

In the reign of Edgar the Peaceable – grandson of Alfred the Great – records specify a stream to the east called the Schadfleet, meaning shallow river. Historians conclude this gave its name to Shadwell. Local people, though, have always believed the name originated from St Chad's Well, a spring discovered by St Chad, who assisted in the re-conversion of England to Christianity. Ratcliffe means red cliff, but it is hard to believe that any part of the terrain along this stretch of the river ever resembled red cliffs. Therefore, it is more likely that the name derives from that of a landowner. The name surfaces as La Rede Clive in 1294, and prior to that, in 1182 as Radeclive. It is believed to originate from Radclive in Lancashire which is recorded in the Domesday Book as *Radeclive*.

In 1148, Queen Matilda founded the Royal Hospital of St Katherine on the site where St Katherine's Marina now stands. It was a benevolent institution in keeping with philanthropic traditions of the Middle Ages. Matilda granted twenty pounds a year to subsidise the hospital's commitments which lay in observing Mass and providing for thirteen destitute people selected from among the impoverished.

Bermondsey Abbey was established in 1182, its monks possessing land around St Saviour's Dock. To the west, much of Horselydown and Shad Thames was owned by the Priory of St John of Jerusalem. The most developed district was Tooley Street. By the fourteenth century, river-front locations were inhabited by shipwrights, breweries, watermills and wharfs. Many of the early immigrants settled here. Areas of exceptional development apart, the predominant description of Medieval Docklands is as a stretch of river peppered with small hamlets on the firmer tracts of ground. The marshes, created by breaches in the river bank, continued to be unpopulated and essentially remote until land reclamation work in the thirteenth and fourteenth centuries. Once drained, the land was employed as cornfields, grassland, and pasture.

The Age of Discovery

The Port of London had, by Elizabethan times, grown in importance and accounted for at least fifty per cent of the nation's commerce. In 1558, Elizabeth I authorised the construction of 20 'legal quays', each 1,400 feet long, through which all dutiable goods had to pass. These extended along the river for about a quarter of a mile, between London Bridge and the Tower. The owners of these quays were to enjoy a state-backed monopoly until the beginning of the nineteenth century.

This was the dawning of the age of discovery. Many ships set sail from east of London on bold voyages of exploration. One such venture, from a reach of the Thames near Ratcliff, was captained by Sir Hugh Willoughby in the 'Bona Esperanza', with a second ship, the 'Edward Bonadventure', under Richard Chancellor. They had intended to find a northeastern passage to Cathay – China – but misfortune struck when the vessels became separated in a squall and Willoughby and his crew froze to death in the Arctic winter. Chancellor, however, found his way to Russia, the land of Ivan the Terrible, then almost unknown to the rest of Europe. He returned with tales of the court of the Czar where courtiers gorged themselves from dishes of pure gold while the peasants were wretchedly poor. Returning from a second expedition to Russia, three years later, Chancellor was shipwrecked off the Scottish coast and drowned. Despite his untimely death, Chancellor's voyages laid the foundation for a trading relationship between the two lands.

Sir Martin Frobisher continued exploration of the northern seas in 1576. He made three voyages, all of which blundered in their major objectives, but which led to additional discoveries in Canada during the latter half of the sixteenth century. Blackwall emerged as a point of embarkation for many merchant venturers. Three small ships sailed from here in 1606, captained by John Smith. Those on the expedition established the first enduring colony in America, at Jamestown Harbour, Virginia.

A few years later in 1620, Captain Christopher Jones sailed the 'Mayflower' from Rotherhithe via Southampton and Plymouth before leaving on the voyage that delivered the Pilgrim Fathers to America.

Little more than a century later, James Cook, destined to become one of the world's unequalled explorers, sailed as an apprentice to John Walker, shipowner of Grape Lane, Whitby. He remained with Walker until 1749, transporting cargoes of timber between Norway and London.

By the 1650s, the river bank had been greatly developed. Shipyards, rope-walks, timber yards and smithies competed for space with housing, as neighbourhood trade and the population expanded. Shadwell, which had, for example, been thinly inhabited in the 1500s was almost entirely developed by the mid-1650s. Of a local population some 10,000 strong, around 70 per cent of men were employed in river-related work. Taverns and chapels were erected all over the area. Civil engineering projects were tackled as well: the wet dock at Blackwall was extended, the Shadwell Waterworks Company was established and the Howland Great Wet Dock was built at Rotherhithe for the East India Company.

Dutch engineers made drainage dykes, or 'dijks', in marshland at Wapping and the Isle of Dogs. Experts believe that the name of the latter area is derived from these dykes and not from any association with dogs. Indigenous folklore, however, explains the name very differently: it recounts the story of a merchant and his dog. When the merchant was murdered by pirates on the isle, the hound is said to have swum to and fro across the divide in order to draw attention to the plight of his master. A second local explanation for the name is that noblemen with a passion for hunting in the parkland around Greenwich used to kennel their hounds on the isle. The animated life of the area with its many river-side drinking houses and the renowned pleasure garden at Rotherhithe enticed many revellers from London, including the diarist Samuel Pepys. Entries in his diary during the latter half of the seventeenth century describe the dirt and squalor of Wapping, congestion of the river due to thriving trade, and mention riots for higher pay among seamen in 1666 and 1667.

In addition to being a leading marketplace for foreign trade and an embarkation point for exploration, the Thames soon became a vital waterway for coastal vessels transporting merchandise to and from the capital. London's population had grown from a mere 40,000 or so in the early sixteenth century to almost 600,000 by the turn of the eighteenth century. For adequate provisions to be available to such a large number of people, supply-routes had to improve. Grain and coal came by coastal ship to the capital – it is calculated that London was burning in excess of thirty per cent of the million tons of coal produced by north-eastern collieries each year. London was also a great provider. Foreign imports –

luxuries from India, China and the East Indies – were much sought after. Sugar, tea, and spices, silks and linens were delivered right up to the capital and shipped back around the coast and inland.

One exceptionally lucrative trade was in slaves. It flourished from 1713 onwards with an average turnover of some 70,000 slaves a year. Most of these people were abducted from West Africa. Many were sold in the West Indies for about 30 pounds a head. Jamaica was the major market but other unfortunates were taken to the American mainland.

In fact, slave-traffic proved so profitable that captains of common merchant vessels frequently returned to port with a few slaves for sale. Captives were doubtless sold at one of the slave markets run at two Wapping inns – or kept as personal servants by the sea captains who lived in fine houses on the river. A newspaper advertisement from the 1760s reads:

> Run away from his master about a Fortnight since, a lusty Negroe boy, about 18 years of Age, full of pock holes: had a silver collar about his neck engrav'd Capt. Thos. Michel's Negroe, living in Grifith St in Shadwell.

Slave ships were often to be seen anchored off Wapping and Shadwell in the spring. On board were the ill-gotten gains bought or bartered as a result of their trade: molasses, rum, ivory, gold and redwood – all were easily sold.

Slavery in Britain was only formally abolished by a ruling in 1772 which outlawed the resale abroad or recapture of slaves who had deserted their masters. Many freed blacks continued to live in the East End where they eked out a living as musicians, entertainers and servants.

Despite intensive trading, the East End was still a number of small, separate communities. An eighteenth century map would show most of what is nowadays Tower Hamlets as grazing land and pasture. Bethnal Green was already a neighbourhood of weavers, dyers and shoe-makers; Limehouse another independent settlement involved in lime-burning and brewing. Wapping's reputation for all things filthy, foul and dangerous came from the combination of sailors on leave, poverty, easy availability of alcohol, smuggling and piracy.

The village of Hackney became notorious around 1732 for its very own desperado, horse-thief, bandit and murderer – Dick Turpin. Turpin was seen by most as a cavalier scoundrel rather than a brigand. Even so, he was no Robin Hood. He robbed, raped, pilfered and murdered with a band of smugglers now known as the 'Gregories Gang'. One account tells how he held the landlady of a north-east London inn over a burning fire-grate until she revealed where she had concealed her valuables. The band was responsible for several attacks, many brutal, in the vicinities of Hackney, Walthamstow and Stamford Hill.

As the list of their offences lengthened, a reward of a hundred guineas was offered for their seizure, while a King's pardon was promised to any member of the gang who would stand in evidence against Turpin himself. Having avoided detention by officers of the peace at an ale-house in Westminster by vaulting through a window, Turpin took to the highway with Thomas Rowden and later, when Rowden was hanged, with another notorious highwayman, Tom King. These two brigands, with Turpin on his horse, Black Bess, rode together for three years.

In March 1739 Turpin was captured, found guilty of horse-stealing and sentenced to death. While awaiting execution, he put his roguish skills to work by imposing an entrance fee on visitors wishing to view the legendary outlaw. He used the money gained to buy a new suit to be hanged in, and to hire mourners to follow him to the gallows. He died on the scaffold at the age of thirty-three.

Life in Docklands was often corrupt and violent. Child labour, drunkenness, crime and execution – usually carried out publicly – were facts of life there. Pilfering from the cargoes of moored ships and barges was widespread, as was smuggling. River pirates would loot by whatever means necessary: violently during the day and by stealth at night.

Congestion on the river during the eighteenth century was intolerable, especially between July and October. It was not uncommon for there to be a queue of 3,500 ocean-going vessels and 10,000 coastal boats awaiting their turn at the quays. With the minimal provision of warehousing facilities, the laden cargo ships were easy prey. Pirates and thieves caught in these nefarious but profitable activities faced transportation or death by hanging at Execution Dock at Wapping. It was at these gallows that Captain Kidd was hanged in 1701.

Those who survived attacks by the many brigands, pirates and tricksters working along the river may not have been fortunate enough to escape another danger – the press gangs. These prowled the streets in the eighteenth and nineteenth centuries around Wapping and Shadwell, cudgelling common villagers and sailors on shore leave as they reeled home from the taverns.

Once men were in the navy, their life expectancy was short. Conditions afloat were loathsome with stinking drinking water, weevil-infested food and the inescapable scourges of typhus and scurvy. Britain was at war with France and Canada and able-bodied men were in short-supply. Unfortunately, most were quite unused to a seafaring life and perished fast. Men from all ports were pressed into service and it was a hazardous time to be seen on the streets. It is said that many men from Wapping and Shadwell resorted to dressing in female garb in order to avoid detention.

The nineteenth century Port of London was still the largest in the world both as regards volume of goods handled and in dock area. It was handling all but a small portion of Far Eastern trade, fifty per cent of the Caribbean and over thirty per cent of the Baltic. Sailors from the world's harbours caroused in the Thames-side taverns and brothels and new roads were named after exotic destinations such as Havana and Malabar.

Immigration

The burial register of Limehouse Church of St Anne's records in 1730 that among the first to be interred there were two negroes, an Asian seaman, a Dane and two Venetians. The East End has served as a gateway for immigrants since the great sailing ships of the sixteenth century began to sail from there to far-off lands. Sailors, exiles, merchants and emigrés have arrived and settled there through the ages. Their assimilation has produced in the East End, a mish-mash of every colour and creed – a vast working class of multiracial nonconformist character, quite unlike any other in the capital or the country as a whole. Almost 150 languages are spoken here by people from five continents.

In the sixteenth century, as the French wars raged, Flemish brewers had arrived in London and they were responsible for the introduction of hop-brewed beer which came to replace that made with malt. French silk-weavers came in the seventeenth century, making Spitalfields a centre for fabric manufacture. It was they who discovered how to make taffeta shine and how to design fine-patterned brocades. They also made the fortunes of their Huguenot masters who built grand houses just off Brick Lane, some of which have recently been beautifully refurbished.

The Huguenots

The Huguenots – many quick to achieve affluence – were rapidly absorbed into the English middle classes. They were noted for their aptitude at innovation and new technology as well as for their manufacturing skills. Many moved smoothly into the City, insurance, and property markets. The name *Huguenot* is actually a corruption of the disparaging old Swiss-German term *eidgenosse* – meaning 'member of a clique'.

The Protestants in France had been severely mistreated. They were prohibited from following certain trades – such as banking; their children were pressed to enter Catholic convents; they were put to death for their beliefs. Catholic partisans killed at least 3,000 Huguenots in the Massacre of St Bartholomew's Day (1572), while subsequent massacres in Bordeaux and Lyon claimed the lives of 10,000 more. Initially, most Huguenots endured the persecution and remained in France – worshipping in secret. However, the political and social climate deteriorated still further in the late 1680s, and in 1685 immense pressure was put on French Protestants to convert to Catholicism. Their priests were granted two weeks to leave the country. Lay Protestants, discovered attempting to flee, were either condemned to the galleys or to a convent for life. The majority of those incapable of securing a trustworthy escape route had no choice but to disown their faith and take part in public conversions.

About a quarter of the exiles came to England – with large numbers going to Switzerland, Germany, Ireland and North America. The majority of those who arrived in London were skilled craftsmen and were soon offered official refuge by Charles II. They took control of the weaving industry in Spitalfields and the manufacture of luxury goods in Soho, producing items much in demand by the Court. They were awarded full naturalisation in 1709.

The Irish

The next significant flood of immigrants, the Irish, were given a very different reception. They disembarked in the eighteenth and nineteenth centuries, impoverished and starving, having been forced from their homeland by famine, English landlords and Irish commercial backwardness. Regarded as 'Papists', they were looked upon with great suspicion and blamed for virtually every crime and job loss in the East End. Despite toiling in the docks in the most degrading conditions, they were regarded as scroungers and beggars with loose morals. Many of the women went into service or sold sundry items in the streets. Those of the men not working in the docks became coal-heavers, agricultural

workers on the farms of Hackney, or cutters of the Rotherhithe tunnel. The East End Irish should also be noted for the
leading role they played in the establishment of the Labour
and Trade Union movement.

A significant Irish community remains in the East End –
swollen by many newcomers attracted by the construction
boom of the 1980s. The barn-like Irish pubs, many surviving
from earlier times, are social centres where adults and children come to mix with friends, relations and neighbours.

Here there are always ready volunteers to join in a sing-
song, or volunteer a tip for the horses or the dogs. Sunday
drinking has not stopped the community from remaining
devout. Many Catholic churches have survived in the East
End, including the colossal St Joseph's Basilica in Poplar.

The East Europeans

During the seventeenth and eighteenth centuries, immigration from the German-speaking parts of Europe led to the
founding of a German community in London many thousands strong, but it was in the second half of the nineteenth
century that this community really started to grow. Information collected by the Census of 1851 confirms that some
9,500 residents of London had been born in Germany; forty
years later that figure had leapt to almost 30,000 – the Census
of 1901 registers 95,425 Russians and Poles in England.

The greatest influx of strangers was between 1860 and
1914. It was during this period that some 120,000 east Europeans – mainly Russians and Poles – arrived. A further
20,000 German, Austrian, Dutch and Rumanian Jews entered Britain after the turn of the twentieth century. The
principal districts in which these communities took root
were Whitechapel, St George-in-the-East and the western
part of Mile End Old Town. The concentration of east
Europeans in this sector was so intense, in fact, that it was
sometimes known as 'Little Germany'.

The three principal explanations for this massive influx of

Germans into London were: a quest for greater religious and political freedom, the political bond that existed between the British and Hanoverian Kings between 1714 and 1837, and probably most influential of all, poverty. Many of those who settled in England may have been *en route* to America, the land of new opportunity, which took in some three million Germans between 1855 and 1890. Many of the east Europeans, America-bound, may have been stranded in England due to lack of funds – or simply have found work in the capital and decided to stay.

The bulk of the Germans were Lutherans. There was a substantial group of Catholics too, (mostly from Bavaria and the Rhineland) and of course, a large minority of Jews. Lutheran, Reformed (Calvinist), Roman Catholic and Wesleyan (Methodist) churches were soon created. The original eighteenth century building of St George's Lutheran Church in Alie Street still stands and looks much as it did when it opened in 1763.

It is estimated that between a quarter and a third of all Germans living in East London during the eighteenth and nineteenth centuries, worked in the sugar industry, refining the raw cane imported from the West Indies. This was both hard and physically dangerous work, performed for low wages. Conditions were scorchingly hot and hazardous to the health. Sugar-bakers were unquestionably the largest single occupational group in the German community, but other trades employed tailors, shoe-makers, bakers, carpenters, butchers, dressers and dyers and cigar makers. Community records kept at the German churches list a large proportion of the worshippers as ex-farmers.

In due course the Germans introduced their music. Henry Mayhew[9] records in 1861, an interview he conducted with members of a German street band in London. There were seven in the group: two French horns, one tambourine, one saxhorn and three clarinet players. One of the clarinetists, a 'flaxen-haired and fresh-coloured German', said that they managed to earn between 7 and 8 shillings each a day –

mostly by playing at private parties. They were all single men
– except one who had brought his wife along to cook and
clean for them. They shared cheap lodgings near Whitechapel and ate, 'goot meals every day'. They knew of thirty-
seven performers – four other German brass bands working
in the area. While they appreciated English beer, they did
not mix with the local people, preferring instead to keep to
the German community of sugar-bakers, and to drink in one
of the three public houses run by their countrymen.

Such was the Victorian passion for European music that it
is said that piano-teaching German refugees came especially
to middle-class districts such as Hackney. Here the more
opulent houses had a piano in the parlour. Children of the
household were taught to play as a symbol of their social
standing.

The Jews

Jewish immigrants to Britain, though often seen as a threat,
have contributed to the host community in several ways.
They are largely responsible for a superficial form of national
identity in the form of cheap mass-produced clothing. They
brought with them indisputable commercial and business
acumen of great value. They have joined the ranks of artists,
poets, philosophers, musicians, lawyers and doctors.
Prompted by their own sufferings, they have been active in
politics and pioneering struggles such as the Labour movement. They have enriched the cynical, witty humour of the
East End community which has supported them, often in
times of intense hardship.

The Jewish presence in the capital dates back to medieval
times when a community of some 5,000 inhabited a settlement in the area of Old Jewry in the heart of the City – just to
the west of where the Bank of England stands today. Existence for them was not always an easy matter; they had few
legal rights and were often the victims of mob violence and
persecution. Thirty Jews were burnt alive in their homes on

the day of Richard I's coronation in 1189. All Jews were imprisoned in 1290 while their financial affairs were investigated and many were subsequently hanged or forced to flee. Left behind was a small Jewish community made up of Sephardic (Spanish) Jews who had submitted outwardly to forcible conversion and integration. These survivors finally managed to secure permission from Cromwell to start celebrating Jewish rites openly again. The Ashkenazis – newer immigrants from the ghettos of Poland, Germany and the Netherlands – were less prosperous to begin with. They established trade in diamond, watch and jewellery markets around Aldgate. The Great Synagogue, opened in Aldgate in 1690, was later destroyed in the Blitz.

By 1791, there were an estimated 11,000 Jews living in London, polarized into two groups with radically different lifestyles: the prosperous Anglo-Jewish community with famous members such as the Rothschilds and Montefiores, and the poverty-stricken Austrian and north German emigrants engaged in humble occupations such as the collection and resale of old clothes.

At the end of the nineteenth century, the still relatively small Jewish community in the East End was inundated by a surge of impoverished refugees from Russia and Poland. They had been driven to emigrate by the hardships they suffered under Nicolas I, following an outbreak of anti-semitism, which brought about the worst persecution of Jews until the Nazi Holocaust. Between 1881 and 1905, a million Jews left Russia and Poland – and 100,000 of them came to Britain through the London docks.

Most arrived by boat at Irongate Stairs, now the site of the Tower Hotel at St Katherine's Dock. The established Anglo-Jewish community, securely settled and already well-integrated into the English bourgeoisie, were appalled. Most of them bitterly resented the new inflow of impoverished immigrants with their old-fashioned ways and reluctance to abandon them. It is thought many newcomers were persuaded to extend their journeys to America, but as widespread persecution of the Jews continued in western Russia, the numbers arriving in the East End of London went on growing.

The newcomers – 'greeners' – remained to a large extent in close-knit communities which worked and socialised independently of the existing mainstream of London life. Mostly destitute, they had no alternative but to enter into the sweat shops. Soon, however, they had formed their own small, house-based synagogues, their own stores, and their own workshops. By 1900, there were small industries from Shoreditch and Spitalfields through to Whitechapel. Dressmakers, shoe-makers, printers and cabinet-makers emerged – many even prospered. The skin trade was based in Fournier Street, the jewellery trade in Black Lion Yard (which sadly no longer exists), and the ready-made clothes industry was located at the corner of Great Garden and Greatorex Streets, and on Whitechapel Road.

As the Jewish residences edged westwards so did their way of life. Several of their shops and studios survive. The trimmings, leather and cloth retailers along Brick Lane, for example, may well be the great-grand-children of settlers at the turn of the century. So too may the clothes and accessory merchants of Wentworth and Middlesex Streets, and many other streets around Aldgate and Whitechapel stations. Petticoat Lane, Brick Lane and Whitechapel markets, once predominantly Jewish, still flourish today and are noted for clothes, fruit and vegetables.

The Wintergarten store, four floors laden with watches, clocks, jewellery, silverware, fine china and crystal, illustrates the success of one family of Polish Jews. Asher Wintergarten arrived in England along with countless other Jews seeking religious asylum. He initially supported his family by repairing watches in Black Lion Yard, but died early – aged just 40 years. The oldest son, aged 19, succeeded his father as the breadwinner. His skilled repairs led to a stall in Petticoat Lane and later to a shop in Widegate Street. The shop moved to Bishopsgate as World War I developed and sustained a direct hit in World War II. It is said that this explosion, in the Blitz of 1941, blew the safe – still locked – onto a platform of Liverpool Street station.

The Jewish presence in the East End remains strong and vivid. It is readily apparent in numerous Jewish eating-houses: the Brick Lane bägel shop, Blooms Restaurant with Sid Bloom's salt-beef speciality and atmosphere of smooth cynical banter. But it is also reflected in the several charitable organizations which remain active today. The Jewish Board of Guardians, founded in 1859 (which changed its name in 1963 and merged with the Jewish Blind Society in 1990), still offers a wide range of community care. This institution did much to assist immigrants and transmigrants in their struggles to survive. It endeavoured to prevent them ending up in the Poor Law Workhouses, where they would be unable to maintain Jewish laws or obtain kosher food. It provided a Yiddish-speaking doctor, dispensary and mid-wife to administer basic medical care. It also encouraged 'greeners' to learn to write and speak English and taught trades such as machining, vital to the existing Jewish employment sectors. The Jews' Temporary Shelter also remains as a philanthropic body. Established in 1885 through a need to accommodate refugees from Eastern Europe, it has more recently supported immigrants from Central Europe and the Middle East.

The Jews' Free School, founded around 1821, was for a time the largest school in England; having around 3,000 pupils. Famous ex-students include Barney Barnato. Born the son of a small Whitechapel trader, he emigrated to South Africa in 1873 with $50 in his pocket. Twenty-two years later, he sold his company, De Beers Consolidated Mines, the largest diamond corporation in the world, for $5 million.

The Chinese

The Chinese community in London's East End, traditionally self-sufficient and self-confident, was evident as early as

1880. The founders of London's Chinatown came to the capital as cooks and sailors on ships of the East India Company. The community expanded in the late nineteenth century as seamen were stranded ashore due to the sale or scrapping of their ships. Originally, it was a close-knit group much associated with drug-dealing and organised street crime. The Chinese, themselves from an ancient and advanced culture, tended to resettle in Britain according to the areas of their own origin. Shanghai sailors, for example, habitually installed themselves around Pennyfields, while those from Canton resided mainly in Gill Street and Limehouse Causeway. (Sax Rohmer's invention, Fu-Manchu, the Asiatic master criminal, is first located on Gill Street.) The Chinese occupied entire districts and, by 1915, Chinatown had extended through large parts of the East End.

Association with other social groups seems to have been common. Frequent Anglo-Chinese and Jewish-Chinese marriages have taken place. The first Chinatown was razed during the Blitz, but Chinese boarding houses, clubs and missions have been rebuilt and remain. Likewise, countless Chinese restaurants are evident, their national dishes having proved extremely popular with European East-Enders.

The Chinese Information and Advice Centre renders support services including advice on national benefits available to members of the community – many of whom appear disinclined to claim, due to the assistance which exists within their community.

Commonwealth Immigrants

In the early post-war period, immigrants poured into London from what were still, at that time, the colonies of the West Indies, India and Pakistan. These most recent arrivals relied on a 1948 reform of the then existing immigration laws. After the Second World War, the British workforce had been greatly depleted by war deaths, civilian casualties and the emigration of British nationals to the 'White

Commonwealth'. Despite entering a greatly diminished workforce, the Commonwealth arrivals, perhaps due to the huge numbers in which they came, were soon caught up in a social minefield where physical attacks on coloureds became common and prejudice was deep-rooted.

The rapid intake of Indians and Pakistanis in the late 1950s and early 1960s fanned the flames of racial resentment. Accommodation recently vacated by the Jews was rapidly filled by the newcomers, the latest settlements being in Spitalfields and Whitechapel. Many of the Indians and Pakistanis took over the trade which had been passed to the Jews by the Huguenots, namely the rag-trade. It was not long before the sewing machines humming in the workshops off Brick Lane, were being guided by the dextrous fingers of those flooding in from the Commonwealth.

The East End today bears the signs of a stable Asian community: Halal butchers have replaced many of the Jewish stores, while the Machzikei Hadath is now the Great Mosque, packed to overflowing in Ramadan as it used to be on Yom Kippur.

There have been Asians in the East End since the first voyages of the East India Company, whose monopoly was established in 1600. Asians arrived then as *lascars*, or seamen and *ayahs*, nurses to the children of white colonials. Many of these early pioneers had no choice but to remain in Britain if they had been stranded ashore or dismissed from service. Of these men and women, the majority were from Sylhet in the flood delta of the Bay of Bengal. First through trade and later through conquest, the East India Company effectively controlled Bengal. The Company succeeded the Mughals in utilising the area for the extraction of lime and the collection of taxes and land rents. The Sylhetis, famous for their bold adventurous nature, often went to sea as a means of financial survival. By 1939, 50,000 of the 190,000 sailors in the British Merchant Marine were lascars. Large numbers perished in torpedo attacks on the wartime North Atlantic and Baltic convoys.

After the war many Bengalis sought their fortunes in Britain. It was the old story of legendary streets 'paved with gold', a capital filled with opportunities for those desperately seeking to escape from a land where floods brought home-lessness, poor work opportunities, starvation and eternal strife. The new reality however, made a far less attractive picture. The immigrants became labourers in the cotton mills of Oldham, steel workers in Sheffield and the foundries of Leeds and porters, boilermen and cooks in the East End of London. The London community, only 300 strong in the early 1950s had swollen to 5,000 by 1962. By 1985, a fifth of Britain's 100,000 Bangladeshis lived in Tower Hamlets.

Another large group of immigrants from the British colo-nies were the West Indians. The first pioneers arrived by boat with few contacts in the capital and visions of eight-eenth-century slavery fresh in their minds. The first Jamai-can settlement was founded in Brixton and, once again, the newcomers were blamed for social and financial decline. Blame for every ill from the shortage of housing and employ-ment to the dirt and squalor of the streets, was laid at their door. In short, the West Indians and later the Somalis, Ethiopians and East Africans experienced and still experi-ence today the social resentment previously shown by the host community to the Jews, the Germans and the Irish.

Development

The Birth of the Docks

By 1800, the monopoly of those owning the legal quays and sufferance wharves was broken, as pressure increased to extend the Port of London. The sheer volume of shipping had outgrown the limited cargo-handling facilities and, as Britain industrialised, there followed a boom in dock-build-ing. In 1800 William Pitt the Younger, then Prime Minister, laid the foundation-stone for the West India Dock, the first of the enclosed docks that were to form the Port of London. The 30-acre import dock and the 24-acre export dock, were

opened in 1802 and 1806 respectively. The 20-acre London
Dock was opened in 1805, the East India Docks in 1806, and
St Katherine's in 1828.

Urban space is perpetually created and recreated according to the economic, political and social requirements of any
given era. As work commenced, many homes and small
businesses were simply swept away. Tenants of rented accommodation received no compensation. Development
companies drove hard bargains with the owners of property.
Valuations were generally about half those estimated by
owners. St Katherine's Dock is notorious for having brought
about the displacement of some 11,000 people and the demolition of the Church and Hospital of St Katherine. Plans to
destroy St Katherine's met with violent opposition from
those inhabiting the surrounding area. Threatened with
eviction, they argued furiously that destruction of the ancient property was contrary to 'every principle of propriety
and decency'. Unfortunately, their endeavours to save the
site were futile – their homes were levelled. Relatives of those
buried in the graveyard of St Katherine's were awarded the
equivalent of up to $10 with which to pay for reburial, but
had to finance the removal of the headstones themselves.
Wapping became an isolated area once more, cut off from the
rest of Stepney. The docks which brought wealth to the rest
of the country took up so much room that there was little left
for the inhabitants. The local population decreased dra-
matically to be replaced by labourers brought in to do the
heavy construction work required. They came from most
parts of England, Scotland and Wales, but mainly from
Ireland.

By virtue of the docks, London soon became the warehouse of the world. Massive fortress-like storage houses,
some seven storeys high, rose sheer from the quaysides of
Limehouse and Rotherhithe upto London Bridge. They
were built for security. Towering walls surrounded the
docks – especially those handling imports subject to duty,
such as tobacco and liquor. The new wharfs, planned by

large companies, replaced the smaller existing wharfs with houses attached, where the owners used to live on the premises. Along the docksides, there grew related industries such as refineries and processing plants, which made use of the imported goods and cheap immigrant labour. The wholesale demolition of housing to make way for the docks meant that the space remaining became intolerably overcrowded. In many cases, houses became multiple tenancies – often with a whole family to a room.

By 1870, the middle and upper classes had fled, leaving the East End an almost exclusively working class area. Never had the chasm between rich and poor been as wide. Poverty among the workers was aggravated by intense competition between dockyard companies and by the introduction of an exploitative casual labour system. Work was scarce and a man dared not question the shameful working conditions nor the minimal wage he was paid. Men had to beg for as little as an hour's employment.

The Blitz and Beyond

It was from the dire circumstances of the eighteenth and nineteenth centuries that Cockney cheerfulness, warmth and humour derives. It arose from the streets as a shield in the collective battle to survive. Cockney resilience was severely tested by the Blitz of World War II. No area in Britain was as intensively and systematically bombed as the London docks. Again and again, the German Luftwaffe returned, dropping explosive and incendiary bombs on the docks and the chemical and munitions factories clustered around them. Deaths and injuries were high, but the destruction to housing was phenomenal. Three and a half million homes were destroyed in London – and the East End bore the brunt of this.

The density of postwar council housing was made possible by the extent of the bomb damage, but replacement housing took a very different form from the old-style terraces and streets in which Eastenders had previously lived. Estates and high-rise flats grew from the rubble during the 1950s and 1960s, 'sanitising' entire districts. For the first time, many local people experienced the luxury of an inside toilet or of central heating. By the mid-1960s, Tower Hamlets, at the heart of the working-class East End, had 90 per cent of its inhabitants living in council housing. The old 'unhygienic' terraces were now in such short supply that, ironically, they became dwellings for the richer middle class.

The transformation of the East End in two decades had many social implications. While the terraces had lacked the comforts initially offered by the estates, they had offered limitless opportunities for social interaction. The old-style streets were the 'village greens' of urban life. Generations were born and raised there, surrounded by friends and relatives. The support system was unfailing: children were left next door on occasions when both parents had the chance of a day's work. The front doorstep – a symbol of pride – was scrubbed twice a week, this ritual itself presenting a chance for a regular chat with the woman next door.

The shops were all within easy walking distance: grocers, greengrocers, butchers and pie-shops used to be filled with people chatting and catching up on the latest gossip.

The stark concrete jungles of the new estates and high rises robbed the community of this easy camaraderie. A new generation grew up, shut away in apartments; mothers struggled with their infants up six flights of stairs when the lifts failed; youngsters played in the barren concrete wastelands and teenagers experienced their first kiss on the fire-escape. Despite the bleakness of the new environment, local community life continues to be played out in the streets. The pubs, markets, bingo halls, betting shops and chippies remain and serve the community well, even now when many are surrounded by new constructions attached to the latest Docklands development.

The Docklands Development

By 1969, the docks were closed as the working port moved progressively further downstream. Little redevelopment took place in the 1970s but in 1981 the government formed the London Docklands Development Corporation (L.D.D.C.). The Corporation had comprehensive planning powers to regenerate the derelict eight square miles of land on the edge of the City – the largest urban redevelopment project in Western Europe.

Docklands is once more in the throes of change and upheaval. The area now shimmers with mirror glass and tubular steel. A space-age light railway runs along its own computer controlled elevated track. Shopping malls complete with rippling fountains and piped music have superseded the corner shops of previous years. The vast majority of new accommodation is for private sale. Converted warehouses are now luxury flats on the river front, pieds-à-terre for the massive influx of professional workers recruited by incoming firms.

In many ways the rebirth of Docklands is altering the physical and social structure of the area in much the way the earlier docks had done. A new townscape, economy and population has been imposed. Commerce has once again intervened in the destiny of the East End. Developers again labour against considerable local opposition to their plans for its transformation. Once again the area that was London's dockland is entering upon a new phase in its long history. This time the goal of developers is to establish a financial capital on the edge of the capital – a 'Wall Street on the water'.

The East End has shaped successive generations of immigrants and has itself been remade by them. The community has survived poverty, overcrowding, unemployment, the Blitz and the decline of the docks with a spirit quite unlike any other in the country. No doubt the East End will deal with upheavals caused by the

278   CULTURAL RESEARCH

redevelopments of the last decade with a similar fortitude. In time *Yuppies*, their warehouse conversions, winebars and passion for wind-surfing on the Thames will be absorbed with a spirit of resignation and humour characteristic of the East End.

SELECT BIBLIOGRAPHY

1 *From Whitby to Wapping – The Story of the Early Years of Captain James Cook*, Julia Hunt, Stepney Historical Trust, London, 1991.
2 *Waeppa's People: A History of Wapping*, Madge Darby, Connor & Butler, Colchester, 1988.
3 *East London Record*, (Volumes 13 & 14), 1990–1991 East London History Society, edited by Colm Kerrigan.
4 *Developing London's Docklands*, Sue Brownill, Paul Chapman Publishing Ltd., London, 1990.
5 *The Streets of East London*, William Fishman, Duckworth & Co. Ltd., London, 1979.
6 *Some Lives! A.G.P.'s East End*, David Widgery, Sinclair-Stevenson Ltd., London, 1991.
7 *Dockland: An Illustrated Historical Survey of Life & Work in the East End*, North East London Polytechnic in conjunction with the Great London Council, edited by S.K. Al Naib/R.J.M. Carr, London 1986.
8 *Making Sense of the London Docklands: Processes of Change*, Dennis Hardy, Middlesex Polytechnic, 1983.
9 *Mayhew's London*, edited by Peter Quennell, Bracken Books, London, 1984.
10 *They came to Britain: The History of a Multicultural Nation*, Phillip Page & Heather Newman, Edward Arnold Ltd., London, 1985.
11 *The Port and Trade of Early Elizabethan London*, Brian Dietz, London Record Society, London 1972.
12 *Looking back: A Docker's Life*, Joe Bloomberg, Stepney Book Publications, London, 1979.